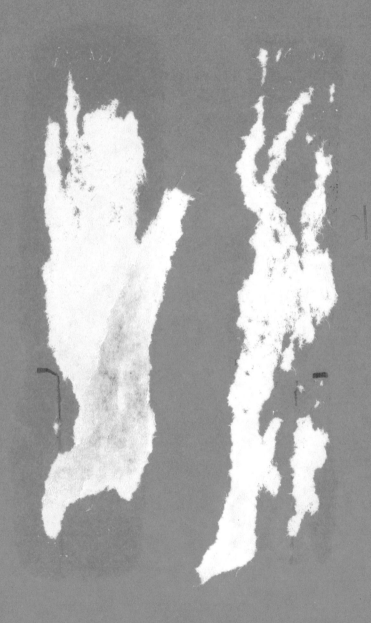

Page i: A spectacularly colored, young Central Plateau dusky rattlesnake, *Crotalus triseriatus triseriatus.*

Pages ii–iii: Although closely related to the neotropical rattlesnake, *Crotalus durissus durissus,* the Uracoan rattlesnake, *Crotalus vegrandis,* has been elevated to species status by several researchers over the past decade.

Opposite, and below: Two distinct color and pattern variations of the Mexican dusky rattlesnake, *Crotalus triseriatus armstrongi.*

Left: As its scientific name implies, the New Mexican ridgenose rattle-snake, *Crotalus willardi obscurus* (*obscurus* is Latin for "indistinct"), has the most weakly patterned and striped face markings of any subspecies of the ridgenose rattle-snakes.

Opposite: The spectacular, uniquely patterned Mexican lance-headed rattlesnake, *Crotalus polystictus,* is arguably the most beautiful of the Mexican high plateau forms.

RATTLESNAKE

PORTRAIT OF A PREDATOR · MANNY RUBIO

SMITHSONIAN INSTITUTION PRESS • Washington and London

Copy editor: Debbie K. Hardin
Production editor: Deborah L. Sanders
Designer: Janice Wheeler

Library of Congress Cataloging-in-Publication Data
Rubio, Manny.
    Rattlesnake : portrait of a predator / Manny Rubio.
        p.   cm.
    Includes bibliographical references (p.   ) and index.
    ISBN 1-56098-808-8 (hardcover : alk. paper)
    1. Rattlesnakes.   I. Title.
  QL666.069R835   1998
  597.96—dc21   98-22935

British Library Cataloguing-in-Publication Data available

Manufactured in Italy, not at government expense
05 04 03 02 01 00 99 98 5 4 3 2 1

∞ The paper used in this publication meets the minimum
requirements of the American National Standard for Information
Sciences—Permanence of Paper for Printed Library Materials ANSI
Z39.48-1984.

Pages viii–ix: Found almost exclusively within the confines of the Grand
Canyon, the Grand Canyon rattlesnake, *Crotalus viridis abyssus,* is rarely
seen. Its cryptic coloration, the gamut of pastels, allows it to blend
extremely well into its rocky habitat.

Opposite: An adult Arizona black rattlesnake, *Crotalus viridis cerberus,* is
usually a very deep, rich, brown color with indistinct blotches edged in
gold or silver.

Overleaf: With its fully extended tongue searching for, and capturing,
miniscule particles from the air, this Arizona ridgenose rattlesnake,
Crotalus willardi willardi, is alert to something within its environment.

In memory of

Charles M. Bogert,

for motivating me by consistently challenging and probing.

For forcing me to continue, to persevere, to research,

to find answers, to think!

Carl F. Kauffeld,

for opening the door, not only to rattlesnakes, but also to all of nature.

Perhaps most important, for always having time

to answer a fledgling naturalist's questions.

Charles Bogert holding a Oaxacan blacktail
rattlesnake, *Crotalus molossus oaxacus,* at his
outdoor laboratory in Oaxaca, Mexico, 1970.

Carl Kauffeld at the Duck Pond Pavilion (made
famous in his book *Snakes and Snake Hunting*),
Okeetee, South Carolina, 1968.

CONTENTS

An aroused western diamond-back, *Crotalus atrox*, stands fully prepared to defend itself.

FOREWORD

The popular understanding of rattlesnakes could use some shoring up. Anyone who is curious about these maligned creatures will be pleasantly rewarded by Manny Rubio's *Rattlesnake: Portrait of a Predator.* This thorough account will arguably become *the* semipopular replacement for Klauber's monumental tome on rattlesnakes. Topics as diverse as the evolutionary origin of rattlesnakes, their sex and growth, their internal functions, their venom and bite, and their role in the environment—all based on the most recent scientific findings—are covered in a relaxed, readable style.

This book will appeal to its two intended audiences: amateur naturalists and technical readers (particularly professional herpetologists). That Latin and common names are used for each rattlesnake species and subspecies will please seasoned veterans, and it will imprint the diversity of rattlesnakes in the minds of a burgeoning number of young herpetologists (who will devour this book).

Rattlesnake is lavishly illustrated with the author's diverse and often unique photographs. All are new, and all were secured specifically for this book. They depict in vivid color most of the major rattlesnake taxa and show many relationships of humans and rattlesnakes. The photographic work alone justifies placing this volume on the reader's shelf.

Coming at a time when the survival of several species of rattlesnakes is precarious, this book is an extremely important contribution to conservation. Rubio's message may do more to save rattlesnakes than anything yet published. Animal rights activists and conservationists will find much ammunition here, especially in the chapters on rattlesnake roundups and the commercial value of rattlesnakes. The rattlesnake roundup must rank among the most disappointing of human social activities. After reading Rubio's powerful firsthand account, one cannot help but conclude that these events propagate misinformation and constitute inhumane exploitation of rattlesnakes. Although Rubio maintains his objectivity and prefers to let the readers form their own opinions, many may find themselves feeling that the rattlesnake roundup is an archaic social institution in dire need of legal prohibition or at least serious reform.

In the chapter on rattlesnakes and religion, Rubio's eyewitness account of a snake-handling fundamentalist congregation is equally impressive for its crisp portrayal of one of the most unusual worship practices of the late twentieth century. Rubio does a masterful job describing these hands-on encounters with live rattlesnakes, and the color photographs vividly transport the reader to the scene. No other source has ever published such a finely written, personal description of this practice.

William S. Brown

A beautiful timber rattlesnake, *Crotalus horridus horridus,* yellow phase, from western Pennsylvania.

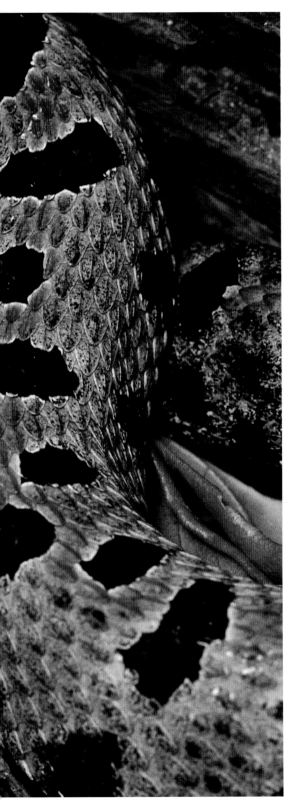

PREFACE

Rattlesnakes have the same appeal for me that hawks and owls have among the birds, the cat animals among the mammals. They are magnificent.

—Carl Kauffeld

Rattlesnake! The mere mention of the word elicits a response—always! There is seldom middle ground. Many persons, twisting and contorting their faces with revulsion, volunteer words of contempt. Snakes in general provoke this negative response, but some people find rattlesnakes particularly loathsome—so much so, they usually kill them on sight.

Regardless of their opinion, people find rattlesnakes fascinating. They are almost mythical creatures, packing venomous fangs at one end and rattling alarms at the other. It is a sound that we all know from movies or life, and we all instinctively react with fear initially.

It is this amazing modification at the end of their tail, the rattle, that makes rattlesnakes unique. All snakes and most lizards completely shed their skin periodically, but only the rattlesnake is left with a permanent, distinctively modified, dead piece of skin (a segment) after each shed. Loosely interlocked with its predecessor, each horny, dry segment produces a characteristic buzzing sound when the tail is vibrated. No other vertebrate animal, no other reptile, has this kind of warning device—the rattle.

Make no mistake, they can back up this warning. The lance-shaped head is formed mainly by underlying venom glands and an elaborate fang-erecting mechanism. The rattlesnake's menacing scowl is enhanced by an elliptical pupil, a protruding scale above each eye, heat-sensitive pits, and a flicking forked tongue. All rattlesnakes have venom and the ability to inject it with a lightning-fast strike. But their venom's toxicity and role have been greatly misinterpreted through unfounded stories, misunderstanding, fear, and prejudice. No animal has been more maligned and persecuted.

Rattlesnakes are both revered and feared. The Hopi have used them in religious ceremonies for centuries, and snake-handling sects survive today in rural Appalachia. The rattlers' remarkableness has attracted people bent on the bizarre, so it is logical that they have found their way into the occult. They have been employed as weapons—for real and fictional murders and suicides. A raid of a crack cocaine house in Colorado in 1989 uncovered a large western diamondback protecting the stash (the snake must have been imported because the species is not found in Colorado). A few years ago, a minister of a snake-

Although widely ranging through Louisiana, Mississippi, Arkansas, eastern Texas, and Oklahoma, the western pigmy rattlesnake, *Sistrurus miliarius streckeri*, is rarely encountered.

handling church in Alabama was convicted, and is serving time, for forcing his wife to be bitten by a rattlesnake as punishment for her infidelity.

Since the earliest European explorers returned from the Americas, they enthralled and frightened people with stories of a fantastic snake with a "bell" on its tail. From that earliest time, inaccurate observations and unexpected confrontations made understanding all but impossible. American folklore is rich with hundreds of accounts of rattlesnakes. Cowboys recounting experiences around the campfire, particularly secondhand accounts of unusual happenings embellished with exaggeration, helped elevate many rattlesnake stories to myths. Rattlesnake lore eventually came to be a vital part of Americana.

Here are some of the more widely repeated, fallacious rattlesnake tales:

- A tortured or restrained rattlesnake will strike itself, committing suicide.
- A rattlesnake will not cross a horsehair rope, a line of burned gunpowder, or a white chalk line; surrounding a ground-sleeping camper with one of these will protect him or her.
- White ash, onions, lead beads, snake bones, burned old shoes, and soil from Ireland are rattlesnake repellents.
- A rattlesnake's age can be told by the number of segments on its rattle.
- Rattlesnakes always rattle before striking.
- Rattlesnakes cannot bite under water.
- Carefully aiming a revolver at a rattlesnake is unnecessary because it will align its head with the barrel.
- A 15-foot-long rattlesnake from Texas weighed 58 pounds.
- Old rattlesnakes grow feathers on their bodies.
- Hybrids of bullsnakes and rattlesnakes lack rattles but maintain the venom and have the speed of the bullsnake.
- The strong smell of cucumbers discloses the presence of a rattlesnake den.
- Wearing a string of rattlesnake rattles around the neck is a general disease preventative and good luck charm. More specifically it prevents rheumatism, smallpox, and sunstroke.
- A fatally injured rattlesnake will not die until sundown.
- Killing a rattlesnake will bring revenge from its mate.

There is another, more positive opinion of rattlesnakes. When viewed objectively, with an aesthetic eye, rattlesnakes are beautiful—exquisite examples of form and symmetry. Nature has supplied them with a full palette of color and a beguiling array of patterns to provide an unequaled display of camouflage. A 6-foot eastern diamondback disappears among dried grasses and fallen pine straw, masked by a patchwork of bright yellow and white diamonds on a somber background of black and browns. Random flecks of pastel pinks, browns, and yellows conceal the speckled rattlesnake, even when it lies fully exposed among the granite rocks of its habitat.

Rattlesnakes are found only in the Americas. They range from southwestern Canada to central Argentina. At least one form is established in every contiguous state, except Delaware, Rhode Island, and (most likely) Maine. Occupying habitats from wet, dank swamps to dry, hot deserts, from sea level to mountain elevations higher than 14,000 feet, they have adapted to an amazing range of conditions. High-elevation and northern-latitude populations may be active for fewer than five months of the year, spending the rest of the year hidden away from the deadly cold. Those from desert areas may never drink water; rather, they absorb and assimilate fluids from the lizards, mammals, and birds they eat. There are small stocky species barely 2 feet in length, massive giants reaching nearly 8 feet, and a plethora in between.

More than eighty different living species and subspecies are recognized currently. Some are abundant, spread over vast geographic ranges. Others are rare, limited to isolated pockets in specific mountain ranges. One is known only from the original specimen, discovered dead on a road in western Mexico.

I was fortunate to have lived throughout my teens within walking distance of the famed Staten Island Zoo. During the late 1950s through the early 1970s, it was known around the world for being the first zoo to exhibit a thriving collection of every described U.S. rattlesnake form, as well as a wide variety of Latin American ones. Many had never been displayed previously. I was captivated to the brink of obsession, spending countless hours after school and on weekends observing and studying their habits, as well as reading everything I could find about them. My curiosity was fed and grew through active conversations with the dedicated keepers. At first they thought of me as one of those inquisitive (annoying) kids who hang around asking a zillion questions. In time, they befriended me, realizing the seriousness of my interest was as great as theirs. These friendships continue today.

I clearly remember once, after I had just spent several hours watching a pair of prairie rattlesnakes mate, Carl Kauffeld, the curator of reptiles, approached and invited me to his office to discuss what I had observed. That was the beginning of a friendship that lasted until his death in 1974. During that time many of the keepers, and occasionally Kauffeld himself, shared dozens of rattlesnake-collecting trips throughout the United States and Mexico to maintain the zoo's collection. I maintained an active interest and collected snakes throughout my college years, when I majored in biology. Although photography became my vocation, I have sustained a nearly lifelong relationship with rattlesnakes.

Scope of the Book

Since its inception, I intended to produce a visually exciting, readable book composed of current factual, interesting information on rattlesnakes. This was never intended to be a definitive technical study of rattlesnakes. Howard Gloyd ("The Rattlesnakes, Genera

The pattern and coloration of this southwestern speckled rattlesnake, *Crotalus mitchellii pyrrhus,* allow it to blend extremely well with its rocky habitat in Arizona's Harquahala Mountains.

Sistrurus and *Crotalus,*" *Chicago Academy of Science Special Publication* 4:1–266 [1940]) and Laurence Klauber (*Rattlesnakes: Their Habits, Life Histories, and Influence on Mankind,* Berkeley: University of California, 1956) did that long ago. It was my intention only to augment Klauber's work and to fill the void by presenting new information and color images of most rattlesnake taxa. I have tried to make this an entertaining book without jeopardizing substance—to present biological facts succinctly and comprehensibly for the precocious lay person and naturalist. Many scientists will certainly question my occasional anthropocentric approach to rattlesnakes. I found it difficult to divorce myself from a human reference point because I have been so closely involved with rattlesnakes for so many years. In contrast, portions of the text may appear too advanced, overly technical, or complicated for some readers, but I feel the inclusion of this material was mandated by the scope of my commitment.

Necessarily much of the information relates to all snakes and is presented as somewhat general statements. Regardless, the text is most specifically steered toward rattlesnakes.

A glossary explains the meanings of many scientific terms as they relate to rattlesnakes. In some cases, to maintain a flow, an explanation has been included in the text as well.

The quotations at the beginning of each chapter were chosen for their relationship to the material that follows them. I assume the reader will be able to discern that many early ones are less-than-accurate observations.

Whenever a rattlesnake taxon (a species or subspecies) is identified in the text, its common (vernacular) name is accompanied by its scientific name. I mostly chose to follow the designations of J. T. Collins's "Standard Common and Current Scientific Names for North American Amphibians and Reptiles" (*Society for the Study of Amphibians and Reptiles Herpetological Circular* 12:1–41 [1990]), J. A. Campbell and W. W. Lamar's *Venomous Reptiles of Latin America* (Ithaca, N.Y.: Cornell University Press, 1989), and E. A. Liner's "Scientific and Common Names for the Amphibians and Reptiles of Mexico in English and Spanish" (*Society for the Study of Amphibians and Reptiles Herpetological Circular* 23 [1994]). Standardization of common names is yet another subject that stimulates debate among herpetologists.

One pitfall of a book of this genre is satisfying systematists. Considerable research is still being undertaken in rattlesnake taxonomy, and there may never be agreement about relationships or nomenclature. In some instances it was necessary to take sides and borrow conclusions from the work of others. Campbell and Lamar suggested that certain taxonomic changes are warranted. Although more evidence to support their ideas needs to be presented, I feel their proposals will be endorsed. No doubt, many of the taxonomic assignments I have accepted will be modified. Change typifies the evolving discipline of systematics.

Under no circumstances can rattlesnakes be considered pets, so there is no discussion about maintaining them in captivity. I have left husbandry to herpetoculturists specializing in that area. I never

recommend that private parties attempt to keep venomous snakes. Anyone who keeps rattlesnakes, or any venomous animal, should do so only with full understanding of the dangerous implications and very serious liability. Simply put, keeping venomous snakes is an accident waiting to happen!

In essence—paraphrasing what Richard Shine said of his book *Australian Snakes: A Natural History* (Ithaca, N.Y.: Cornell University Press, 1991)—I have produced a book I wish had been available when I was growing up.

About the Photography

For those enamored with photographic trivia, all of the images were taken as 35mm transparencies with Canon cameras and lenses. The bulk were produced with 100mm and 200mm macro lenses, but 50mm macro lenses, as well as 17, 24, 28, 35, 300, 400, and 80–200mm lenses, were used for the effects they create. When needed Vivitar 283, Metz 45C, or Canon 480EG flash units were used in the field to provide fill-flash or main light. Close-ups and setups demanded more power; they were lighted with Dynalite 1000 professional units, mostly with one or two umbrella reflectors or "soft" boxes. An array of other inconsequential paraphernalia expedited and solved myriad problems that arose. A tripod was used occasionally. Fuji 100 Professional and Provia 100 films were chosen for their saturation, color rendition, consistency, and sharpness.

Great pains were taken to use "real" furnishings in setups. In every case the created environment is as realistic as possible. Toward this end, a light-handed approach to propping was employed. If a specific item was needed, but unavailable, it was "suggested" in the form of an unidentifiable, out-of-focus substitute. Over the years I have collected and maintained a large selection of rocks, sand, and dried vegetation from various habitats for use in photography. Because the welfare of the snakes was always paramount (there is a pervasive threat of disease contamination), many zoos preferred that I use their props.

Although I have been photographing snakes for more than thirty years, I approached this as a special project. To wit, nearly all the images have been taken specifically for this book during the past twelve years. I must admit that (on more than one occasion) I rethought the ideal, feeling my commitment was—well, stupid! This was particularly apparent when I discovered many species were unavailable in any private or zoo collection; when specimens I traveled a great distance to photograph were not the subspecies that they were claimed to be; and when hours of fieldwork, mostly in isolated, far-off regions, failed to produce the desired rattlesnake sighting.

From the outset, I never planned to photograph all the forms. It was impossible for several reasons. Live specimens of many rattlesnakes were unavailable or unobtainable. Heavy enforcement of state and city ordinances against keeping venomous snakes has severely limited rattlesnakes in private collections. Paramyxovirus (a deadly virus specific to certain snake species) killed many species that were common in zoos during the late 1980s. Also, there is a recent trend away from keeping large numbers of a particular taxonomic group (such as rattlesnakes). Most institutions and exhibitors prefer to maintain a more diversified collection.

One form, the Autlan rattlesnake, *Crotalus lannomi,* is represented by a lone, partially smashed, preserved specimen housed in Brigham Young University Museum. It was found dead on a Mexican road in June 1966 by an old friend, Joe Lannom. Since then, many skilled and hard-working field herpetologists have scoured the area, but no additional specimens have been found. At least three other Mexican montane forms (*Crotalus pusillus, Crotalus stejnegeri,* and *Crotalus transversus*) have been rare in collections, with fewer than two dozen specimens having been collected alive.

Over the past decade the growing expense and bureaucratic difficulties in acquiring Mexican collecting permits have all but stopped the flow of Mexican specimens into the United States. I hope that provisions can be added to the North American Free Trade Agreement (NAFTA) to expedite and simplify the procedure.

Several alleged members of the neotropical group *Crotalus durissus* are taxonomically dubious, but very few (if any) of these have been imported into the United States alive in the past ten years. Further study needs to be done to see if *Crotalus vegrandis* and *Crotalus unicolor* are full species or subspecies of *Crotalus durissus.*

I did, in the end, manage to photograph all U.S. rattlesnake species and subspecies. Perhaps a future edition will be even more inclusive.

I invite you to join me on a photographic and written tribute to these special American natives. I expect you will lose some fear, while gaining respect and the knowledge that these magnificent predators are considerably more fascinating than the unfounded stories so often ascribed to them.

The desert-grassland massasauga, *Sistrurus catenatus edwardsii,* appears to live in dry environments. However, research with radio-tagged specimens in western New Mexico has shown that they actually spend a great deal of time beneath the surface in the moist burrows of various small animals.

ACKNOWLEDGMENTS

My nearly lifelong preoccupation with rattlesnakes has not survived without the continuing support of many relatives and friends. The women in my life—my mother, Bessie, my ex-wives, Melinda and Susan, and my three daughters, Kim, Stephanie, and Jill—accepted and (frequently) overlooked what they believed, beyond doubt, was some ongoing, eccentric, primeval, male craving. My very good friend Gin Ellis has had a profound effect on the completion of this book. During my many bouts with burnout and frustration, she was totally supportive and provided needed inspiration and motivation. She accompanied and assisted me on many photographic excursions, and her literary advice and editorial skills were influential in fashioning a readable text.

I am forever indebted to William S. Brown for his enthusiastic support and scrupulous and impeccable editing skills and for the time he took from his busy schedule to write the foreword. Martha (Mickey) Bogert, Roger Conant, Don Hahn, Jim Murphy, Laura and Gordon Schuett, and an anonymous reviewer read major portions of the text and offered considerable, warranted criticism. Also, special thanks to Bern Bechtel, Dave Hardy, Dennis Herman, Howard Lawler, and W. H. (Marty) Martin for their expertise, critiques, and remarks.

Without the enthusiastic acceptance and prodding of Robb Reavill this book may have taken several more years to be completed. I also thank Peter Cannell, director of Smithsonian Institution Press, for giving me additional time when I pushed deadlines because a needed specimen was located or when I wanted to add just one more photograph; Kate Gibbs, for her youthful exuberance, understanding, and calming words in times of perceived deadline pressure; and Janice Wheeler, designer par excellence, for using her special magic to mesh a few hundred images and thousands of words into a book that went beyond my expectations.

Of the dozens of collecting partners in more than thirty years of traipsing through swamps, mountains, and deserts, I am most grateful to my longtime friends Jim Bockowski, Zig Leszczynski, and Bob Zappalorti. Not only did they share my interests from those early days, but also they provided companionship on collecting trips and nightlong road-cruising stints. These junkets took us throughout the U.S. Southeast and Southwest and to Mexico in the seemingly endless quest for rattlesnakes. On the most recent trips (specifically for this book), Jim Bockowski and newer but no less enthusiastic friends Greg Greer, Jim Merli, Thom Moisi, and Gene Trescott unselfishly helped me collect and pose many of the rattlesnakes. Special thanks are extended to Dave Spiteri and Gary Keasler for sharing the nautical adventure of traveling to Coronado Island to photograph *Crotalus viridis caliginis*.

I am indebted to the reptile keepers and curators

The Totonacan rattlesnake, *Crotalus durissus totonacus*, which ranges fairly close to the southern tip of Texas, is rarely exhibited in zoos.

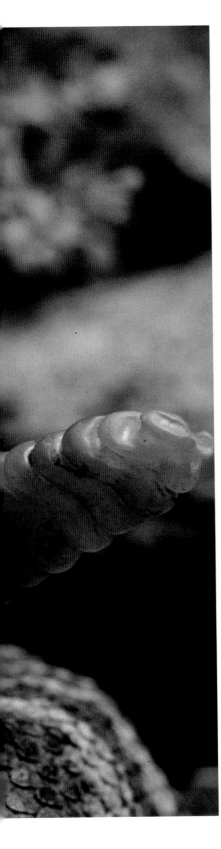

The El Muerto Island rattle-snake, *Crotalus mitchellii muertensis,* is found only on the small island from which it acquired its name. It is one of the smaller subspecies of the speckled rattlesnake but has the characteristic large head proportionate to its body.

who volunteered many hours, at times working overtime, to handle snakes for me: Dennis Herman, Zoo/Atlanta; Carl Alimonti and Dennis Hall, Staten Island Zoo; Matt Finstrom and Craig Ivanyi, Arizona-Sonora Desert Museum; Mike Goode, Columbus Zoo; Donal Boyer, Dallas Zoo; Rick Reed, Fort Worth Zoo; Johnny Arnett, Cincinnati Zoo; Mike Chadwick, Houston Zoo; and Alan Kardon, San Antonio Zoo.

Also, I thank the directors and curators who managed to "grease the wheels," allowing me to upset work schedules and expediting clearance of intricate insurance obstacles that may have impeded photography: Dave Bloady, Vince Gatulla, Howard Lawler, Karl Peterson, and Bill Summerville. And I thank the private collectors who permitted me to invade their homes or schools and disturb their animals: Dick Bartlett, Tom Crutchfield, Doug Foster, Chris Giacoletti, Jim Gerholdt, David Lazcano, Hugh McCrystal, Thom Moisi, Rene Van Swinderen, Barney Tomberlin, and Gene Trescott. I am additionally grateful to Thom Moisi and Gene Trescott for their relentless pursuit of specimens otherwise hidden in private collections and for uncovering a dazzling array of rattlesnake-related literature and ephemera.

I am in awe of the painstaking perfection and unlimited artistic ability of Ellen Foose in producing the magnificent wood-carving of the eastern diamondback head and the construction of the speckled rattlesnake viscera. It would have been very difficult to find a variety of unusual rattlesnake-related items, artifacts, and rare snakes without the help of Bob Meyers and his unique and extensive Rattlesnake Museum in Albuquerque. I thank Garland's Trading Post in Red Rock, Arizona, for allowing me to photograph their kachinas and Native American artifacts.

I would be seriously remiss if I did not acknowledge the ability and tenacity of Paul Gritis, Don Hahn, Pete Strimple, and Eric Theiss in finding obscure and otherwise difficult-to-obtain literature for my library.

I thank Pete Casabonne, owner of Color Genesis (a professional processing lab in Atlanta) for expediting the processing of my film, frequently within a few hours. Also, I thank Lane Thompson for taking great pride in flawlessly processing and mounting more than 1,700 rolls of film for this book.

It is impossible to thank the hundreds of anonymous researchers and writers who supplied the unlimited fodder that so ably overloaded my synapses from the formative years to recent times. My knowledge relies heavily on their contributions and observations. The writers of certain works have had an indelible effect and deserve special recognition: Charles Bogert, Roger Conant, Raymond Ditmars, Howard Gloyd, Carl Kauffeld, and, of course, Laurence Klauber.

The largest island in the Sea of Cortez has an indigenous subspecies that bears the island's name, the Angel de la Guarda Island speckled rattlesnake, *Crotalus mitchellii angelensis*. Compared to the other subspecies, this is an exceptionally large, heavy snake with a massive head.

The vividly patterned Del Nido ridgenose rattlesnake, *Crotalus willardi amabilis*, lives in a remote region of Mexico and is rarely seen in zoo collections.

This bright, orange-phase tiger rattlesnake, *Crotalus tigris*, from near Phoenix, is highly sought by zoos and collectors alike. Tiger rattlesnakes are difficult to find, and state and federal governments protect most of its fragile habitat.

ORIGINS AND CHARACTERISTICS OF RATTLESNAKES

Show me your teeth and I'll show you what you are.
—Baron Cuvier

My eyes locked on it from 30 feet away. There was no doubt. As I moved closer, I realized my fantasy—I was looking at my first rattlesnake, an adult eastern diamondback rattlesnake, *Crotalus adamanteus*. I had read Carl Kauffeld's *Snakes and Snake Hunting* (Garden City, N.Y.: Hanover House, 1957) twice since it was published the previous year, and here I was, reliving Kauffeld's vivid descriptions of just such an encounter with a rattlesnake in the wild. Although I had imagined it clearly, I never anticipated it would happen so soon; this was my first snake hunting trip to the fabled burned fields of Okeetee, South Carolina.

I was transfixed by the snake's bulk (easily as thick as my calf) and attempted to visualize it stretched out. It had to be more than 5 feet (1.5 meters) in length. The bright, hot sun exaggerated the contrasting yellow, black, brown, and white diamonds, and the distinctive white and black facial stripe on its massive head became more vibrant the closer I got to the snake. I approached cautiously, not wanting it to escape, to lunge irretrievably into recesses of the charred stump immediately behind it. Stopping within 6 feet, I slowly, deliberately crouched to relish the experience. I was ecstatic, in awe. My knees wobbled and my heart pounded. As I reached up to wipe the beads of sweat that were streaming into my eyes, the snake reacted, ever so inconspicuously. There was no movement other than its black tongue flicking sinuously, first down, then up above its head. For

This magnificent eastern diamondback rattlesnake, *Crotalus adamanteus*, basks in the South Carolina sun, adjacent to the recesses of the burned-out stump in which it hibernated.

Above: The small, nondescript scales atop the head of a southeastern Arizona phase of the northern blacktail rattlesnake, *Crotalus molossus molossus,* are characteristic of all members of the genus *Crotalus.*

Right: The prominent head scales are clearly visible in this close-up of a Mexican pigmy rattlesnake, *Sistrurus ravus.*

five minutes I remained on one knee, immobile, absorbing everything. The snake was still, except for methodically sampling the air, obviously aware that something nearby was violating its space.

I needed to make a photograph. As I grabbed for my camera and uncovered the lens, my prize made for the stump. With a sweeping motion I reached out with my snake hook and yanked it away from its escape. Its demeanor changed instantly. No more nice guy! It became the stereotypical rattlesnake. Springing into a tight defensive coil, it rattled furiously—first facing me and standing its ground, then rapidly backing toward the stump. I was so startled and overwhelmed that I fell backward. In a blink it was gone—a golden blur pouring into the darkness of the stump hole.

Over the past nearly four decades I have seen scores of eastern diamondbacks in similar situations. Each brought an adrenaline rush, unbelievable excitement, and an undeniable feeling of reverence. I have been extremely fortunate to witness this majestic creature, the king of rattlesnakes, before the rattlesnake and its habitat are gone.

Distinguishing Characteristics

It is the rattle, of course, that makes a rattlesnake unique among snakes. No other snake—no other creature, for that matter—has one. Even a seasoned herpetologist startled by the distinctive rattling of an aroused rattlesnake freezes in mid-step. A chill races through the body. Experience dictates the response to this momentary fear reflex. Regardless, it is an unnerving incident that is never forgotten.

There are other less apparent characteristics that separate rattlesnakes from other snakes. The second most noticeable external feature is the facial pit. These paired openings and associated organs are found on a group of mostly American venomous snakes that share a common ancestry. They are called pitvipers (crotalines). The rattlesnake's body shape, rather chunky toward the midsection and tapering at both ends, and the fairly obvious lance-shaped head are also distinguishing characteristics.

Canebrake, timber, ridgenose, sidewinder, pigmy, long-tailed, midget faded, banded rock, blacktail, red diamond, desert-grassland, prairie, Great Basin, Mojave, Grand Canyon, and Aruba Island are descriptive common names that disclose something about particular rattlesnake forms. The common name of a particular rattlesnake varies from place to place within its range, so each has been assigned a scientific name. This Latin binomial (two names) universally provides a precise designation and provides a tool to finding its place in the grand scheme of living things. It is the only valid name assigned to that taxon. To maintain stability, the naming process follows rules regulated by the International Commission of Zoological Nomenclature. It is based on the tenth edition (1758) of Carl von Linné's *Systema Naturae.* As science advances, classification methods are modified, but the original principles remain largely valid today.

Taxonomists, using embryological, anatomical, morphological, behavioral, and (more recently) chromosomal, molecular, and biochemical similarities and differences have isolated a perplexing diversity of species and subspecies. Herpetologists identify approximately eighty-three kinds of living rattlesnakes. The number fluctuates with the results of new studies.

Laurence Klauber, the late research associate at the San Diego Museum of Natural History and first curator of reptiles at the San Diego Zoo, painstakingly undertook a variety of rattlesnake research projects for more than four decades. Although he was educated as and worked as an electrical engineer, he maintained a lifetime fascination with rattlesnakes. Using statistics, Klauber compared a wide series of variables to establish important relationships and correlations that had not previously been considered. After he published several excellent monographs on rattlesnake biology, natural history, and systematics, his life's work culminated in one of the most extensive studies ever written on any form of wildlife, *Rattlesnakes: Their Habits, Life Histories, and Influence on Mankind* (Berkeley: University of California Press, 1956).

One of his pioneering investigations dealt with the relative size and length of the rattles of different races. He concluded that the primitive forms have proportionately smaller, less-defined rattles. He also deduced that many early rattlesnakes were quite large, with small, nearly silent rattles.

The Two Rattlesnake Genera

The currently accepted thirty-two species (eighty-three subspecies) of rattlesnakes are divided into two genera, *Sistrurus* and *Crotalus,* visibly distinguished by the size of the scales on the crown of the head. Rattlesnakes with a series of small, similar shaped scales belong to the larger genus known as *Crotalus*. Those with a less uniform group of nine large scales (arranged in cross-rows from front to back as 2-2-3-2) characterize the genus *Sistrurus*.

There is one known, notable exception. Examples from a population of Guerreran pigmy rattlesnake, *Sistrurus ravus exiguus,* have divided parietals, resulting in eleven head scales. The *Sistrurus* head scale arrangement is similar to their colubrid snake ancestors and suggests they are more primitive (less derived). Data from DNA analysis have substantiated the relationship between the two genera (A. Knight and D. P. Mindell, "Substitution Bias, Weighting of DNA Sequence Evolution, and the Phylogenetic Position of Fea's Viper," *Systematic Biology* 42:18–31 [1993]).

Crotalus is derived from the Greek, *krotalon,* meaning "little bell" or "rattle." *Sistrurus* is derived from the Latin, *sistrum,* which in turn is from Greek, *seistron,* meaning "small religious" or "child's rattle," and Greek, *oura,* meaning "tail."

Species

Although rattlesnakes maintain the primary physical characteristics of their kind, a variety of traits distinguish the separate rattlesnake

Other than subtle differences in pattern, there is a great similarity among the three subspecies of sidewinders. *From top:* Mojave Desert sidewinder, *Crotalus cerastes cerastes;* Sonoran Desert sidewinder, *Crotalus cerastes cercobombus;* and Colorado Desert sidewinder, *Crotalus cerastes laterorepens.*

species. The biological species concept (one widely recognized definition of a species) suggests that species remain (generally) genetically isolated by having restricted gene flow and are thus incapable of bearing viable offspring from matings with other species. In rare instances successful interbreeding occurs, producing hybrids with characteristics of both parents or hybrids with strange pattern anomalies. In theory, the offspring of such matings are incapable of reproduction. When viable and more widespread hybridization occurs, a new species could develop. This process likely would involve other isolating geographical and ecological factors that would prevent a further gene flow with other unrelated species. In addition, it would probably require thousands of years.

Subspecies

There are two interpretations of subspecies. One assumes that the rattlesnake in question demonstrates geographical, color, or size variation with no defined lineage at all. The other assumes that the lineage is defined, but not well defined.

There has been considerable debate about the validity of subspecies. Some scientists feel that acceptable subspecies (representing true lineages) should simply be named as species, and geographic variants should not be recognized. Others believe that even the subtlest phenotypic criteria may be useful in disclosing more complex genetic variation. This is a view that would require naming additional subspecies. I follow the consensus view that recognizes subspecies when useful in describing the geographical variation within a species.

Numerous, wide-ranging species have spawned variant forms with modified physical attributes necessary to better invade and survive in an assortment of environments. These forms (subspecies) are often found at the periphery of a species' range or occur in those species that contain populations isolated by geological or geographical barriers. They are similar to the parental stock but demonstrate noticeable disparity in scalation, pattern, coloration, or size. The major distinction between a subspecies and a species is that different subspecies are recognized portions of a single species and thus are expected to freely interbreed. The best-defined subspecies are those that are so geographically isolated from other subspecies that interbreeding in the wild can no longer occur. At this point, many taxonomists feel these populations are distinct species. So goes the debate.

Beyond Subspecies

In regions in which two subspecies meet in a contact zone, many rattlesnakes bear a perplexing array of characteristics inherent to both forms. It is difficult to assign these individuals to either taxon, so they are called *intergrades*. Identification becomes more difficult if the area of intergradation is broad and ill defined.

The yellow and black variants of timber rattlesnakes, *Crotalus horridus horridus,* are seen side by side. It is not uncommon to find both color variants in the same brood, such as these from central Pennsylvania.

Within the realm of subspecies are groups that have evolved subtle, superficial differences. Most commonly these differences are in coloration, size, habits, and food preferences. The extent of these dissimilarities may or may not be great enough to support subspecific recognition. These groups are known as *demes, local breeding populations,* or *subpopulations.*

Still another level of variation is found among species and subspecies. Those animals bearing unique patterns and coloration within a brood (on a regular basis) are referred to as *morphs.* Color morphs are prevalent in some species, such as the timber rattlesnake, *Crotalus horridus horridus.* It has both a yellow morph and a black morph. The latter is most prevalent in more northerly altitudes. Certain populations of the eastern massasauga, *Sistrurus catenatus catenatus,* are almost completely black, obscuring the normal blotched pattern.

Species Groups

Some rattlesnakes show many similar morphological and physical characteristics and yet are distinct species. These affinities usually indicate recent divergence from a common ancestor. Systematists often disagree on the relationships of these similar looking species.

Hybridization, a rare event in the wild, occasionally occurs when two different species live in close proximity. Here are two such hybrids *(from top):* panamint rattlesnake, *Crotalus mitchellii stephensi,* x Great Basin rattlesnake, *Crotalus viridis lutosus,* from Esmeralda County, Nevada; and red diamond rattlesnake, *Crotalus ruber ruber,* x southern Pacific rattlesnake, *Crotalus viridis helleri,* from Orange County, California.

At various times they have been described as subspecies of one another. There is little doubt that they are closely related, so they are considered as a species group. For example, three western species demonstrate a common lineage with the western diamondback, *Crotalus atrox,* and are known as "the *atrox* group." These are the western diamondback; the red diamond rattlesnake, *Crotalus ruber,* with its three subspecies; and the Tortuga Island diamond rattlesnake, *Crotalus tortugensis.* The Santa Catalina Island rattlesnake, *Crotalus catalinensis,* has recently been placed within the *atrox* group as well. Several other rattlesnake species groups have been proposed and named.

By closely examining the biogeography of monotypic species (those that include no recognized subspecies), their specialization or isolation from others is evident. These isolated populations are frequently called *relics* because they are the remains of former rattlesnake taxa that had a much wider original range. They have become isolated over thousands of years by a variety of physiographic, geologic, and ecologic barriers. For example, some montane forms were affected by glaciation. They were cut off, confined to remaining suitable habitat by retreating glaciers. Additional ecological changes in the valleys prevented further dispersal. In some instances of geological or geographic isolation, new subspecies within a species were founded.

The Number of Rattlesnake Taxa

The genus *Crotalus* has twenty-nine species, with a total of seventy-four subspecies, and *Sistrurus* consists of three species and nine subspecies. Of the accepted *Crotalus,* thirteen species are monotypic (including no recognized variant forms), and the other sixteen species include a total of sixty-one subspecies (including the nominate form). In total, eighty-three living forms, or named taxa (either species or subspecies), are recognized by scientists. There are another half dozen or so forms that are possible additions to the list, but these require further research. In a few cases additions will be accepted once they are reviewed by peers and these reviews are published in professional journals.

Sistrurus demonstrates several affinities with certain *Crotalus* species, but the difference in the size of the head scales is a principal physical characteristic for the generic division. One puzzling disparity is the larger size of the rattles of the Mexican species of a pigmy rattlesnake, *Sistrurus ravus,* when compared to those of the other *Sistrurus* species; they are more proportionate to those of *Crotalus.*

Hybrids

It is uncommon for different rattlesnake species that are sympatric (living in the same general region) to hybridize in the wild, but it does occur. Some reported interspecific breedings are Mojave rattlesnake, *Crotalus scutulatus scutulatus,* x sidewinder, *Crotalus cerastes;*

There is some question about the derivation of this brightly patterned hybrid, an eastern diamondback, *Crotalus adamanteus*, x canebrake rattlesnake, *Crotalus horridus atricaudatus*.

Mojave, *Crotalus scutulatus scutulatus*, x prairie, *Crotalus viridis viridis;* northern Pacific, *Crotalus viridis oreganus,* x southern Pacific rattlesnakes, *Crotalus viridis helleri;* red diamond, *Crotalus ruber ruber,* x western diamondback rattlesnakes, *Crotalus atrox;* red diamond, *Crotalus ruber ruber,* x southern Pacific rattlesnakes, *Crotalus viridis helleri;* eastern diamondback, *Crotalus adamanteus,* x canebrake rattlesnakes, *Crotalus horridus atricaudatus;* eastern diamondback, *Crotalus adamanteus,* x western diamondback rattlesnakes, *Crotalus atrox;* and New Mexican ridgenose, *Crotalus willardi obscurus,* x banded rock rattlesnakes, *Crotalus lepidus klauberi.*

Rattlesnakes (many snake species for that matter) hybridize fairly commonly when brought together under the unnatural situation produced by captivity. Several of the previously mentioned rattlesnake crosses were bred in captivity, and their offspring have produced viable young. To further complicate the matter, the phenomenon occurs when species from totally distinct geographic regions are brought together. Such hybridization could never happen in nature. As an example, offspring were produced from mating an Aruba Island rattlesnake, *Crotalus unicolor,* and a Mojave rattlesnake, *Crotalus scutulatus scutulatus,* at the San Diego Zoo. Even more thought provoking, the second-generation hybrids of these totally unrelated and geographically distinct species were capable of reproduction.

There are reports of intergeneric hybrids, crosses between certain closely related snake genera. Although it was disputed at the time

Right: Captivity brings together species that would never meet in nature, and occasionally hybridizing occurs. In this case, the unusual hybrid is a western diamondback, *Crotalus atrox*, x eastern diamondback, *Crotalus adamanteus.*

Below: Although this hybrid, western diamondback, *Crotalus atrox*, x Mojave rattlesnake, *Crotalus scutulatus scutulatus,* was produced in captivity, such a cross is possible in the wild, because the habitats and ranges of these snakes overlap throughout Arizona, adjacent New Mexico, and part of northern Mexico. There have been several unsubstantiated reports of wild hybrids.

Opposite: Because of its endangered-species status and a captive-breeding campaign, the Aruba Island rattlesnake, *Crotalus unicolor,* is well known among snake enthusiasts.

of its description in 1942 (the specimen was captured in 1895), there is one reported case of a hybrid of an eastern massasauga, *Sistrurus catenatus catenatus,* and a timber rattlesnake, *Crotalus horridus horridus* (R. M. Bailey, "An Intergeneric Hybrid Rattlesnake," *American Naturalist* 76:376–85 [1942]).

Island Populations and Some Isolating Characters

Many island forms most likely originated as waifs, carried to the island on debris or by swimming. Others were separated when the islands became isolated from the larger landmasses. Although insular forms retain some characteristics of mainland relatives, thousands of years of isolation and lack of gene flow resulted in sufficient changes that support specific or subspecific recognition. Eleven insular forms of rattlesnakes are currently recognized. All are Mexican taxa except the Aruba Island rattlesnake, *Crotalus unicolor,* which lives on this small Caribbean island off the coast of Venezuela. As they have done for many island races, taxonomists have reclassified the Aruba Island rattlesnake as a species or as a subspecies several times. Other mainland taxa have colonized islands, but they do not appear to demonstrate characteristics warranting taxonomic acceptance and a special scientific name. Eventually, DNA analysis will settle many of these taxonomic debates, at least for a while.

A Brief Look at Rattlesnake Evolution

Skeletal remains are the principal physical evidence used by paleontologists to organize relationships among "higher" (more derived) forms of vertebrate life. Unfortunately, snake bones are small and delicate and do not fossilize well. The shortage of adequate snake fossils has left sizable gaps in the paleontological record. Lacking this extensive tangible osteological evidence, paleontologists must use other approaches, such as comparative anatomy, embryology, zoogeography, biochemistry, and ecology, in its place.

Most herpetologists accept that the earliest rattlesnakes originated and radiated from north-central Mexico. This idea is strengthened by the wide variety of similar taxa that thrive in various parts of the Mexican plateau. It appears that over the millennia they dispersed north and south, becoming established in most habitats suitable for snakes.

The entire population of the Coronado Island rattlesnake, *Crotalus viridis caliginis (above)*, lives on the largest of the three small turtle-shell-shaped islands *(below)*. Because the island's sides are so steep, the snakes are mostly limited to a square mile of viable habitat.

Opposite, and above:
Most island forms are constantly being assessed and reassigned as species and subspecies. Five of these (all of which are from Mexico) are, *clockwise from top left,* the Tortuga Island diamond rattlesnake, *Crotalus tortugensis,* believed by many to be a subspecies of the western diamondback, *Crotalus atrox;* the red diamond rattlesnake, *Crotalus ruber ruber;* an unnamed subspecies of the speckled rattlesnake, *Crotalus mitchellii,* from Cerralvo Island; the Cedros Island diamond rattlesnake, *Crotalus exsul exsul,* believed to be a subspecies of *Crotalus ruber;* and the Cerralvo Island rattlesnake, *Crotalus enyo cerralvensis.*

The closer the body scales of this Guerreran pigmy rattlesnake, *Sistrurus ravus exiguus,* are to the rattle, the smaller they are. The closest (and smallest) are called fringe scales. The scales of all rattlesnakes are arranged in this pattern, and the number of fringe scales is frequently used as a characteristic in distinguishing subspecies.

In the western United States some rattlesnakes can be found inhabiting extremely different, seemingly inhospitable environments. Sidewinders, *Crotalus cerastes,* can be found in hot, sandy regions from below sea level in the Mojave Desert, and northern Pacific rattlesnakes, *Crotalus viridis oreganus,* have been captured in rocky areas at 11,000 feet (3,350 meters) in the Sierra Nevada Mountains.

Adequate fossil evidence shows the eastern diamondback, *Crotalus adamanteus,* became established in the moist U.S. Gulf Coast states during the Pleistocene era. For many years, it was believed these fossil vertebrae were those of an extinct species, *Crotalus giganteus.* Currently, that form is considered to be an extinct relictual population of the eastern diamondback. These very early examples were larger, perhaps 8 feet (2.4 meters) in length, with a diameter of 12 to 18 inches (30 to 46 centimeters). Some herpetologists consider the other large U.S. rattlesnake, the western diamondback, *Crotalus atrox,* to be closely related to the eastern form, but there are several conspicuous differences. Aside from the disparities in head scale configurations, body proportions, and coloration, the western diamondback migrated northward much later and preferred dryer climes.

Although there is recent evidence to disprove the hypothesis, it is believed that Viperidae (the family to which pitvipers belong) evolved from a branch of Colubridae, the largest family (3,000 forms) of mostly nonvenomous or weakly venomous snakes. There is additional debate about whether Viperidae is composed of two subfamilies, the true vipers (Viperinae, approximately 40 species) in Africa and Eurasia and pitvipers (Crotalinae, approximately 142 species) in Eurasia and the Americas, or if they are separate families, Viperidae and Crotalidae. Yet another hypothesis, that Viperinae are paraphyletic (not directly derived from a single common ancestor) somewhat complicates matters. For now, I have accepted the consensus and consider them subfamilies.

Although all the members of Viperinae and Crotalinae have a venom-injecting apparatus and hollow fangs, only Crotalinae have facial pits. Because rattlesnakes have facial pits, they belong within Crotalinae. Of all snakes, pitvipers are probably the most derived or specialized group, having a facial pit, long movable fangs, specialized venom glands, and venom. The rattlesnake's rattle shows further refinement.

Most sources trace the first modern pitvipers to Europe and the central United States as recently as the late Tertiary period, in the Pliocene epoch (12 million years ago). In 1993, using molecular analysis, A. Knight and colleagues ("Choosing among Hypotheses of Rattlesnake Phylogeny: A Best-Fit Rate Test for DNA Sequence Data," *Systematic Biology* 42:356–67) estimated a much earlier origin for rattlesnakes, the Oligocene epoch (30 million years ago), of the Tertiary period.

There are no fossils to demonstrate the direct relationship between pitvipers and the other vipers, but most zoogeographers agree they are directly related. Their ancestral stock evolved in Eurasia, and the two subfamilies split there. Members of Viperinae dispersed west and south, settling in Africa (part of Eurasia), and ancestors of Crotalinae followed the Bering land bridge from the west to the Americas. This was not a rapid movement of pitvipers but one that progressed over millions of years as living conditions became favorable for them.

During the late Tertiary period (Oligocene and upper Miocene epochs), the earliest forms of rattlesnakes branched off from other still dispersing and evolving pitvipers. It is theorized that by the mid- or late Pliocene epoch most current rattlesnake species were in existence. It appears rattlesnakes had little competition from other venomous snakes and were able to diversify and dominate in favorable American habitats. Rattlesnakes today are endemic to the Western Hemisphere.

The South American Rattlesnake and Some Close Relatives

Only the neotropical rattlesnake, *Crotalus durissus,* was able to establish a foothold in South America where it inhabits grasslands, savannas, and dry forests. The periodic disruption and discontinuance of the Panamanian land bridge dating back to the middle Tertiary may have stalled the southerly progression of the neotropical rattlesnake, while allowing a less eventful migration of other pitvipers.

Unlike most rattlesnakes, other pitvipers adapted well to the humid tropical Americas. Many remained terrestrial: lance-headed pitvipers, *Bothrops* (thirty-one species); hognosed and montane pitvipers, *Porthidium* (eight species); Mexican horned pitviper, *Ophryacus* (one species); and newly reassigned and named mesic lowland pitvipers, *Atropoides* (three species). Forest pitvipers, *Bothriopsis* (seven species), became predominately arboreal, and palm pitvipers, *Bothriechis* (seven species) chose an exclusively arboreal lifestyle. In their 1989 book *The Venomous Reptiles of Latin America* (Ithaca, N.Y.: Cornell University Press), Campbell and Lamar proposed a new genus of small, terrestrial mountain vipers, *Cerrophidion,* assigning to this genus three species previously considered *Porthidium.*

The bushmaster, *Lachesis muta,* is another fascinating pitviper found in tropical America. It has a common origin with other crotalines but remains less derived. Although closely related to other crotalines, it has anatomical characteristics that warrant special generic positioning. Its reproductive mode is unique among American pitvipers, for rather than bearing live young *(viviparous)* it lays eggs *(oviparous).* Bushmaster also has the greatest length of any living viper, attaining 12 feet (3.66 meters).

The bushmaster's tail terminates in a pronounced horny spine that could be the precursor of the rattle—that is, the living bushmaster retains a tail structure possibly reminiscent of an early rattlesnake. Nearly all terrestrial pitvipers today have prominent pointed tail tips. A small Argentinean viper, *Bothrops ammodytoides,* has a blunted tail most similar to the rattlesnakes, although it lacks a rattle.

More Research Needed

In 1965 there were forty-six recognized species and subspecies of rattlesnakes; today there are more than eighty. Much work needs to be done on the isolated Mexican populations of the western diamondback, *Crotalus atrox,* and on its relationship with the Tortuga Island diamond rattlesnake, *Crotalus tortugensis.* Some believe an additional western subspecies of timber rattlesnake, *Crotalus horridus,* are warranted. The validity and complexity of western rattlesnake subspecies have been speculated on for some time, as have the three subspecies of sidewinder. Legitimacy of the monotypic island taxa is frequently debated. Questions remain about the relationship between Mexican west-coast rattlesnakes, *Crotalus basiliscus,* and blacktail rattlesnakes, *Crotalus molossus.* Some believe they should be treated as subspecies of a single species. The subspecific relationship of rock rattlesnakes *(Crotalus lepidus)* is a perplexing situation that needs reevaluation, as does their connection with Mexican dusky rattlesnakes, *Crotalus triseriatus armstrongi.* Support for conserving three sidewinder subspecies has also been questioned. These are but a few of the perplexing challenges confronting taxonomists and systematisists of rattlesnakes.

Molecular biologists, using sophisticated genetic and biochemical analyses involving DNA, proteins, and other molecules, are able to show affinities and dissimilarities at the molecular level, opening an exciting new frontier in taxonomy. Biochemical analysis of venoms has disclosed some unexpected affinities. Although there is no recent geographical link, components in their venom have shown

Only one rattlesnake species ranges into South America: the neotropical rattlesnake, *Crotalus durissus.* Most herpetologists recognize nine South American subspecies and four others in Mexico and Central America. This is *Crotalus durissus durissus.*

A taxonomically perplexing form *(left)* is found in extreme southern Sonora and adjacent Sinaloa, Mexico. Its pattern, coloration, and scutulation appear to be of a hybrid between the Mexican west-coast rattlesnake, *Crotalus basiliscus (below)*, and the northern blacktail rattlesnake, *Crotalus molossus molossus (opposite)*. Differing herpetologists have considered it nothing more than a variant of either of these two taxa, rather than a hybrid or a distinct subspecies.

that timber rattlesnakes, *Crotalus horridus*, appear to be closely related to neotropical rattlesnakes, *Crotalus durissus*, and to blacktail rattlesnakes, *Crotalus molossus*.

Compared to the long-employed methods, molecular research is in its infancy. For rattlesnakes, current findings and proposed systematic assignments (although presently somewhat controversial) have become grounded in these modern techniques, which have been used as important tools in differentiating many other animal species. It is only logical that these methods have found a place in rattlesnake systematics. Additional research undoubtedly will provide evidence to stabilize and, taxonomists hope, to clarify some puzzling rattlesnake relationships. The new methods will help classify all the forms of *Crotalus* and *Sistrurus* according to their evolutionary relationships. New taxa will be described and others will be suppressed. One must accept that there are few absolutes in the natural sciences, because our methods of classifying nature are only our best scientific attempts to reflect the evolutionary forces that shaped the diversity of life.

HOW AND WHERE RATTLESNAKES LIVE

One of the most spectacular aspects of nature is its diversity. This diversity has a very special property that it is not continuous, but consists of discrete units, species.

—Ernst Mayr

Over millions of years rattlesnakes have adapted to a variety of areas, many of which appear to be inhospitable. They are found at extremes, exemplified by sidewinders in the hot, barren, arid Mojave Desert, and Central Plateau dusky rattlesnakes, *Crotalus triseriatus triseriatus,* at elevations above 14,000 feet (4,270 meters) on Mount Orizaba, in the eastern part of the Transverse Volcanic Cordillera, where snow and freezing temperatures prevail for more than half of the year. In between, rattlesnakes are found nearly everywhere.

The two U.S. species of *Sistrurus (Sistrurus miliarius* and *Sistrurus catenatus)* are small and stout bodied and have tiny rattles. They range throughout the central and southeastern states as far west as extreme southeastern Arizona. Another species, *Sistrurus ravus,* is isolated on the Mexican plateau.

Crotalus are found in all the contiguous states except three. Timber rattlesnakes, *Crotalus horridus horridus,* once inhabited Rhode Island and the southern tip of Maine, but they have been exterminated from these states. There are no records of them ever inhabiting Delaware. In Rhode Island, farming, urbanization, and habitat destruction were the culprits; in Maine, they appear to have succumbed to natural changes in climate and the environment as well as to human predation. Their survival throughout New England is

Had it not started rattling, this western diamondback rattlesnake, *Crotalus atrox,* probably would not have been detected in the partial shadow of the creosote bush.

Opposite, in background: The Tucson Mountains and the adjacent Avra Valley to the west are unique in the variety of rattlesnakes inhabiting the area. Although the snakes' elevation ranges overlap considerably and they may be found in close proximity, each species lives within a limited geographical area, likely within a preferred microhabitat. *Opposite, inset:* Northern blacktail rattlesnakes, *Crotalus molossus molossus,* are more prevalent among the larger higher rocky outcrops. *Left, from top:* Tiger rattlesnakes, *Crotalus tigris,* live within the rockier territory. Western diamondbacks, *Crotalus atrox,* are abundant throughout the scrub desert. Mojave rattlesnakes, *Crotalus scutulatus scutulatus,* are much more common a few miles south of the area of the background photo, in slightly more open, predominately creosote-bush desert. *Below:* Likewise, Sonoran Desert sidewinders, *Crotalus cerastes cercobombus,* prefer the sandier, more open desert in the western part of the valley.

highly tenuous, but they persist in a number of localities in Connecticut and Massachusetts and a few localities in Vermont and New Hampshire.

Many rattlesnake species are wide ranging, with no respect for national boundaries. Mexico is truly rattlesnake paradise—all but three species are found there. The eastern diamondback, *Crotalus adamanteus,* timber, *Crotalus horridus,* and the pigmy rattlesnakes, *Sistrurus miliarius,* are found only in the United States. Although rattlesnakes have a limited range in southern Canada, they are far reaching in Latin America.

The twelve currently recognized subspecies of the neotropical rattlesnake are the most wide ranging. They spread in suitable habitat from eastern Mexico, throughout Central America (except Panama), into northern and eastern South America, as far south as northern Argentina. Four races of the neotropical rattlesnake are represented in Mexico, but none are found in Chile and Ecuador. Excluding Isla de Margarita and Islas los Testigos off the coast of Venezuela and the unique Aruba Island form, there are no rattlesnakes in the West Indies.

Modification and Adaptability

Two species typify geographic variation, the western diamondback, *Crotalus atrox,* and the western rattlesnake, *Crotalus viridis.* The western diamondback has the widest geographic range of all rattlesnake species that are monotypic (lacking subspecies). It lives in ten southwestern states and in most of the northern half of Mexico. A wide assortment of terrain is populated. Although preferring drier lowlands, western diamondback can be found from coastal plains to rocky, steep hillsides. Along the Gulf Coast it has been found near the beach. Excepting a few isolated colonies in north-central Mexico, it is rare above an elevation of 4,000 feet (1,220 meters). In some areas, notably portions of central and western Texas, impressive population densities are attained. Estimates of seventy-five snakes per square mile are cited. During the cold winter months huge numbers gather to den.

Western diamondbacks from southeast Texas and the lower Rio Grande Valley are second only to the eastern diamondback in size. A 7-foot (2.1-meter) monster came from south of Dallas, and larger examples are recorded. However, in the western, more desertified parts of its range, specimens as large as 5 feet (1.5 meters) are uncommon.

Western rattlesnake, *Crotalus viridis,* is the polytypic antithesis of

Florida palmetto scrub *(above)* harbors the largest rattlesnake, the eastern diamondback, *Crotalus adamanteus (opposite),* and the smallest, the Florida pigmy rattlesnake, *Sistrurus miliarius barbouri (right).*

the western diamondback. It has seven subspecies ranging through-out all the western states. One subspecies is restricted to the tiny Coronado Island, off the Pacific coast of Baja California. Other races are found from northern Baja and extreme north-central Mex-ico to southwestern Canada. Ranging from sea level to elevations near 11,000 feet (3,350 meters), the western rattlesnake, *Crotalus viridis,* demonstrates the greatest versatility in habitat choice and physical characteristics of any rattlesnake species.

None of the western rattlesnake races are giants, but size varies greatly between the subspecies. Four subspecies—the southern Pacific rattlesnake, *Crotalus viridis helleri,* northern Pacific, *Crotalus viridis oreganus*, Great Basin, *Crotalus viridis lutosus,* and prairie rattlesnake, *Crotalus viridis viridis*—each have attained slightly more than 5 feet (1.5 meters) in length, but they are exceptions. The Ari-zona black rattlesnake, *Crotalus viridis cerberus,* and Grand Canyon rattlesnake, *Crotalus viridis abyssus,* reach just beyond 3 feet (1 me-ter). The midget faded rattlesnake, *Crotalus viridis concolor,* as its common name implies, is a small form, rarely reaching 24 inches (61 centimeters). The Hopi rattlesnake, *Crotalus viridis nuntius,* and Coronado Island rattlesnake, *Crotalus viridis caliginis,* are only slightly longer, measuring just beyond 2 feet (0.6 meter).

The stunted forms of the western rattlesnake typify most smaller rattlesnake taxa, living in areas that are heavily affected by adverse weather, short growing seasons, or limited food supplies. The midget faded and Hopi rattlesnakes inhabit high deserts with long, dry seasons and lengthy, cold winters. These snakes aestivate in the summer and hibernate in the winter for long periods, restricting their growing seasons. Coronado Island is cloud shrouded and dank for weeks at a time, limiting foraging and food intake by its endemic form. Conversely, the mid-sized forms generally live in relatively temperate climates with a balance of suitable climatic conditions. The subspecies that attain the largest size live within areas having the best overall climatic conditions and food supplies.

Research is being done on the status and validity of the *viridis* group. Over the years scientists have claimed the Hopi rattlesnake, *Crotalus viridis nuntius,* to be nothing more than a stunted popula-tion of the western rattlesnake, *Crotalus viridis,* and suggest it be placed into synonymy. Certain venom properties have given cause to more closely scrutinize the midget faded and Grand Canyon forms.

Habitat

Rattlesnakes are found in nearly all types of habitats that support populations of terrestrial, ectothermic ("cold-blooded") vertebrates. The majority live near fairly open, rocky areas. Rocks supply excel-lent cover and retreats, an abundance of food animals (e.g., lizards, rodents, birds, arachnids, insects), and open basking sites. Several taxa seek outcroppings or talus, and others inhabit gaps between boulders, ledges, and fissures in the ground. The type of rock may

or may not be important. Limestone, sandstone, granite, and lava beds can harbor populations. The availability of open areas, which allow periodic basking, is a universal requirement.

This is not to suggest that all forms live near rocks. Some are found in savannas, prairies, scrubby desert, sandy areas, pinelands, deciduous forests, and marshy areas. Western rattlesnakes *(Crotalus viridis),* timber *(Crotalus horridus),* canebrake *(Crotalus horridus atri-caudatus),* and eastern diamondback rattlesnakes *(Crotalus adaman-teus)* spend the majority of their active lives on the surface, shel-tered among grasses, shrubs, fallen leaves, and other ground litter. Likely other species do as well. When weather demands it, they hibernate or aestivate in suitable underground refuges supplied by the eroding root systems of fallen or dead trees, in rock cavities, or in animal burrows.

Certain taxa have very specific habitat requirements. Many live only within particular plant associations and at extremely narrow ranges in elevation. This specificity is not unique to snakes; most forms of life dwell in distinctive environments. A thorough under-standing of the principles of ecology (e.g., community interactions, niche dimensions, faunal assemblages) are beyond the scope of this book. One point is clear, however: Environmental components are extremely important in limiting the distribution of rattlesnakes.

Sympatry

Although they may be sympatric (inhabiting the same region), it is highly improbable that two species of rattlesnakes have identical ecological needs and share identical niches. In the mountains of southeastern Arizona, northern blacktail rattlesnakes, *Crotalus*

Eastern massasaugas, *Sistrurus catenatus catenatus,* are commonly asso-ciated with swampy, boggy areas in the north-central United States. Al-though they hibernate in these areas, foraging and most summer activi-ties are undertaken in nearby grassy areas. This specimen, like many others found in Ohio, is nearly melanistic.

In the highlands of Oaxaca, Mexico, this abandoned and overgrown field *(left)*, with rock piles and walls, provides excellent cover, basking sites, and available prey for the Oaxacan small-headed rattlesnake, *Crotalus intermedius gloydi (above)* .

Humans have unknowingly embellished habitat in some rural areas. Clearings for roads, power lines, and fire trails provide openings in forested areas that are readily infiltrated by a variety of animals. This road cut in Hidalgo, Mexico *(left)*, produced talus enabling the indigenous colony of Central Plateau dusky rattlesnakes, *Crotalus triseriatus triseriatus (above)*, to flourish.

Opposite, top:
A grassy slope with rocky outcrops in San Luis Potosi *(background)* is habitat for the Mexican blacktail rattlesnake, *Crotalus molossus nigrescens (inset)*. This magnificent specimen has exceptional, contrasting black and white markings; most are greener with a less distinct pattern.

Opposite, and below:
The open limestone ledges along the Pecos River in Val Verde County, Texas *(opposite, bottom)*, are excellent habitats for the mottled rock rattlesnake, *Crotalus lepidus lepidus (below, top)*, and the gray-phase northern blacktail rattlesnake, *Crotalus molossus molossus (below, bottom)*.

molossus molossus, are frequently found in rock slides with much smaller banded rock rattlesnakes, *Crotalus lepidus klauberi*. The latter most likely live their entire lives in the slide, finding all their needs satisfied. Talus provides food (a plentiful supply of small lizards and centipedes), water (pockets of rainwater), mates, and retreats for protection and hibernation.

Northern blacktail rattlesnakes, *Crotalus molossus molossus*, use the rock slide mainly for basking. It would take scores of the small indigenous lizards to supply enough nourishment (their usual fare is small mammals and birds), and the fissures in the rock slide are in general much too narrow to accommodate their robust bodies. More likely, they are visiting from nearby haunts among larger boulders or ledges. These rocks may be sheltered from the sun by dense vegetation and evidently harbor larger prey, such as rock squirrels. Also, the northern blacktail rattlesnake's home range and foraging area is much greater than that of its smaller congener.

Perhaps the most curious example of sympatry is the association between western diamondback, *Crotalus atrox*, and Mojave rattlesnakes, *Crotalus scutulatus scutulatus*. The two forms look much alike (they are often confused by naturalists and herpetologists), and they have many similar habits. Their geographic ranges overlap extensively, but they remain separate by preferring slightly different habitats. In certain portions of their overlapping ranges, minor alterations of the habitat reveal one species is slowly replacing the other. Shifts in precipitation levels and the introduction of cattle are considered major variables instigating this transformation. But it is important to note that, as in most of nature, these changes are extremely subtle, and the process of snake species replacement will take many years.

Grazing destroys plant associations in southeastern Arizona and southwestern New Mexico, where a more desertified environment prevails. The Mojave rattlesnake, *Crotalus scutulatus scutulatus*, appears to be better suited there and is becoming the dominant species. The opposite is true in the Sonoran desert near Tucson, Arizona, where, in areas of greater slope and rocky substrate, the expansion of less xeric and more brushy and grassy habitat with friable soil, ground cover, and rodent burrows for refuges is producing more suitable haunts for the western diamondback, *Crotalus atrox*.

Other animal and plant relationships are undergoing changes along with the rattlesnakes. Because different mammal and lizard species prefer different insect and plant foods, the entire food chain is being altered. Although both species of rattlesnakes consume a variety of similar small mammals, the larger western diamondback, *Crotalus atrox*, is capable of eating rabbits that are more prevalent in grassland habitats. Also, it is believed that Mojave rattlesnakes, *Crotalus scutulatus scutulatus*, consume a greater number of lizards, more common to drier areas. Overall, the Mojave rattlesnake appears to be more readily adaptable to the habitat changes.

Montane Rattlesnakes

Many montane (mountain-dwelling) taxa appear to have wide distributions but actually live in isolated pockets. These "islands" are mostly vestiges of vast areas cut off during glacial periods that occurred thousands of years ago. For a variety of reasons, the land between them remains inhospitable to these snakes and prevents their reuniting. Prolonged isolation has led to changes, warranting recognition of subspecies. The various subspecies of the ridgenose rattlesnake, *Crotalus willardi,* are perfect examples. They are scattered about in restricted areas in several mountain ranges in northeastern Mexico and extreme southeastern Arizona and southwestern New Mexico.

The suitable microhabitat of montane rattlesnakes is open rocky areas surrounded by pine–oak, pinon pine–juniper, or fir forests. Some rattlesnakes, like the previously mentioned banded rock rattlesnake, *Crotalus lepidus klauberi,* live in very steep talus slopes with southern exposures. When disturbed, they quickly disappear into the labyrinth of crevices. Faint buzzing of their diminutive rattles is the only clue disclosing their presence. Other mountain forms avoid hillsides, taking more readily to valleys and stream beds, with nearby permanent water. There are several rarer Mexican species that have similar habitat preferences.

Of the eleven rattlesnake species that are considered montane, six are monotypic: the Queretaran blotched (*Crotalus aquilus*), Autlan *(Crotalus lannomi),* tancitaran dusky (*Crotalus pusillus),* Mexican lance-headed *(Crotalus polystictus),* long-tailed (*Crotalus stejnegeri),* and cross-banded mountain rattlesnakes *(Crotalus transversus).* All but the Queretaran blotched rattlesnake are considered primitive, because they evolved very early in the rattlesnake evolutionary process. The other five species, *Crotalus lepidus, Crotalus willardi, Crotalus intermedius, Crotalus triseriatus,* and *Crotalus pricei,* are polytypic—that is, they have one or more subspecies.

Desert Rattlesnakes

Only desert-dwelling sidewinders, *Crotalus cerastes,* appear to exist in open, barren, sandy country. Although they will travel (mostly at night) over extensive areas of loose windblown sand and have the ability to partially bury themselves in it, they prefer scrubby, sandy areas near washes. This habitat offers some shade along with rodent and lizard burrows as retreats. During hotter periods they are not found very far from this type of cover. Rodents rarely dig

Above:
Although synonymous with hot arid areas such as the White Water Canyon *(background),* sidewinders, *Crotalus cerastes (inset),* are not the only rattlesnakes that live in that seemingly foreboding environment. Each desert has its own highly adapted forms.

Opposite, clockwise from top:
Rocky deserts in southern California harbor the red diamond rattlesnake, *Crotalus ruber ruber,* and the panamint rattlesnake, *Crotalus mitchellii stephensi.* Also, this area is the westernmost range of the western diamondback, *Crotalus atrox.* This brightly colored and patterned specimen is from the Cochella Valley, near Palm Springs, California.

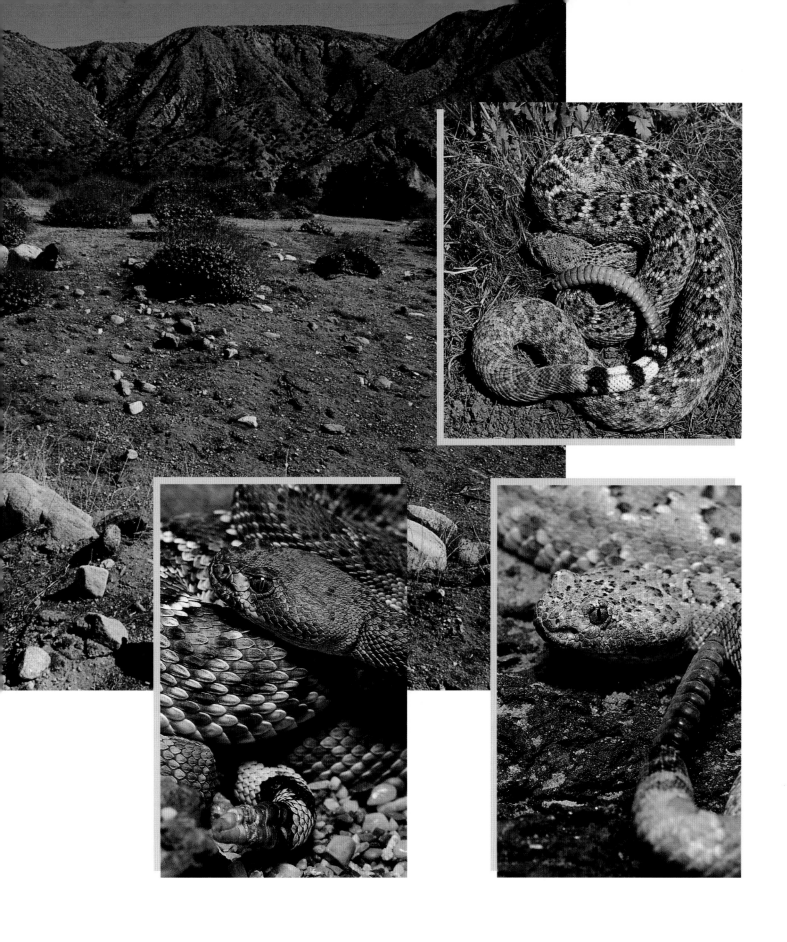

In Baja California del Sur *(background)*, subspecies of the red diamond and panamint rattlesnakes, the San Lucan Island diamond rattlesnake, *Crotalus ruber lucasensis (left)*, and the San Lucan speckled rattlesnake, *Crotalus mitchellii mitchellii (opposite, top)* live in similar habitat, with the Rosario rattlesnake, *Crotalus enyo furvus (opposite, bottom)*.

burrows in rocky, impermeable, alluvial areas; correspondingly, adult sidewinders find little refuge there. Young sidewinders are able to use smaller hiding places, so they are more commonly found in these areas. Unlike most desert snakes, sidewinder activity periods are not totally reliant on rain and are only partially diminished by wind.

During warmer months, a tightly coiled sidewinder may be found buried in sand with little more than its head, neck, and partial upper back exposed. Looking like a saucer tossed aside, an almost perfect ring of disturbed sand encircles the otherwise cryptically patterned, tan body. Using a side-to-side shuffling, rocking motion combined with a series of rippling muscular contractions, it digs laterally, moving the sand out and aside, forcing itself into the soft ground, settling with the dorsal surface just slightly above the substrate surface. The head and neck may be used to pull sand over the outer body. Wind-blown sand may bury them further. If the temperature is suitable and it is not prowling for ten minutes or more, a sidewinder will generally assume this cratered resting position. It occasionally spends the night in this cratered coil, awakening and warming with the early morning sun.

Cratering is an excellent method of thermoregulating. With the potentially dangerous, rapid heating from intense, late morning sun, a sizable amount of body heat is dissipated through the ventral area lying in contact with cooler subsurface sand. The opposite is true at night. The subsurface zone retains a considerable amount of daytime heat, slowing down cooling from the falling evening air temperatures. By using the ventral and dorsal blood vessels, a sidewinder can achieve an excellent temperature balance. Slight changes in skin color, either lighter or darker depending on the

temperature and color of the sand, may also help in thermoregulation. During the somewhat cooler spring and fall, a sidewinder may spend the entire day on the surface in a cratered coil. A large percentage of daily activity is spent thermoregulating to keep the snake alive and alert and to expedite digestion.

It is likely that considerable feeding is done by ambush from the sidewinder's cratered position. As the environment becomes hotter, the snake seeks shade provided by shrubs large enough to cast a sufficient shadow, and the snake may once again crater. This may prove even more advantageous for ambush predation. Like sidewinders, foraging lizards escape the sun when they become overheated. Should the two choose the same shrub, the result would be unpleasant for the lizard.

When it is too hot, the uncomfortable rattlesnake retires to the stable, cooler recesses of animal burrows that pockmark this part of the desert. It resurfaces at dusk to continue nocturnal foraging. Following a meandering course, a sidewinder may travel hundreds of feet during the night. Using its unique sidewinding locomotion, the snake stays on the move, cruising over open sand with ease. When grass or shrubs are encountered, it changes to a rectilinear mode to weave through them. Sidewinding continues when open sand is again available. Unlike most snakes, sidewinders appear not to tire readily. They may stop to rest in thirty-minute intervals. Regardless of the season, for some reason most movement ceases about midnight.

Four other species also are considered desert rattlesnakes, because they live almost exclusively within hot, sparsely vegetated, sandy, or rocky areas receiving extremely low, highly seasonal, and rapidly evaporating rainfall. Unlike the sidewinder, they prefer boulder-strewn, hot, dry foothills commonly found within deserts.

The monotypic tiger rattlesnake, *Crotalus tigris*, is found in localized pockets in south-central Arizona and Sonora, Mexico. An isolated pocket has been discovered recently near the New Mexico–Arizona border. Little is known about this rattlesnake's natural history. Because its head is proportionately smaller than that of any other rattlesnake, it is believed it can more readily probe into constricted areas in search of lizards. Tiger rattlesnake venom is highly toxic, but the amount injected is usually small. It is more than adequate to subdue any of the numerous suitably sized saurians that share its range. Captive tiger rattlesnakes readily consume lizards but will eat small rodents as well. Although they may be observed basking throughout the warm months, they are most active for a brief few weeks in August during the summer monsoon season. Because the majority found wandering about are males, it is a logical assumption that they are seeking mates at this time.

The five subspecies of the speckled rattlesnake, *Crotalus mitchellii*, resemble the tiger rattlesnake in coloration and habitat preference but have larger and more distinct heads. They seem to prefer small mammals and birds but will eat lizards. Their venom is relatively potent. Fairly large numbers have been found hibernating together

among the deep fissures of the rocky, dry foothill canyons they inhabit. They are more wide ranging than the tiger rattlesnake, preferring hotter and drier rocky parts of the Sonoran and the Mojave deserts to the north and west.

The three forms of Baja California rattlesnake, *Crotalus enyo*, live strictly within the boundaries of that Mexican peninsula. One is an insular form. Again, dry and hot rocky canyons are the habitat of choice, but some specimens have been found in chaparral and at the fringes of the tropical deciduous forest. When hurriedly traveling across sandy stretches, they may employ sidewinding. This type of locomotion is commonly used by neonates. The Baja California rattlesnake has large eyes, most likely enabling them to more readily see movement of lizards and small mammal prey. Like the tiger rattlesnake, this species has a proportionately smaller, narrower head than most other rattlesnakes. (Incidentally, many nocturnal snakes have disproportionately large eyes.)

The two subspecies of Mojave rattlesnake, *Crotalus scutulatus*, are desert dwellers throughout most of their range, but brushy grassland and semidesert areas are also chosen. Because of the variety of habitats and similar food preferences, they are a major competitor of the other desert rattlesnakes. In some places they are extremely common, whereas sympatric species are rare or absent. Distinct variations in the quality and toxicity of venom have been found in populations from different parts of the range. This may be somehow correlated with the habitat, or it may be a signal of additional genetically separable subspecies or demes.

Several other rattlesnakes are closely allied with desert environments in parts of their range but inhabit more diversified niches elsewhere. Most notable are the western diamondback, *Crotalus atrox*, the desert phase of the red diamond rattlesnake, *Crotalus ruber ruber*, and a lowland morph of the northern blacktail rattlesnake, *Crotalus molossus molossus*.

Mesic Rattlesnakes

Concordant to popular opinion, very few species of rattlesnakes live in permanently wet, marshy environments. Nearly all are *Sistrurus*. Although the eastern massasauga, *Sistrurus catenatus catenatus*, is commonly seen in lower wetlands only during the early spring and late fall, it is rarely encountered in water, preferring the drier tussocks and grassy islands with a preponderance of crayfish burrows within the wet zones. There is a higher concentration of them there at those times because the boggy areas are the preferred hibernation sites. They commonly hibernate in crayfish burrows.

A unique subspecies of rock rattlesnake, the Tamaulipan rock rattlesnake, *Crotalus lepidus morulus*, inhabits isolated talus in that Mexican state.

North of Monument Valley *(above)* and throughout most of Utah, the small, subtle-colored midget faded rattlesnake, *Crotalus viridis concolor (left),* is found.

Lack of foliage and more barren ground make the snake more visible. With spring warming, massasaugas move into more productive foraging areas afforded by higher ground. Incidentally, *mississauga* (massasauga) means "great river mouth" in Chippewa, probably referring to the snakes' tendency to inhabit swamplands at the mouths of rivers.

The two western massasauga subspecies, the western massasauga, *Sistrurus catenatus tergeminus,* and the desert-grassland massasauga, *Sistrurus catenatus edwardsii,* live in grassy areas that retain a higher percentage of moisture than the surrounding open environment. At the western edge of its range, in extreme southeastern Arizona, the desert-grassland massasauga has been able to survive (but is uncommon) in heavily desertified places. It spends a great deal of time in moist rodent burrows among the grasses. This may be found to be typical behavior of both of the western massasauga races.

The closely related eastern pigmy rattlesnakes, *Sistrurus miliarius,* show an affinity for wet habitats. The Florida form is most commonly encountered adjacent to swampy areas. Populations of the Mexican pigmy, *Sistrurus ravus,* however, are found in arid environments as well as moist cloud forests, at much higher elevations than the U.S. forms. They are often quite far from water.

Habitats

A few varieties of neotropical rattlesnake, *Crotalus durissus,* have been encountered in rain forests and, more rarely, in cloud forests. These are exceptions, because this taxon favors drier savannas and grasslands. In fact, its range appears very wide (like montane taxa), and its distribution is extremely spotty. It is usually limited to suitable, open, frequently grassy, drier tracts scattered about and within rain forests.

Rattlesnakes may be found traveling through almost any type of terrain, but the greatest concentration of actual habitat is in fairly open territory or areas bordering it. Canopy (trees and shrubs blocking direct sunlight) can be influential because it inhibits basking. The availability of suitable ground cover and retreats that provide shelter are more significant factors. Timber rattlesnakes, *Crotalus horridus horridus,* spend most of their summer months foraging in fairly dense eastern forests with a modicum of brush, fallen leaves, and decaying logs. During the warmer months, eastern diamondbacks, *Crotalus adamanteus,* live within a dense understory of palmetto and scrub.

Banded rock, *Crotalus lepidus klauberi,* and western twin-spotted rattlesnakes, *Crotalus pricei pricei,* abound on certain rock slides in southeastern Arizona. Massive, sprawling prairie dog colonies frequently harbor great numbers of prairie rattlesnakes, *Crotalus viridis viridis.* Northern Pacific rattlesnakes, *Crotalus viridis oreganus,* although fairly large, have managed to maintain sizable densities in large urban parks.

When habitat is ideal and food is abundant, it is not uncommon to find rattlesnakes living in groups. In parts of Florida, dusky pigmy rattlesnakes, *Sistrurus miliarius barbouri,* can be plentiful in a small area but be totally lacking in nearby sites. Dozens have been observed within an area of 350 square feet (100 square meters). As many as 500 to 600 have been estimated to inhabit a 20-acre (8.1-hectare) plot near Jacksonville, Florida.

The pigmy rattlesnakes' habitat selection and population density have produced serious consequences for humans. The following example is little more than the obvious result of human's interrelationship and conflict with nature.

Weather in portions of southern Florida is ideal for cultivating a variety of plants. Nurseries grow shrubs, almost unattended, in expansive tracts of fertile land. For expediency they are grown in partially buried containers. The moist conditions attract insects, which attract frogs and lizards, which in turn attract dusky pigmy rattlesnakes, *Sistrurus miliarius barbouri.* The conditions are so favorable, rattlesnake populations may attain exceptional density in a few years.

When the plants reach sufficient size, the containers are extracted and shipped to nurseries and garden supply stores. Because they are small and secretive in nature, some rattlesnakes remain hidden within these containers. Essentially, this has been a portion of their habitat for a great part of their lives. In recent years, on different occasions, while inspecting plants in the nursery departments of variety stores, at least three Floridians have been bitten by sequestered rattlesnakes.

FROM HEAD TO TAIL: THE RATTLESNAKE'S EXTERIOR

"The Crotalus" is the largest of our rattlesnakes, reaching even to the length of eight feet. . . . I have seen others over seven feet long; a more disgusting and terrific animal can not be imagined than this; its dusky colour, bloated body, and sinister eyes of sparkling gray and yellow, with the projecting orbital plates, combine to form an expression of sullen ferocity unsurpassed in the brute creation.

—John Edwards Holbrook

No one can deny that the symmetry, pattern, and color woven throughout the bodies of the various rattlesnakes place them among nature's most simplistically designed and beautiful animals. Over thousands of years, many rattlesnake races developed unique coats with color and pattern that work as effective camouflage within their habitat. Known as *cryptic coloration,* this phenomenon is the product of natural selection. Those selected have a more successful rate of survival to sexual maturity, and pass on these traits via genes to their offspring.

Rattlesnakes have evolved some of the most intricate patterns of all snakes. They have crossbands, chevrons, diamonds, blotches, spots, and mottling, but none is solely and completely longitudinally striped.

The exceptions are some of the timber rattlesnakes, *Crotalus horridus horridus,* that have an almost continuous, rust-colored vertebral stripe.

The prominent supraocular scale over each sidewinder's eye (here a Sonoran Desert sidewinder, *Crotalus cerastes cercobombus*) provides protection for the eye. When the snake burrows in loose sand, the soft, elongated scale is forced down, partially covering the lidless eye. Other rattlesnakes have similar, but smaller, less-flexible supraocular protuberances. Although their function is frequently debated, these scales are generally believed to act as eye shades, enabling the snake to see while prowling in bright sunlight.

Lack of pattern is an uncommon aberrancy among rattlesnakes. These unusual specimens of the western diamondback, *Crotalus atrox (left)*, and the red diamond rattlesnake, *Crotalus ruber ruber (below)*, have similar brownish coloration and completely lack their distinct diamond-shaped markings. On closer examination, faint longitudinal stripes can be seen. The otherwise prominent black and white banded ("coon") tails are darker and longitudinally striped.

However, the dark chevrons and crossbands still dominate. Most timber rattlesnakes from the northeastern United States and Appalachian Mountains lack this trait. The stripe is most obvious in southern examples and is a characteristic of the lowland subspecies, the canebrake rattlesnake, *Crotalus horridus atricaudatus*.

In other taxa the colors may contrast boldly, fuse into an unpretentious blanket, or be so faded the snake appears almost patternless. Frequently, all the members of a particular population are patterned and colored to blend with the soil and rocks of that location. This is clearly seen in speckled rattlesnakes, *Crotalus mitchellii*, where individuals living in pinkish quartz rock are almost always pink, those inhabiting tan rocks are tan, or grayish ones are mostly gray. It is believed that offspring born without this matching coloration are selected against by being more vulnerable to predators and will likely eventually be eliminated from the population.

Unlike the brightly colored red, yellow, and black banded coral snakes, and their tri-colored milk snake mimics, rattlesnakes have few showy, vibrant colors (reds, yellows, blues) to draw attention to them. Most brilliantly colored snakes are mostly small and fossorial, rarely out on the surface. Their color is a surprise or warning device (apposmatic or phaneric coloration). A potential predator capable of seeing color is so startled by a flash of color, it stops and shies away for a brief second. At the same instant, the snake bolts, making a speedy escape. Most rattlesnakes will take flight only if their pattern has failed to camouflage them. Most wild eastern massasaugas, *Sistrurus catenatus catenatus,* go undetected by people because they remain motionless, refusing to rattle when casually approached to within 18 inches (46 centimeters). It is even more interesting that they refuse to strike defensively until they are restrained. This provocation initiates repeated strikes.

Typifying other wide-ranging forms, the western diamondback, *Crotalus atrox,* maintains its distinctive pattern of large white and black or brown diamonds throughout its range. However, the suffused background varies from silvery gray and white to an array of subtle pinks, tans, yellows, and greens, closely matching the dominant colors of the surrounding countryside. Lying coiled in the bright morning sun, with the broken shadows of a creosote bush adding to its disruptive pattern, a full-grown adult is easily overlooked. This same rattlesnake crossing a road stands out from 50 yards (46 meters) away.

The finely stippled blue-green background with contrasting, almost black crossbands or blotches permits the banded rock rattlesnake, *Crotalus lepidus klauberi,* to blend so well with the crumbled, lichen-covered rocks of its habitat that most are heard buzzing before they are seen.

The color of a rattlesnake's tongue ranges from light pink to rich black, differing with the species. Some have a varying amount of pigment, becoming darker toward the tips. So far, no explanation or correlation has been given for the differences in tongue coloration, but it may serve a cryptic function.

Pigmentation

Color and pattern in reptiles are dependent on special pigment cells (chromatophores) found in the deep layer of the skin, the dermis. These color-producing cells are called *melanophores, xanthophores,* and *iridophores*. Melanophores synthesize black and brown pigments called *melanin,* and xanthophores synthesize reds and yellows. Some scientists separate the red-synthesizing cells, calling them *erythrophores*. Iridophores contain granules that are highly reflective to thermal and light waves. They contribute to the color production by reflecting available light, accounting for subtle hues such as tans, grays, blues, and greens.

Melanophores are the most prevalent pigment cells. There are two types, dermal and epidermal, depending on their location in the skin. The individual cells are variable in shape with cytoplasmic, branch-like processes. The amount of melanin, interacting with the other pigments and reflections of the iridophores, produces the overall variety of color and pattern.

Melanin performs other perhaps more important functions, shielding and protecting the internal organs from solar radiation while helping in thermoregulation. Iridophores and xanthophores appear to play an additional role in thermoregulation. Dark skin is beneficial for absorbing radiant energy. Most high elevation and northerly forms are more deeply pigmented. Except for one New Mexican population of the western diamondback that inhabits dark lava fields, no low-desert dwelling rattlesnakes have normal melanistic phases. They are predominantly light colored to better reflect the harsh sun, and the paler hue also contributes to their camouflage.

A pituitary hormone, MSH (melanocyte stimulating hormone), stimulates the dispersion of melanin granules. Several species have the ability to contract and expand their melanophores, lightening or darkening the basic pigmentation. In addition, this appears to be a regulatory function involved with body temperature control. Some melanin is transferred from the melanophores into the epidermal cells and is shed with the outermost keratinized layer. This accounts for some of the coloration and pattern that is discernible in the shed skins of many snakes.

Melanism

Of all the rattlesnakes, the eastern massasauga, *Sistrurus catenatus catenatus,* the northern Pacific, *Crotalus viridis oreganus,* the Arizona black, *Crotalus viridis cerberus,* and the timber rattlesnake, *Crotalus horridus horridus,* have normal melanistic (darkly pigmented, almost completely black) adult phases. They are born with a vivid normal pattern, typical of those taxa. Maturation brings an overall darkening of the skin. Frequently, it is so deep and rich that it resembles black velvet. Because they are not born black they are not truly

An amelanistic western diamondback, *Crotalus atrox*—offspring from several generations of such animals bred at the Dallas Zoo.

melanistic. Colonies of nearly all-black adult eastern massasaugas and northern Pacific rattlesnakes have been found.

There are examples of denning colonies of timber rattlesnakes, *Crotalus horridus horridus,* that comprise only dark-phase snakes, including a New York population and a colony remaining in New Hampshire. Except for Alabama and south-central Tennessee (where timber rattlesnakes are all pale), most Appalachian colonies have light (yellow-morph) and dark (black-morph) examples. Dark snakes are associated with damp, cool forests.

At least one small population of the southern Pacific rattlesnake, *Crotalus viridis helleri,* from west of Los Angeles, has an overall gray appearance. Other pigment cells are greatly reduced, but the pattern (produced by the melanin) is vivid and bright. Known as *axanthism* or *anerythrism* (reduced red pigmentation), it has been noted in examples of several other snake taxa as well.

In many cases, the Arizona black rattlesnake, *Crotalus viridis cerberus,* is a misnomer. Although very dark as an adult, most specimens are a deeply saturated brown. The bright silvery white, gray, and black pattern of the juvenile changes drastically in its second year, achieving a full somber hue with distinct narrow crossbanding in its third season.

Aberrant Coloration

Distinct from rattlesnakes that darken as adults, truly aberrantly colored ones are occasionally born. Abnormal production or varying amounts of pigment are responsible. In the wild, these genetic

Above: **A spectacular amelanistic southern Pacific rattlesnake, *Crotalus viridis helleri.***

Below: **The same amelanistic specimen that is shown above, along with another of the same subspecies that has an axanthic (gray) aberrancy and is from near Lake Elsinore, California.**

anomalies are usually short lived. Their colors are so strikingly different that they may afford little camouflage from predators.

Albinism is probably the most common color aberrancy. Albinism (more properly called *amelanism* in reptiles) is a biochemical defect in the synthesis of melanin caused by a genetic mutation and is a consistently heritable recessive trait. It results in the absence of, or diminished, black or brown pigment in the skin and eyes. Because the xanthophores (xanthophore–erythrophore complex) are not affected by the albino mutation, most individuals are actually partial albinos. They have a yellow background color with a red or orange pattern and pink eyes. This is unlike albino birds and mammals that are pure white with pink eyes. The lack of eye pigment impairs their vision because a great deal of light is reflected and scattered, rather than absorbed and passed into the visual receptor cells.

In theory, an all-yellow or all-red rattlesnake could be produced provided that, along with amelanism, the complementary pigment is lacking. These color aberrancies have been found in other snakes, but to date not in rattlesnakes.

Examples of amelanistic eastern diamondbacks, *Crotalus adamanteus,* are seen from two distinct areas. The younger one *(top)* is from near Fitzgerald, Georgia, and the slightly larger one *(bottom)* is from near Ocala, Florida. Over the years, several other examples have been captured from the same regions.

A very rare abnormality is a snow-white snake with normally pigmented eyes or, as in one recorded case, blue eyes. This genetic mutation is known as *leucism.* Leucistic snakes lack functional melanophores and xanthophores and have a reduced number of iridophores.

Once again, with the topic of coloration, we are confronted with biochemistry, a complex science beyond the scope of this book. However, some basic explanation is warranted. *Tyrosinase* is a major enzyme responsible for catalyzing and metabolizing the amino acid tyrosine into melanin. Although there is no way to visually distinguish

Right: This axanthic red diamond rattlesnake, *Crotalus ruber ruber,* was captured near Lake Elsinore, California.

Below: The Houston Zoo has bred several generations of xanthic, hypomelanistic northwestern neotropical rattlesnakes, *Crotalus durissus culminatus.* One is pictured here with a normal specimen.

This is probably the only known living example of an axanthic, hypermelanistic eastern diamondback, *Crotalus adamanteus*.

Another aberrant eastern diamondback, *Crotalus adamanteus*. The pale coloration from lack of vivid black and yellow pigments (hypomelanism and hypoxanthism) has led herpetologists to call this mutant a "ghost" morph.

between them, two forms of genetic mutations have been uncovered that cause albinism. One that prevents the synthesis of tyrosinase produces tyrosinase-negative albinos. The other, capable of synthesizing tyrosinase but unable to manufacture melanin, produces similar appearing tyrosinase-positive albinos.

Additional color abnormalities involving other chromatophores have been recorded. The most common is a genetic mutation that prevents the proper functioning of xanthophores. *Axanthism* is a decrease or absence of the pigments synthesized by the xanthophores. Axanthic snakes contain no reds or yellows; the color pattern is determined solely by melanophores and iridophores.

Hypomelanism, a drastic but incomplete reduction in black pigment, is another variation found in some individuals. A reduction but not complete lack of yellow is *hypoxanthism*, and reduction of red is *hypoerythrism*. The opposite, an increased amount of a pigment, would assume the prefix "hyper-." Hypermelanistic examples were discussed previously. A colony of otherwise normally patterned Carolina pigmy rattlesnakes, *Sistrurus miliarius miliarius*, from eastern North Carolina (known as the Hyde County morph) has a very high percentage of bright red pigment caused by hypererythrism.

Above: A beautiful hypererythristic morph of the Carolina pigmy rattlesnake, *Sistrurus miliarius miliarius,* is found in Hyde County, North Carolina. Habitat destruction and overcollecting have seriously reduced the wild population. Fortunately, it is being successfully bred in captivity.

Right: In certain parts of northern Florida, hypermelanistic dusky pigmy rattlesnakes, *Sistrurus miliarius barbouri,* are occasionally found.

A truly unique, actually rather weird, pattern-aberrant prairie rattlesnake, *Crotalus viridis viridis*. There are small patches of pure white (piebaldism) on the sides and an amorphous pattern and mixture of colors. Nothing is known about this particular specimen other than it was caught in the wild in North Dakota. Pythons that have been bred with a similar aberrant pattern are called *calico* by herpetoculturists.

Areas of snow-white skin interspacing amorphous or unpatterned darker areas constitute yet another rare abberancy: piebaldism. This red diamond rattlesnake, *Crotalus ruber ruber,* was caught at a dry lake, Lake Chapala in Baja California, as a youngster.

Aberrant Patterns

Perhaps the most bizarre color abnormality is piebaldism—normally colored snakes containing random, distinct, white, patternless patches. Unusual patterns, like striping, zigzag, or longitudinally connected blotches or diamonds, are infrequent but have been documented. Genetic mutations, abnormal temperatures during thermoregulation, or other stress factors while in utero are known to cause color-pattern anomalies. More research needs to be done to determine the origin and development of these aberrations.

Patternless rattlesnakes have also been found. A diffused dark color predominates. The lack of any pattern tends to support the hypothesis that melanin for pattern and coloration are genetically independent.

A portrait of this hypererythristic, cranberry-colored Humantlan rattlesnake, *Crotalus scutulatus salvini,* appears elsewhere in this book, but this animal has such an amazing appearance that it merits a full-body illustration.

Head

When viewed close up a rattlesnake's head is seen in all its beauty. Portraits disclose delicate nuances with a palette of bright, showy colors and markings not seen in many animals. Discerning herpetologists have favorites, but many feel the ridgenose rattlesnake, *Crotalus willardi,* has the most eye-catching head of all the rattlesnakes.

Applying minimal imagination, one can readily see the uncanny resemblance to Apache war paint. Two bold, snow-white stripes splashed across the plain reddish-brown head delineate a darker, mask-like section. One line extends diagonally from the tip of raised nose scales (the *canthus rostralis*), along the entire face, below the eye, to the junction of the jaw. Here it joins the other that shadows it, closely following the line of the lower lips. An equally bright, white, vertical line bisects the snout. There is no documentation, but it is conceivable that Apache warriors chose their vivid facial markings from this little rattlesnake. Surely their paths crossed, because its habitat is well within the Apache mountain hunting grounds.

Head Scales

Unlike other snakes with modified head scales to facilitate burrowing in loose sand or gravel, the ridgenose rattlesnake's rostrum (from which its common name is derived) appears to have no evident function. There are no records of burrowing proclivity, and the surface of the rocky forested areas they inhabit is difficult to penetrate by burrowing. The ridge might facilitate moving through leaf litter or probing the head into tight areas between rocks and debris. It is puzzling that the nominate form, the Arizona ridgenose rattlesnake, *Crotalus willardi willardi,* has only a minor protrusion, and the most recently derived subspecies, the New Mexican ridgenose rattlesnake, *Crotalus willardi obscurus,* has the most prominent. Generally, this type of variation implies an adaptation that is still evolving.

Normally, the pattern of a Central Plateau pigmy rattlesnake, *Sistrurus ravus ravus,* is a series of blotches. This aberrancy (blotches connected into longitudinal stripes), although very unusual, has been observed in several other snake taxa.

Taxonomists employ the distinctive patterns and the configuration of head scales of the various rattlesnake taxa to differentiate forms. Each type of head scale is named for its position and shape. Their arrangement and number remain fairly constant within the same species. When that information is combined with other attributes, such as overall color and pattern, size, and number of body scale rows, similarities and differences have been defined. These scale patterns often justify subspecific designation.

As we have seen earlier, the two rattlesnake genera are distinguished by the size and grouping of the scales on top of the head. Those with a crown covered with a series of small similar-sized scales belong to the larger genus *Crotalus*. The others, with a grouping of nine larger symmetrically arranged scales, belong to the more primitive *Sistrurus*.

The paired supraoculars appear to have adapted to assist the snake's lifestyle. Situated directly above each eye, they act as visors, shielding the sun. They are more prominent on desert and prairie forms, but others have them as well. Among rattlesnakes, the supraoculars of the sidewinder, *Crotalus cerastes,* are uniquely modified. Elongated and pointed, they extend well over each eye and are

responsible for its other common name, horned rattlesnake. Their specific name, *cerastes,* means "horned." The scales are soft and fleshy and are pressured into folding over, partially covering the eye, when the snake is burrowing in sand or moving through rodent or lizard burrows. This prevents sand, roots, and debris from scratching the transparent eye covering.

Skin

A rattlesnake's skin is shaped as a series of roughly textured scales that overlap at the posterior edge and cover the entire body dorsally. It is important to understand that snake and fish scales are not homologous. Snake scales originate in the epidermal layer and are texturized folds in a continuous covering, whereas fish scales originate in the dermal layer and are separate and removable. Snake scales are a major protection against many life-threatening hazards, such as desiccation and direct physical damage. All rattlesnake dorsal scales have an elevated central ridge (a keel) running their length. The one or two most lateral rows lack keels. The keels add strength and elasticity to the scales. When large prey are

Each ridgenose rattlesnake subspecies has slightly different facial markings. Differences in physical factors such as facial striping, size of the canthus rostralis (the scales forming the ridge along the "nose"), and pattern are used to distinguish the subspecies and partially demonstrate the evolution of their lineage. *Clockwise from top left:* The Arizona ridgenose rattlesnake, *Crotalus willardi willardi,* has the most vivid and defined facial markings, and the New Mexican ridgenose rattlesnake, *Crotalus willardi obscurus,* has the least. The other subspecies include the southern ridgenose, *Crotalus willardi meridionalis,* the Del Nido ridgenose, *Crotalus willardi amabilis,* and the western Chihuahuan ridgenose, *Crotalus willardi silus.*

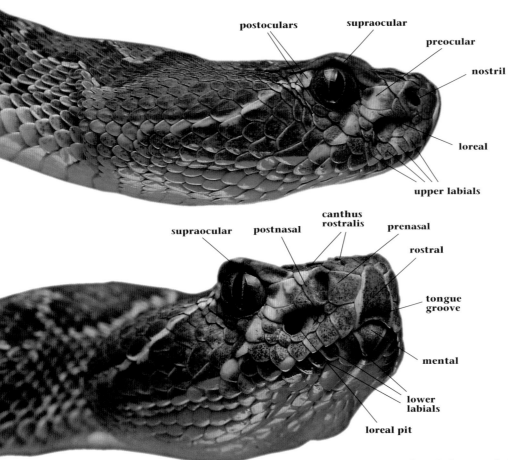

postoculars   supraocular

preocular

nostril

loreal

upper labials

supraocular   postnasal   canthus rostralis   prenasal

rostral

tongue groove

mental

lower labials

loreal pit

The position and number of various rattlesnake head scales are clearly seen on this prairie rattlesnake, *Crotalus viridis viridis*. These are important characters in defining many rattlesnake forms.

ingested, creases between the scales unfold, permitting food animals larger than the snake's girth to be accommodated. The skin appears to be greatly stretched, but in fact it is barely taxed. Also, keels reduce shininess, thereby enhancing cryptic coloration.

Ventral scutes, long plate-like scales that run almost completely across the belly, are highly modified to aid in locomotion. Unlike dorsal scales, they are smooth, flat, and elongated and run singularly and transversely across the venter. They are attached and hinged anteriorly. The free, posterior edge is rather thin, almost sharp, and slightly overlaps its successor. When the snake is moving, muscles elevate the loose edge, providing additional traction on any textured surface. Daily movement against the ground, rocks, branches, and the like produces extensive wear to the snake's ventral scutes.

A large, specially modified scale, the anal scute, covers and protects the vent. The cloaca, which receives the terminal ducts of the digestive, reproductive, and urinary tracts, terminates in the vent. Unlike other ventral scales, the subcaudals are on the underside of the tail, distal to the cloaca. Arranged as singular, transverse scales, they are occasionally and randomly paired or divided into two rows as they are in colubrid snakes.

The snake's ability to shed its outer layer of skin has long fascinated people. Ancient religions of the Americas bestowed supernatural abilities on snakes, believing them to have the power of rebirth. All in all, shedding is a necessary, reasonable process. Vertebrates normally shed the outer layer of skin cells (the epidermis) as part of growing and to repair the surface. In humans, shedding is an ongoing but difficult to detect process, because the cells flake off in microscopic quantities. A trauma to the skin, such as acute sunburn, presents more graphic sloughing.

The innermost layer of the skin, the dermis, is the thickest. It supplies most of the integrity and support, as well as accommodating pigment cells. The horny outer epidermis of reptiles is developed with a thick layer of keratin that encases the body, shielding the thin sensitive growing layer, the inner epidermis, directly beneath it. Snakes' eyes are also covered with this layer, an important adaptation because they do not have movable lids. The lower lid fuses with the upper during development, forming a transparent scale called the *spectacle*. Although this scale protects the sensitive underlying cornea from abrasion, it hampers the snakes vision, especially as it becomes worn from daily activities and just prior to shedding.

Damage to other parts of the skin is inflicted by bites from both prey and predators and by minor accidents. Many adult snakes have scars of varying sizes. In the southeast, where burning underbrush is part of successful tree farming, luckless eastern diamondbacks, *Crotalus adamanteus*, canebrakes, *Crotalus horridus atricaudatus*, and dusky pigmy rattlesnakes, *Sistrurus miliarius barbouri*, frequently have burn scars. From time to time, cactus spines pierce the skin of desert snakes. Some spines fall out from the attrition of movement; others are pulled out with the shed skin. After a time, deeply embedded spines will wear off at the surface but remain internally. Most cause no further damage.

The basal (inner) layer of the epidermis is constantly producing new cells that move up toward the surface. As they approach the surface, they are keratinized into an expendable dead outer epidermal layer that is periodically shed. In warmer regions, shedding (also known as *molting* and *sloughing*) occurs as often as three times a year. Timber rattlesnakes, *Crotalus horridus horridus,* in the northern states normally shed once or twice a year. Injured snakes, particularly those with skin damage, shed more frequently as the body attempts to repair itself. Young snakes will undergo additional molts if growing conditions are ideal. Captives raised under prolonged favorable conditions shed as many as six times during the first year. More commonly, juvenile timber rattlesnakes in northern regions shed once or twice a year, whereas those with longer, warmer growing seasons in the south may shed up to four times in a year.

Approximately ten days prior to shedding, fluid is formed between the living and dead layers to facilitate shedding. The snake takes on a dull milky or cloudy appearance, most noticeable in the eye and the basal rattle segment. Vision is impaired by the cloudy liquid, forcing the snake into inactivity or hiding. During this period the snake is said to be *opaque* or *blue* or *cloudy*. Most of the fluid dissipates a few days before shedding. Sloughing begins when the snake finds a rough surface on which to rub its snout and loosen the edge of the skin.

The noticeable milky cast in the eye of an eastern massasauga, *Sistrurus catenatus catenatus,* discloses that it is a few days from shedding its skin. The cloudy appearance is caused by fluid produced between the entire old outer layer of skin and the new one beneath it. Herpetologists say a snake in this state is *opaque* or *blue*. The eye will clear when the fluid passes through the outer layer in a few days, just before the snake sheds.

Shedding begins when the skin covering the head has been rubbed and lifted from the labials and has begun to be pulled back. Note that the transparent covering of the eye is part of the shed skin. The snake will continue to rub the loosened end of the shedding layer until it catches on a branch, twig, or other stable object. Once caught, it will continue to peel back and away. Eventually, the snake will move out from within the skin, leaving the shed skin inside out.

The shed is usually in one piece, starting at the lips (labials) and snout. With continued rubbing and crawling, the loose end is caught on a branch, rock, or similar object, is forced backward, and peels off inside out. Exercising caterpillar movement, the snake appears to be walking out of its old skin. The entire process is best likened to removing a sock by peeling it from the ankle downward and off.

For several minutes the shed skin remains moist and elastic. It is a complete replica, like a casting, of the snake. Every scale and contour is there, including the spectacle and lining of the pit cavity. The only openings are at the mouth, anal scute (covering the cloaca), nostrils, and end of the tail. Scars are evident. Traces of pattern can be discerned in the sheds of some taxa, and others are vividly marked.

In short order the shed will be recycled. It will dry out and disintegrate, be eaten by a variety of scavengers, or (ironically) be used by birds and rodents (frequently the prey of rattlesnakes) in building their nests.

The new skin offers the snake in all its beauty. Its color and pattern will not be as bright and radiant again until immediately after the next shed. In the mating season, females' skin pheromones (sex attractant odors) are most intense immediately following a shed and are invaluable in attracting and stimulating males. Nevares and Quijada-Mascarenas ("*Crotalus scutulatus scutulatus:* Mating Behavior," *Herpetology Review* 20:71 [1989]) reported that a pair of juvenile Mojave rattlesnake yearlings were housed together and engaged in prolonged coitus (7.5 hours) initiated by the female's shedding.

Incidentally, not unlike most other vertebrates, cells lining the mouth are sloughed somewhat indiscriminately and pass into the alimentary canal. But those covering the tongue are shed together. In captivity, it is not uncommon to find a tongue shed, usually split nearly in half, in a water dish.

Rattle

Among all snakes only the shed skin of a rattlesnake has an opening at the tip of the blunt tail as a distinguishing characteristic. The missing piece of skin is left as another segment to the rattle. In other snakes the scale at the tip of the tapered tail is sharply cone-shaped and shed as part of the skin.

In rattlesnakes this terminal scale is much larger, thicker, and peculiarly shaped with two annular constrictions. These indentations provide the two, three, or four grooves and ridges that enable a loose interlocking of the previous hollow rings. They are better described as shells, or most preferably as keratinized segments. Similar to human fingernails, the dry material is tough and pliable, as keratin is its chief constituent.

Rattlesnakes are born with a prebutton, a skin cap on the tail tip of the newborn snake. The prebutton differs little (except for its slightly larger size) from the terminal scale of other snakes. At the first shed a few days after birth, the prebutton is molted with the skin and is replaced by the underlying button that was present within the skin cap. With each subsequent shedding throughout

This larger-than-life cross-sectional model of a rattle shows how each segment interlocks with the previous one. Also, it shows how these hollow lobes loosely overlap to enable movement but fit tightly enough to not fall off when the tail is shaken. Rattle segments are made of dry, horny, keratinized skin (much like human fingernails).

The variation in size and shape of rattles of different species and genera. *From left:* eastern diamondback rattlesnake, *Crotalus adamanteus;* western diamondback rattlesnake, *Crotalus atrox;* northern Pacific rattlesnake, *Crotalus viridis oreganus;* mottled rock rattlesnake, *Crotalus lepidus lepidus;* eastern twin-spotted rattlesnake, *Crotalus pricei miquihuanus;* and dusky pigmy rattlesnake, *Sistrurus miliarius barbouri.* The only complete string (with a terminal segment) here is the western diamondback's. The rattles have been arranged in an erect position. The shape of the segments causes them to lean away from the direction in which the rattlesnake would be moving.

Above: A close-up of the rattleless Santa Catalina Island rattlesnake, *Crotalus catalinensis.* Likely, there is no need for a rattle as a warning device because there are no animals on the island large enough to step on the rattlesnake accidentally, and it therefore has evolved away from having one.

Right: Many examples of another island form, the San Lorenzo Island diamond rattlesnake, *Crotalus ruber lorenzoensis,* are maturing without rattles, probably for the same reason as for the Santa Catalina Island rattlesnake.

the life of the snake, a new rattle segment is added to the chain, while another is formed inside it, at the base of the rattle.

A complete rattle string is identified by the tapering series of rings (segments) terminating with a smooth, conical button. As the snake reaches maturity and growth subsides, new segments are almost equal in size to their predecessor, eliminating the taper. The snake's daily activity and accidents that cause breakage to its rattle determine the number of segments retained. In the wild, more than ten segments are exceptional, but sedentary zoo specimens may have two dozen or more. While traveling, the rattle is held vertically, which affords some protection.

Regularly, segments toward the tip of the rattle break off from wear. Sometimes an accident or genetic mutation will render a rattlesnake permanently incapable of producing the appendage. One insular form, the Santa Catalina Island rattlesnake, *Crotalus catalinensis,* has evolved without a rattle. It has been postulated that in this species the rattle has atrophied, is now vestigial, and no longer has a function.

The San Lorenzo Island diamond rattlesnake, *Crotalus ruber lorenzoensis,* commonly matures without a rattle. Several examples of the San Esteban Island blacktail rattlesnake, *Crotalus molossus estebanensis,* have been found without rattles as well. Perhaps in a few thousand years these two other insular rattlesnakes may be completely rattleless as well.

Sound of a Rattle

When frightened, rattlesnakes are quick to react by vibrating their tails. The loose, interlocking segments click and clack against each other like castanets, producing the characteristic rattling sound. Observers have likened the noise of various species to whizzing, whirring, clattering, buzzing, hissing, escaping steam, shaking seeds in a pod, sizzling bacon, grinding a knife blade, running water, or the vibration calls of various insects. None of these sounds is exactly like a rattling rattlesnake, however. I consider it is mostly a buzzing sound. The range of sounds, rate of vibration, and loudness are governed by the species, temperament, size, number of segments, and ambient temperature.

A large aroused eastern diamondback, *Crotalus adamanteus,* in a warm environment produces a distinctive, deep, resonating cacophony that carries many yards. There is little chance it would go unheard. Under similar conditions, a prairie rattlesnake, *Crotalus viridis viridis,* one of the more excitable mid-sized forms, emits a higher pitched, more rapid, distinctive whirring. It too would be quite audible but would not carry nearly as far. Of the small, sometimes diminutive varieties, the pigmy rattlesnake, *Sistrurus miliarius,* would not be heard more than a few feet away (about a meter), if at all. Its buzzing compares with that of small insects.

A very specialized shaker muscle is responsible for the tail's movement. Physiologically, the muscle contracts at a rapid and consistent rate and is extremely slow to fatigue. If provoked, some species can maintain a full rattling for nearly three hours. A rich supply of blood vessels, permitting rapid oxygen transfer, is a major adaptation enabling this action by the shaker muscle. Temperature is the primary factor in the rate of vibration. The warmer it is, the more rapid the vibration. At full tilt, with the ambient temperature about 90°F (32.2°C), the rattle is a blur, moving at more than sixty cycles per second. The same animal, when cooled to 55°F (13°C), responds with a rattling as low as twenty cycles per second. Personalities also affect a snake's propensity to rattle. Red diamond rattlesnakes, *Crotalus ruber,* are generally quite placid, rarely choosing to display. Western diamondbacks, *Crotalus atrox,* are the antithesis, rattling with a fervor that coincides with their irascible dispositions.

A magnificent, exceptionally long string of rattles of a captive red diamond rattlesnake, *Crotalus ruber ruber.* The rigors of daily living would make it impossible for a wild rattlesnake to maintain a rattle of this length. Even with its remarkable length, this example is missing a few terminal segments.

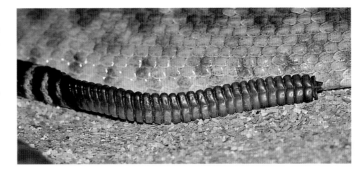

Exceptionally long rattle strings defeat the purpose of having a rattle. Weight and number of segments slow down the action, asynchronizing the movement. The sound is diminished by moisture when the segments become waterlogged. A wet rattlesnake caught out in a heavy rain or swimming long distances is almost mute.

Functions of the Rattle

The most widely accepted hypothesis for the evolution of the rattle is that the rattle is a warning device for predatory animals that might be a threat to the rattlesnake. It produces a signal to drive them away. Its effectiveness varies greatly with the situation. On the tranquil open range where free-roaming cattle, through their constant meandering and browsing, could easily trample a snake, the strident sound of an irate rattlesnake would send them scrambling. Surely bison would have a similar reaction.

Incidentally, many of the more nervous, harmless snake varieties (colubrid snakes) vibrate their tails when disturbed. In dry leaves the sound produced by them is very similar to that of a rattlesnake. Predators most likely respond as though they were encountering one of their venomous cousins.

It is little wonder that the rattle's uniqueness has encouraged many people to view it as having mystical properties. Many Native Americans, although they generally fear snakes, wear rattles around their necks as talismans or charms. They are believed to protect the wearer from his or her enemies (including snakes), giving them great strength in battle, warding off evil spirits and disease, and appeasing the gods. Some credit the rattle with aphrodisiac and fertility properties.

Certainly, rattling and the accompanying menacing exhibition deter most trespassers. However, in some instances these behaviors are counterproductive, disclosing the snake's presence and advertising them to enemies. Deer, elk, antelope, and hogs might react by dispatching such a noisy menace with a few well-placed fore hooves. Predators such as owls, hawks, ravens, coyotes, and javelinas, bent on a meal, might accept rattling as the dinner bell. Humans, quick to protect anyone and anything from perceived danger, will almost surely choose to kill an unfortunate rattlesnake on sight, regardless that it may be miles away from any form of civilization and not be a realistic threat. The act of "plinking" (shooting the heads off aroused rattlesnakes) is "sport" to some misguided outdoorsmen.

As might be expected, many hypotheses regarding the function of the rattle have been proposed, ranging from reasonable to preposterous. The most widely accepted idea is that the rattling sound is a successful way of alerting and warning hoofed mammals (e.g., bison) that they are too close to the snake.

Tales have been related of male rattlesnakes attempting to lure the opposite sex with a nocturnal chorus, like that of anurans (frogs and toads). Another equally unfounded story claims rattling is used in courtship to stimulate the potential mate. Still others see it as an alarm, warning other snakes of pending danger, in essence acting as sentries. Baby rattlesnakes are claimed to be called and soothed to sleep by their mother's rattle. However, serpents cannot hear, so the rattle has no use as a love call or as an auditory signal in any interaction with other snakes.

A less romantic, more mystical story is that rattlesnakes have the ability to fascinate and charm their prey. An animal is attracted and mesmerized by the rattle, permitting it to be further influenced by the snake's hypnotic eyes. Transfixed, it is bitten and killed without effort. An offshoot of this myth, still believed by many, is that the sound is so startling, so frightening, that the prey is paralyzed.

These rattlesnake stories have all been debunked in one way or another. No valid reports have been submitted to fortify any of these claims by any of the naturalists who have spent time in rattlesnake country.

Perhaps the most plausible of the unusual offerings of the rattle's function is that rattling (particularly that of immature and smaller forms) attracts birds, because it sounds like a calling insect. Studies show certain snakes actually use their tails as a lure to attract overly curious prey. Neonate copperheads (*Agkistrodon contortrox)* and cottonmouths (*Agkistrodon discivorous)* have vividly colored greenish-yellow tail tips that are waved rhythmically to attract unsuspecting small frogs and possibly insects.

Massasaugas, *Sistrurus catenatus*, pigmy, *Sistrurus miliarius,* rock, *Crotalus lepidus,* and ridgenose rattlesnakes, *Crotalus willardi,* are born with brightly colored, greenish-yellow tail tips that have been observed in a luring posture. Observations of dusky pigmy rattlesnakes made under laboratory conditions proved that both immature and adult snakes lured and captured small frogs (J. F. Jackson and D. L. Martin, "Caudal Luring in the Dusky Pygmy Rattlesnake, *Sistrurus miliarius barbouri," Copeia* 1980:926–27 [1980]). The tactic started only when the snakes became aware of the presence of the anurans. Because no sound was produced by the rattle, tail color and movement must have been the enticement.

Reports of other types of snakes known to use the tail tip as a caudal lure, as well as those of the copperhead and cottonmouth, disclose the tail is waved in a slow, flag-waving manner, from side to side, while held in an almost vertical position. A slightly different method is used by rattlesnakes. Their tails are undulated and moved laterally (dragged) along the ground, like a small crawling insect. Although they do not have brightly colored tails, immature sidewinders, *Crotalus cerastes,* use caudal luring to attract lizards into striking range. The swaying motion of their tiny rattles must appear very insect-like to a foraging lizard.

Above: The tail of a newborn banded rock rattlesnake, *Crotalus lepidus klauberi,* is distinctly bright yellow. It is strongly believed to be used as a lure to small prey, likely lizards.

Right: The western diamondback rattlesnake, *Crotalus atrox,* is known to stand its ground when actively provoked. This is its standard stance when aroused.

After considerable provocation this northwestern neotropical rattle-snake, *Crotalus durissus culminatus,* lowers its head, spreads its ribs, and attempts to back away. The flattening of the body makes the snake appear larger, and its head is more difficult for a predator to grab when it is closer to its body.

Provocation and Display

The initial reaction of a startled western rattlesnake lying in a loose resting coil is to freeze, relying on cryptic coloration for conceal-ment. Further provocation leads to rattling, with little change in position. If the intruder is not frightened off, an ensuing threat posture fortifies the snake's intent to defend itself. Whipping into a spectacular display, its head menacingly poised aloft and atop a sin-uous S-shaped coil, the snake is now ready to strike at anything in range. Flattening its body, alternately inhaling and exhaling great quantities of air through its slightly opened mouth, producing a series of loud, violent hisses, and furiously rattling gain the neces-sary attention. As the snake faces the intruder, its tongue waves constantly, tips set widely apart, methodically testing the air. The snake continues its violent exhibition while carefully backing away toward the nearest retreat.

An aroused or suddenly disturbed timber rattlesnake uses the rapid inhalation of air to produce a louder, more forceful hissing sound. It may be audible from as far away as 15 feet (4.5 meters). In full defensive display, the resonant sound, combined with signifi-cant, rapid inflating and deflating of the lung, makes the snake appear much larger and more formidable.

Other Displays

Other highly specific defensive (warning) displays have been observed in provoked rattlesnakes. When taunted, the Mexican blacktail rattlesnake, *Crotalus molossus nigrescens,* will gape, turning toward the threat. The fangs are not erected. If the fangs were erected, it is believed that the maxillary bones would force the lateral facial skin up and back, effectively blocking the receptive ability of the facial pits. Although the mouth is not opened as prominently as is that of a cottonmouth in a defensive posture, its interior is clearly revealed.

The Humantlan rattlesnake, *Crotalus scutulatus salvini,* has shown a display unusual among rattlesnakes. It is a lateral flattening and widening of the neck immediately behind the head, hooding, with-out affecting the rest of the body. This neck-flattening is combined with a typical defensive posture (S-shaped striking coil), while the snake backs away with the fore-portion of its body at a 30-degree angle above the ground. Although not as pronounced, a similar dis-play is elicited from a few subspecies of the neotropical rattlesnake, *Crotalus durissus,* when they are harassed. Once I observed a partic-ularly stressed, caged, female canebrake, *Crotalus horridus atricauda-tus,* vertically flattening her neck and slightly gaping at the mouth when no escape route or hide box was available.

Although the Mojave rattlesnake, *Crotalus scutulatus scutulatus,* has never been observed hooding, it has responded to taunting by flattening its entire body, including its head, and pressing its body tightly to the ground. Variations of this flattening defense display are fairly common among other rattlesnake species. It makes them appear larger and helps to eliminate the more easily grasped, cylin-drical body shape.

Pigmy rattlesnakes, *Sistrurus miliarius,* are known to bob their heads vertically at closely approaching provokers. If grabbed and tightly restrained, many rattlesnakes will thrash violently, attempt-ing to escape. They will void their cloacas and excrete or spray a vile smelling musk from paired glands near the vent. It has been suggested that under less violent but stressful conditions an alarm scent is excreted from the vent area to warn other snakes, and shaking the rattle likely helps disperse the scent. William S. Brown (personal communication, 1997) related that timber rattlesnakes, *Crotalus horridus horridus,* can "jet-propel musk from scent glands in a stream, much like a water pistol would, or sometimes in a shower of fine droplets. This action is not aided by a vibrating rattle, as it can happen if the rattle is held and restrained from rattling."

Red diamond rattlesnakes, *Crotalus ruber,* frequently form a tight, spring-like, defensive coil. It appears as though they have been carefully wrapped to fit into a tight jar. The head is at the top but may be hidden underneath a coil. A last-resort action taken by

Confronted by the serious threat of becoming a meal to a California kingsnake, *Lampropeltis getula californiae*, this subadult southern Pacific rattlesnake, *Crotalus viridis helleri*, attempts to thwart the predator's aggressive move by body bridging and lowering its head.

overly taunted rattlesnakes with no means of escape is to hide their heads beneath coils, rather than displaying them. Rattling may stop, especially if the rattle is concealed by the coils, and they may strike out from this position. Head-hiding is frequently linked with body bridging to thwart an attack.

Body Bridging as a Defense

Sensing the presence of a kingsnake, *Lampropeltis getula,* by the kingsnake's odor, a threatened rattlesnake initiates a series of postures that appear to be unique to crotaline snakes. The lung is inflated, increasing body mass, and the coil closest to the offender is raised at a distinct vertical angle. While continuing to face and observe its serpentine enemy, the rattlesnake keeps its head pressed against the ground making it less accessible. Movement, including body jerking, that sometimes becomes longitudinal waves, keeps the elevated coil perpendicular to the attacker. This may be likened to a person bringing his arm up, shielding his face from a punch. The procedure produces a sizable frontal barrier, preventing the kingsnake from readily grasping the rattlesnake's head. Its elevated coil may be brought down with considerable force, thumping the intruder.

Recent studies have shown this display may be more important as a deterrent should the confrontation occur in a tunnel or burrow. In tight quarters, the unusual positioning, combined with body inflating, makes it difficult for the attacker to discern the size of the rattlesnake. Also, body bridging and the pressure exerted against the tunnel walls block the tunnel while preventing a kingsnake from grabbing or constricting the rattlesnake.

As an aside, this aversion by rattlesnakes to kingsnake odor has brought about a synthetic product that appears to be the first really effective rattlesnake repellent.

THE RATTLESNAKE'S SEVEN SENSES

There is, however, only one reptile on the desert that humanity need greatly fear on account of his poison and that is the rattlesnake. The rattle is indescribable, but a person will know it the first time he hears it. It is something between a buzz and a burr, and can cause a cold perspiration in a minute fraction of time.

—J. C. Van Dyke

The facial pit (from which the common name *pitviper* was derived) is a small cavity situated between the nostril and the eye on each side of the head. In Latin America the closeness and similar appearance of the four orifices (nostrils and pits) have promoted the widely used common name for many pitvipers, *cuatro narices,* meaning four nostrils.

Within the pit is a heat-radiation-detecting organ. The pit functions as a locating and homing device enabling a rattlesnake to "see" warm-blooded animals. It is a decided advantage when seeking prey at night or within dark hiding places where the snake's weak vision is almost useless. Pits are so sensitive that the body temperature of a mouse can be detected and the distance judged to ensure an accurate strike from as far away as 2 feet (0.6 meter). When the pits are directed upward, they act as a final homing device if the prey moves during the strike, allowing the rattlesnake to make instantaneous changes in direction. This provides yet another advantage to the rattlesnake in procuring food.

Rattlesnakes' pits are deep and irregularly shaped (almost crescent) and are angled in a

Face to face with an alerted neotropical rattlesnake, *Crotalus durissus durissus,* we can clearly see three of its primary sensing devices: its eyes; heat-sensing facial pits; and its extended, bifurcated, pink tongue. Its nostrils are small and somewhat hidden, slightly below the pits.

The head of this San Lorenzo Island diamond rattlesnake, *Crotalus ruber lorenzoensis*, beautiful in its simplicity, shows the shape and position of the snake's nostrils and pits.

more forward direction than the eyes. They are true thermoreceptor organs. Inside, toward the base, lies a pit membrane that is suspended above a highly vascularized cavity. There is a duct leading from this cavity to a minuscule opening in the skin anterior to the eye. Musculature allows closing of the duct. This most likely permits the snake to control the submembrane temperature and regulate the air pressure within the pit.

The pit membrane is riddled with tiny, specific receptive spots that are richly supplied with branching nerve endings. Minutely differing temperatures (as little as 0.003°C) are recorded by these spots, providing a radiation pattern or image of the prey animal. A denser, "hotter" pattern distinguishes the main body of the prey, the ideal target for a successful strike. Thermal receptance is less defined toward the periphery. The two pits, in unison, produce an infrared binocular image, permitting an extremely accurate shadow of a moving animal. This explains why a rattlesnake moves its head from side to side, scanning for a nonmoving mouse that it has initially detected by other senses. Basically, a pit works like a directional dish microphone, seen on the sidelines of a football game, which isolates and picks up the quarterback's calls. Facial pits are purely infrared receptive, responding only to heat and not touch, light, or sound.

Information is passed along one branch of the trigeminal nerve to the optic tectum, the same portion of the brain in which visual data are processed. Like visual impulses, they cross over. The right pit material is processed on the left side of the brain and the left pit on the right. Some of the brain neurons within the optic lobe

accept data from the eyes, some from the pits. Quite probably, the combined input produces a sophisticated, thermally enhanced "visual" image. With a little imagination one could assume the image is similar to the one seen by the alien depicted in the early 1990s science fiction motion picture *The Predator.*

Pits with the same biological function are found in several species of boas and pythons. However, although anatomically similar to facial pits, they evolved independently and are an example of convergent evolution. There are minor differences in their morphology, physiology, and exact function. Called *labial pits,* they are arranged in multiples, in a row along the upper or lower lips, or both. They are much larger, less elaborate, and less sensitive and respond most readily to more drastic changes in temperature. Labial pits sense warm-blooded prey as it moves along the series of pits, whereas in crotalids a single pit serves the same function. Labial pits are sensitive to touch as well as to thermal stimuli.

Additional receptive areas have been located on external labial scales of both boids (a large, mostly tropical group of constricting snakes such as boas and pythons) and crotalines. Investigations may show that they provide some form of microthermal reception. Pit membranes are continuous with the outer skin and are shed as part of it.

An innovative idea suggests the primary function of the facial pits is for protection. The mass of the potential predator is ascertained from the size of its heat image. If presented with a large image, the rattlesnake could avoid a potentially dangerous confrontation with a large enemy.

The Jacobson's Organ

All snakes, and closely related monitor lizards, have a conspicuous forked tongue as one of their primary sensing receptive organs. It is the collector for a sensory apparatus, the Jacobson's organ. Also referred to as a *vomeronasal organ,* it is analogous to a combination of the smell and taste senses of other animals. Scientists disagree about the use of the term *taste* when referring to this organ, preferring to call it a *chemoreceptor* (chemical sensor). Minuscule taste buds have been located on the tongues of some snakes (not in rattlesnakes), therefore some snakes do have a taste sense.

The Jacobson's organ lies within paired cavities in the roof of the mouth. It has long been an accepted hypothesis that each time the moist tongue is extended it captures microscopic particles, and when withdrawn the tips are passed near these orifices, transferring the particles. A recent study on a boa constrictor and Burmese python demonstrated that these snakes do not have adequate muscular control for placing the tongue tips near the openings. K. Schwenk ("The Serpent's Tongue," *Natural History Magazine* 104:48–54 [1995]) suggested that particles are carried into the mouth by the tongue and deposited on a pair of pads on the floor of the mouth, directly beneath the openings, to the Jacobson's

Left: A view of the prominent labial pits of an adult ball python, *Python regius.*

Below: The extended black tongue of this tiger rattlesnake, *Crotalus tigris,* shows the bifurcated tips being fully employed.

Left: The blue basal section of an otherwise black tongue is seen on this Mojave rattlesnake, *Crotalus scutulatus scutulatus.*

Below: The tongue of this incredible and unusually colored Humantlan rattlesnake, *Crotalus scutulatus salvini,* differs from that of the northern subspecies in that its base is red. Most Humantlan rattlesnakes are brown, tan, or greenish, not cranberry. Quite possibly this specimen is hypererythristic.

Opposite: The tongue of the northwestern neotropical rattlesnake, *Crotalus durissus culminatus,* as in the other subspecies of *Crotalus durissus,* is pinkish red.

organ. Contraction of the lower jaw forces the pads in contact with the openings, enabling the particles to contact the Jacobson's organ. Ratsnakes have been shown to have tiny processes in the roof of the mouth anterior to the openings that "scrape" the tongue tips, depositing scent molecules at the orifices.

Preliminary data indicate that tongue scanning is, in part, a receiving of electrostatic energy produced by environmental features. The dry skin of a moving snake produces positive electrostatic charges, is a poor conductor, and has fewer discharge points than provided by the hair and feathers of prey animals. Tongue scanning would repel other positive charges and attract negative charges. The different charges could be detected by an electroreceptor or other sensory cells. The researchers who collected these data further suggested that moist air, which is conductive, also plays a role: "The airborne plumes of moisture exhaled by animals and flowing out from under cover are invaded by static charges from the Earth and could be detected by snakes" (W. T. Vonstille and W. T. Stille III, "Electrostatic Sense in Rattlesnakes," *Nature* 370:184–85 [1994]).

Regardless of the transfer methodology, the transported particles stimulate nerve endings, and the information is transmitted to the brain as electric impulses via a part of the olfactory nerve. During the embryonic development in more derived snakes (colubrids and viperids), this part of the olfactory nerve shows a distinct separation from the other olfactory tissue. By birth the vomeronasal cells have formed an intact columnar structure.

Seeing movement is a likely trigger for tongue flicking. A snake

Left: The Baja California rattle-snake, *Crotalus enyo enyo*, has the largest eyes proportionately of any rattlesnake. It is assumed to have better eyesight than many other rattlesnakes. The eye appears exceptionally large in this speci-men because it is a juvenile.

Below: No reason or function has been proposed for the distinctive, bright orange eye of the Central Plateau dusky rattlesnake, *Cro-talus triseriatus triseriatus.*

uses its Jacobson's organ to discern chemical information about its surroundings, whether the object being confronted is food (e.g., a mouse), a predator (e.g., a kingsnake), a member of the opposite sex, or an unknown impediment in its immediate path.

A rattlesnake that is casually exploring the environment—or conversely fully aroused, coiled and ready to strike at an intruder—exercises full extension of the tongue with long, slow whip-like passes. The snake is laboriously attempting to extract every particle and as much information as it can. Though mostly used in a vertical orientation, the tongue can be steered in any direction. The tips are widely spaced, affording maximum sweep. On occasion, the tongue tips will be tightly pressed against an object, such as a rock or the ground, to ensure capturing as many chemical specks as possible. This prolonged contact appears to be a secondary function to more fully investigate a previously detected airborne cue.

Most snakes, stimulated by food or a mate, use rapid, short, darting tongue movements. Chemosensitive searching, a specific, more intense tongue flicking, is undertaken almost immediately after striking prey. Smaller montane forms use this method almost exclusively.

Other Senses

When compared to the sophistication of the Jacobson's organ, the other primary senses are fairly limited. Snakes have no external ear openings and a poorly defined middle-ear structure, rendering their hearing greatly impaired. Unlike the considerably more derived mammals that have three primary conductive middle-ear bones (incus, maleus, stapes), snakes have one, the slender, rod-shaped columella (a bone somewhat homologous to the stapes).

However, they are not deaf. As in other vertebrates, vibrations passing through the ground are picked up by the body and transferred to bones in the maxillary and skull. The columella contacts the quadrate bone at the rear of the lower jaw and contacts the skull's supratemporal bone at the other. Vibrations stimulate sensory nerve endings that transmit the "sound" (as electrical impulses) to the brain via the auditory nerve. The quadrate bone in certain colubrids acts like the eardrum membrane of other reptiles receiving and transmitting aerial sounds. In both cases, lower pitched resonance is more readily "heard." A dense surface material, such as hard-packed dirt or rock, facilitates the transfer of minor tremors from as much as 15 feet (4.6 meters) away. Some scientists theorize that the lung may act as a receptor for airborne sounds. It is believed that rattlesnakes cannot discern higher range frequency, so they cannot hear the sound of another rattlesnake's rattle.

A snake's vision generally lacks clarity but varies greatly from species to species. It is believed that they differentiate size, shape, light, and shadows, but some see little more than indistinct forms. Moving objects are detected quickly by a snake that is awake and alert. When the snake is asleep, the iris is usually slightly ventral and anterior to the center point.

The structure of the snake's eye differs from that of other vertebrate animals, including their nearest relatives, the lizards. Likely, these differences are part of their evolutionary history. Because it is widely believed that snakes evolved from burrowers, it is logical to assume that their limited vision is a remnant of that lifestyle.

Snakes do not have movable eyelids. Inside the eye, the lens is focused by moving it forward and backward (like a camera lens) rather than by changing its shape. Rattlesnakes lack a fovea or focal point at the back of the eye, so they are incapable of seeing a sharply defined image. They see a wide field, with better acuity toward the center. Their vision becomes almost useless at the periphery. Because rattlesnakes' eyes are set toward the sides of the head, the angle they accept does not completely overlap, giving them mostly lateral, monocular vision. This severely limits their depth perception.

Movement, likely perceived through the reflection of highlights, is the most important stimulus. It initiates response, bringing other senses into play. Snakes' retinas contain a preponderance of rod cells (light receptors). These provide a superior adaptation for twilight and night vision, the peak activity period for most rattlesnakes. Because both rods and cones are present, rattlesnakes must see in some form of color. Some species, notably Baja California rattlesnakes, *Crotalus enyo,* have disproportionately larger eyes than others. Their smaller head, also disproportionate to most other rattlesnakes, causes the eyes to appear even bigger. All rattlesnakes have elliptical pupils. Larger pupils facilitate better overall vision. This is advantageous because a large percentage of their prey is composed of quick, darting lizards during the day and small mammals at night. Large eyes also make them more alert to the presence of predators. Many rattlesnakes react to prey movement immediately with a strike, never employing the vomeronasal tongue-flicking apparatus. They do, however, use it after a strike and for trailing envenomated prey.

The snake's nasal passages are lined with a succession of olfactory cells that are more prominent than those in humans. Unlike other vertebrate predators, however, they do not appear to employ "sniffing" as a specific action. The presence of a kingsnake (a major rattlesnake predator) initiates tongue exploration before the predator is in sight, so olfaction must be an important stimulus, as was discussed in the previous section. Likewise, an unseen mouse provokes the same response. Prairie rattlesnakes, *Crotalus viridis viridis,* have been observed gaping (yawning widely) and shaking their heads horizontally to capture odors.

When feeding, the snake locates the dead prey's head by probing and prodding with its rostrum. It is probable that its nostrils are being employed in conjunction with the vomeronasal apparatus to find the animal's mouth or nose, enabling head-first swallowing. More research needs to be done to establish the nostril's value, other than its role as the major air passage for breathing.

Left: A section of lateral skin of a northern blacktail rattlesnake, *Crotalus molossus molossus,* shows typical rattlesnake body scales. The keel or ridge runs mid-line from the slightly rounded anterior edge to the more pointed posterior edge. Keels add strength to the skin.

Below: Although the scales of this well-fed Angel de la Guarda Island speckled rattlesnake, *Crotalus mitchellii angelensis,* are less defined than in the rattlesnake shown above, a keel is present. The snake's considerable girth, the result of fat stored along the body wall, has stretched the skin. What appears to be a series of scales is actually a continuous covering of skin.

Opposite: An adult Yucatan neotropical rattlesnake, *Crotalus durissus tzabcan,* basks in a typical nondefensive, resting coil.

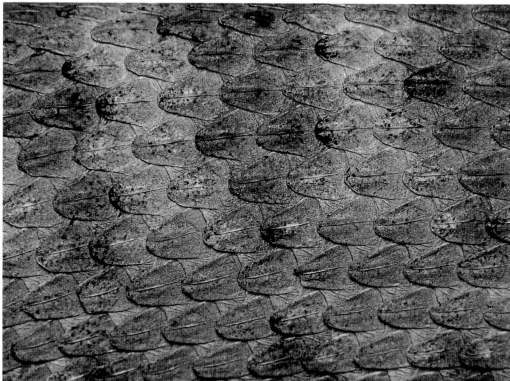

A combination of senses, relying heavily on the pits and Jacobson's organ, make a rattlesnake's tracking ability extraordinarily acute. Until recently, the vomeronasal organs and pits were considered the primary guides for an accurate strike. A study of the prairie rattlesnake, *Crotalus viridis viridis,* under daylight conditions demonstrated that its pits and eyes share equally in the process, and the tongue and Jacobson's organ are rarely involved. The latter are more important as tracking devices.

Skin as a Receptor

Snakes experience the feeling of pain. Although tough and pliable, their skin is capable of feeling the slightest contact, tension, or pressure. Not only are these mechanoreceptors (touch sensors) distributed over most of the body, but they are found in the hinges between the scales as well. Numerous nerve endings detect minute changes in temperature that stimulate thermoregulatory behavior. Tiny, paired, indented areas are found on some dorsal scales. Known as apical pits, they are believed to be sensitive to touch. Prominent near the anal area of both genders, these pits may be used for sexual arousal or they may produce gender-recognition substances during courtship and mating.

The skin's acceptance of radiant energy, its ability to determine the temperature, and the snake's ability to move toward or away from one temperature gradient to another are among the most important behavioral actions in its daily life. In concert with the circulatory system, the skin permits and monitors thermal control. This is why snakes are frequently found basking in early morning or late afternoon, avoiding the potentially lethal rays of the more direct midday sun.

When first emerging from the coolness of a retreat, a snake may simply remain stretched out in a crawling position to quickly capture some radiant energy. After a brief warm-up period, it usually assumes a more protective and cryptic resting coil. Most of the body remains in contact with the warm ground. To maximize the effect, the coils are juxtaposed and concentric, with little overlap. The amount of body facing the radiant energy source is increased by changing position or laterally widening the entire body. This is accomplished by spreading the distal ends of the ribs laterally, essentially flattening the body. Vertical articulation at the vertebrae and lack of connecting ligaments distally enable the ribs to move

Above: A Sonoran Desert sidewinder, *Crotalus cerastes cercobombus*, has formed a crater in loose sand and bedded down for the cool night. It will remain in this position until the morning sun warms it to a temperature that is high enough to force it to seek cover in a nearby burrow.

Opposite: A canebrake rattlesnake, *Crotalus horridus atricaudatus*, has just crawled from its nighttime retreat, and by flattening its body, it is accepting the maximum amount of first warmth of the morning sun. After a few minutes the snake will assume a less dangerously exposed position, the resting coil, and continue basking until it reaches its optimum temperature.

into this position. As the angle of the sun changes or shadows are produced, the snake will reorient itself to attain the greatest benefit.

All snakes are considered "cold-blooded" (ectothermic). Unlike "warm-blooded" (endothermic) animals, they are unable to produce much of their own body heat. To sustain life and to maintain a desirable body temperature, snakes rely on an exchange of body heat with their surroundings.

The circulatory system is the primary vehicle for controlling body temperature. Regulated by peripheral vascular nerves, blood warmed on the surface is carried to the internal organs. Cooling is done in a like manner. An elevated heart rate allows the heart to pump excessively heated blood away from the organs to the skin or lungs.

Because all metabolic and muscular functions depend on body temperature, there is a definite preferred activity range, between 80 and 90°F (26–32°C). There are also tolerance ranges, minimum and maximum temperatures outside of which death will occur. Snakes inhabiting the hottest, driest deserts will succumb when their internal temperature surpasses 110°F (43°C) for as little as a few minutes. It is perhaps surprising that rattlesnakes have more endurance at the lower end of the thermal scale. Temperatures below freezing will not immediately kill. Adult rattlesnakes can recover from brief exposure to temperatures as low as 4°F and can even thrive in temperatures as low as 37°F for several days.

FEEDING AND INNER WORKINGS

The food of the rattlesnake consists of rats, mice, reptiles, and small birds, the latter of which creatures it is said to obtain by the exercise of a mysterious power termed fascination, the victim being held, as it were, by the gaze of its destroyer, and compelled to remain in the same spot until the Serpent can approach sufficiently near to seize it.

—Reverend J. G. Wood

All snakes are carnivorous. Because they must swallow their food whole, snakes prefer prey of size that can be consumed without great difficulty. Stories of devouring huge meals, frequently seen in photographs as massive bulges along the midsection, pertain mostly to boas, pythons, and many species of the extensive family colubridae, and this is not the norm. This is not to say rattlesnakes will *not* consume very large meals if the opportunity presents itself.

A mature canebrake rattlesnake, *Crotulus horridus atricaudatus,* will enter a rodent burrow and effortlessly consume parents and progeny in one meal. However, because many rattlesnakes are on the smaller side, they are partial to conveniently sized quarry. Almost any appropriate animal easily swallowed will be caught and eaten.

Food Animals

Small mammals, birds, and the young of larger warm-blooded mammals are the most frequent prey. However, a variety of animals including

An immature banded rock rattlesnake, *Crotalus lepidus klauberi,* from Arizona eating a large banded centipede, *Scolopendra polymorpha.* Although large centipedes have been found in the stomachs of preserved rock and ridgenose rattlesnakes, the feeding process has not been previously recorded.

This western diamondback, *Crotalus atrox,* was found in the bright early morning sun consuming a white-winged dove, *Zenaida asiatica.* On closer observation, it became evident (from the odor of putrefaction, loose feathers, and attracted flies) that the bird had been dead for several hours or longer. It appeared that the rattlesnake had come upon the dove while foraging and was consuming it as carrion. While attempting to pull the carcass into the shade, the rattlesnake never tried to release it, regardless of my presence or the obvious annoyance of photography.

insects, arthropods, lizards, snakes, frogs, toads, salamanders, and bird eggs are also eaten, mostly by immature and smaller kinds of rattlesnakes. Rattlesnakes are also not beyond cannibalism; neonates and smaller conspecifics are occasionally devoured. Vegetable material is never consumed directly but could be ingested secondarily by being in the stomachs of prey.

Many of the small montane forms frequently prey on lizards, which tend to be easy pickings because they live in the same habitat. Young pigmy rattlesnakes, *Sistrurus miliarius,* consume mostly small frogs and lizards that are readily available in their habitat, but adults prefer voles, shrews, or deer mice. The other U.S. *Sistrurus* species, massasaugas, *Sistrurus catenatus,* most frequently eat small mammals and birds but will accept anurans, crayfish, fish, and lizards, as well as other snakes. Newborns have been found to show a decided preference for smaller or neonate snakes. Although mice are common on Coronado Island, the island's small indigenous rattlesnake, *Crotalus viridis caliginis,* is said to be predominately a lizard eater. Prevailing relatively cool weather conditions force it to

Above: The displacement of the jaw and distention of the skin in the neck area are seen as an immature southern Pacific rattlesnake, *Crotalus viridis helleri,* swallows a rodent.

Opposite: Stretched skin delineates the area of the stomach containing the mouse shown being swallowed in the photograph above.

be diurnal, along with the lizard population. The rodents are mostly nocturnal.

The seasonal availability of various food animals plays an important part in the diet of rattlesnakes. As they grow and mature, most forms alter their diet decidedly. Young rattlesnakes consume a variety of available ectotherms, such as lizards, usually changing to a preference for larger endotherms, such as mammals, as they reach adulthood.

A big western diamondback, *Crotalus atrox,* cannot swallow an adult jack rabbit, but it will gorge itself with a nest of young rabbits. Rabbits, prairie dogs, gophers, and ground squirrels are important food items for larger rattlesnakes, particularly in regions where the snake's activity season is short. These mid-sized mammals have a high protein content, with thin coats and little indigestible roughage. They also are an excellent nutrient source to fortify and

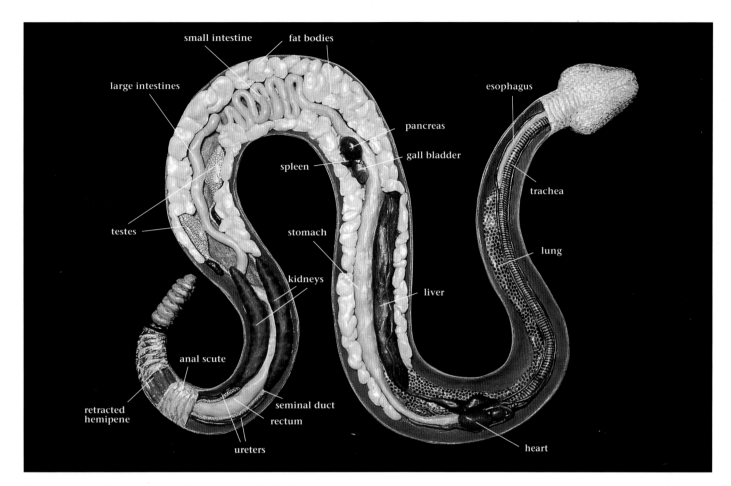

small intestine fat bodies

large intestines

esophagus

pancreas

gall bladder

spleen

trachea

testes

stomach

lung

kidneys

liver

anal scute

retracted
hemipene

seminal duct

rectum

ureters

heart

Above: The ventral view (with the skin cut away) clearly shows the position of the major internal organs of a southwestern speckled rattlesnake, *Crotalus mitchellii pyrrhus.* This carefully constructed replica matches the details of a dissected specimen. Color has been added to some of the major arteries (red) and veins (blue) for better viewing of their placement.

Opposite: This sequence shows an immature banded rock rattlesnake, *Crotalus lepidus klauberi,* from Arizona that has struck a large centipede, *Scolopendra polymorpha,* a few centimeters distal to its head and fangs. The snake's fangs have entered the centipede's body in the soft tissue between the hard chitinous exoskeleton segments. The snake did not release the centipede, retaining its hold for several minutes while the centipede thrashed about trying to escape. Eventually, the effect of the venom quieted the centipede, likely killing it. Without releasing its hold, the rattlesnake began to swallow. The centipede was "folded" at the juncture of the bite and swallowed in that position. The centipede's venom apparatus was never a threat to the rattlesnake.

replenish postpartum females recently depleted of their fat stores by reproduction.

Foraging rattlesnakes, happening on a decaying animal that they have not killed, may make a meal of it. Frequently, the carrion demonstrates such an advanced state of decomposition and putrefaction that the carcass is fragile to the point of falling to pieces.

The permeating stench of carrion appears to be the attractant. The odor carries a great distance and is easily intercepted by the rattlesnake's vomeronasal apparatus. It must be assumed that the snake finds such a carcass by following airborne cues. Because most snakes will readily eat prekilled animals in captivity (sometimes they prefer them), it is likely that scavenging is part of their normal feeding strategy.

Until recently, the method of catching, killing, and consuming one unexpected genus of food animal remained a mystery. Stomach contents of preserved specimens revealed both banded rock, *Crotalus lepidus klauberi,* and ridgenose rattlesnakes, *Crotalus willardi,* regularly eat centipedes of the genus *Scolopendra.* These large and aggressive arthropods have been found in the stomachs of other

Relying on its cryptic coloration, a Carolina pigmy rattlesnake, *Sistrurus miliarius miliarius,* remains coiled, anticipating that an unlucky victim will approach too closely.

rattlesnakes, in allied pitvipers, and in several unrelated snake genera. They are commonly half the length of the rattlesnake, have a rigid chitinous exoskeleton, and possess huge pincer-like fangs that are capable of injecting a lethal dose of their own venom. It is possible the snake has a partial immunity to the centipede's venom.

Color photographs of a confrontation between a rattlesnake and a centipede are shown here for the first time. It appears that the rattlesnake strikes at an area close to the centipede's head. The fangs are imbedded between the segments, and the snake holds on to the struggling arthropod until it stops moving. Most likely this technique prevents the snake from being envenomated or killed by its formidable prey.

Catching Prey

Perhaps befitting their (sometimes) short-term gluttonous habits, rattlesnakes are primarily ambush predators; they sit and wait for a meal. Most rodents and some lizards have a series of pathways that meander throughout their home range. This minihighway system tunnels through high grass, passes between large rocks and boulders, and bypasses cacti, trees, and other obstacles in the terrain. These animals (as well as others) commonly use these routes in their daily activities. They know them so well, they literally speed from one place to another, undaunted, almost unseen. This famil-

A beautiful timber rattlesnake, *Crotalus horridus horridus,* from southern Tennessee lies motionless, nearly concealed, with its head tilted upward in an alert position. It remained in this position for several minutes, and only after several photographs were made was there any response—a tongue flick.

iarity becomes more advantageous to them during the hotter months, when most normal activities become nocturnal.

Applying its smelling, tasting, and seeing tools, a foraging rattlesnake actively searches for, and locates, one of these frequently used trails. Then it nestles back in a shady, secluded spot, motionless, in a resting coil. It remains in that position until it sees, smells, or thermally intercepts an approaching meal. Sight seems to be the stimulating factor during daylight. Once the prey is in range, the snake remains motionless, there is no tongue flicking, and it does not turn toward the prey animal. The unsuspecting

A Great Basin rattlesnake, *Crotalus viridis lutosus,* aware of an approaching mouse, motionlessly awaits its prey in a fully cocked strike position.

mouse, following its daily regimen, passes within striking range, and—wham! Stabbing deeply into the body cavity (usually broadside into the bulkier, more vascularized thoracic region), the snake injects venom and releases the rodent—all within a fraction of a second.

Frightened and dazed, the envenomated animal runs, trying to escape. The rattlesnake immediately turns its head in the direction of the fleeing animal and begins rapid tongue flicking. This is called strike-induced chemosensory searching (SICS). The behavior is inborn and will be followed throughout the snake's life. It is interesting to note that if the strike misses, SICS terminates almost immediately. The mouse may travel several yards, but within seconds the venom takes effect. Quickly losing equilibrium, it flounders about briefly, then dies, usually in less than ten minutes.

With remarkable accuracy, relying primarily on its tongue and Jacobson's organ, the rattlesnake distinguishes the trail of the envenomated animal. Slowly and deliberately, it follows the scent—precisely. As it moves, the trail is scanned with short head-arcing movements (a few inches from side to side) while constantly flicking its tongue. It follows the scent unerringly, occasionally for a hundred feet or more. Once found, the mouse carcass is carefully searched for signs of life. The head is located, and the rodent is consumed.

To increase its odds of making a kill, the timber rattlesnake, *Crotalus horridus horridus,* has a specific strategy while awaiting a squirrel, chipmunk, or deer mouse. These rodents commonly use fallen logs or tree trunks as pathways. The snake lies in a resting coil with its neck slightly withdrawn. Its head is in an elevated position in contact with the log and perpendicular to the potential prey's path. When the rodent enters striking range, it becomes an instant victim.

On four different occasions, two herpetologists saw a marked wild specimen of timber rattlesnake use a variation of this ambush strategy (Brown and

This small southern Pacific rattlesnake, *Crotalus viridis helleri,* has struck a Great Basin fence lizard, *Sceloporus occidentalis biseriatus,* as it attempted to run by. The lizard's momentum caused the rattlesnake's foresection to be twisted into this unusual position.

Greenberg, "Vertical-Tree Ambush Posture in *Crotalus horridus,*" *Herpetological Review* 23:67 [1992]). In each case, they tested the ambush strategy when the snake had positioned itself at the base of a living vertical tree, with its head facing upward and its neck slightly extended in a loose coil, away from its body, and remained motionless. The researchers slowly lowered a freshly killed chipmunk, held by tongs, toward the snake from a distance of 3 feet (1 meter). At approximately 4 inches (10 centimeters), the snake flicked its tongue. As they moved the chipmunk closer, the snake struck and they released it from the tongs. In thirty minutes the snake had swallowed the chipmunk and crawled away from the tree.

The mechanisms of rattlesnake foraging, capturing, and feeding are an extremely complex interaction of mechanical and physiological functions. The most intricate (and yet to be fully explained) is the chemical reaction that occurs in or on the prey animal during the incredibly brief time the fangs and mouth are in contact with it. A chemical "profile" of the prey animal is picked up (and unknown venom components are deposited) during the strike. This information makes the individual dying prey animal distinguishable from others and readily traceable. Also, it has been shown that for a brief period (less than two hours) the rattlesnake can "remember" odors from the rodent's skin.

Usually, the dose of venom is more than adequate for the size of the victim, so a rapid death is all but ensured. There is little chance for escape. Nevertheless, occasionally the fangs do not penetrate thick fur and skin, no venom is injected, or the dose is insufficient, and the bitten animal recovers to make a getaway.

A hungry rattlesnake may abandon the waiting approach and become an aggressive predator. Actively following a normal scent trail, it finds and kills the animal leaving it. Should a rattlesnake, seeking refuge from the sun in a burrow, come on a potential meal, it would certainly take advantage of the offering. Ecologists call this *opportunistic feeding.*

Rattlesnakes do not rely totally on the effect of venom to capture prey. Some hold on. Those that feed mostly on terrestrial endotherms envenomate, release, and track. It is speculated that the sharp teeth of resisting small mammals make them formidable adversaries, and because they run to escape after being bitten, they leave a scent trail and are simple to track. Those preferring ectotherms (frogs, lizards, insects) and flying endotherms (birds, bats) envenomate and retain their grasp until the animal stops struggling. These cold-blooded and flying prey can run, hop, or fly great distances, leaving far less traceable trails or no trail at all. In general they offer little in the way of dangerous opposition.

Rattlesnakes that eat both types of prey adjust, using the technique most appropriate to ensure a meal. Twin-spotted rattlesnakes, *Crotalus pricei,* retain a hold on lizards, their most frequent prey, but release rodents. Sidewinders, *Crotalus cerastes,* also are prone to bite and hold on. Most likely this permits them to remain within the shade of their cratered ambush site, rather than venturing out into open hotter, possibly lethal, areas to find and consume their prey.

Unlike many other snakes, rattlesnakes do not wrap around and constrict and suffocate their victims. A food animal rarely may be pressed against a tunnel wall and suffocated, as a reaction to its annoying movements or the snake's inability to bite it.

There are other exceptions where fangs are not used. Precious venom is not wasted on a nest of newborn or nestling mice or rats. Incapable of much resistance, they are simply swallowed one by one, alive. By contrast, a protective parent would likely be the recipient of a lethal bite and become part of the meal too. Like neonate rodents, the young of ground nesting birds are candidates as dinner, also without the need for envenomation. Because adult birds will take flight after they are bitten, they are more likely to be held. Smaller birds' eggs are part of some rattlesnakes' diets and are swallowed whole, with no need for fangs or venom.

Swallowing

The rattlesnake checks for signs of life in the prey animal by pushing and prodding with its snout, using its tongue, Jacobson's organ, and nostrils to "smell." Simultaneously, by detecting odors emitted from the prey's mouth, its head is sought. Finding the prey's nose, the snake opens its mouth around the nose, and ingestion begins. Head first is the most efficient position for swallowing an animal. As legs, wings, and fur fold backward away from the head, it becomes a relatively unobstructed shape. To further the process, a snake often straightens an extended wing or leg by dragging and rubbing the quarry against the ground. Larger animals may be pushed and forced against the ground or other stable objects to help anchor them.

The skull and mouth structure of the rattlesnake is similar to that of other snakes. It is modified to permit extensive stretching, facilitating the ingestion of prey several times larger than would be expected. Some rattlesnakes are less capable of accommodating very large food items than others. Adult eastern diamondbacks, *Crotalus adamanteus,* regularly eat adult cottontail rabbits. This is possible because the head of a large adult eastern diamondback is as big as a man's fist, and rabbits appear bulkier because of their fur. However, it is no simple feat.

Distention of the head, sometimes to grotesque proportions, is made possible by several skull-joint modifications. The flexibility and resilience of the skin and the remarkable elasticity of ligaments attaching the anterior ends of the lower jawbones accomplish this. There is no bony suture at this juncture to inhibit movement. The opening of the mouth can be extended in almost any direction.

The entire head and neck are distended and tightly constricted while feeding, making breathing difficult. Two modifications solve the problem: the glottis and air storage ability of the saccular portion of the lung.

The glottis, a large opening into the trachea for breathing, lies in the base of the mouth cavity immediately behind the sheath that harbors the tongue. Strong muscles elevate cartilaginous rings permitting passage of air through the trachea. This arrangement for deep breathing while feeding on sizable prey also allows greater quantities of air passage or panting during heat duress.

It is important to understand that rattlesnakes do not chew (masticate) or tear their prey. Rather, four rows of pin-sharp, backward-curved teeth hold and manipulate the prey animal. Most other snakes have two additional rows of teeth along the outer upper jaw. The rattlesnake has only fangs on the movable tooth-bearing maxillary bones.

With a series of twisting, contorting maneuvers, one side of the jaw and skull is thrust forward, enabling the teeth to hook and anchor the food. The action is repeated on the other side. This ratchet-like motion is better visualized as the hand-over-hand tactic used in a tug of war; only here, prey is pulled into the mouth and throat. Snakes have muscular control over skull parts on one side at a time while the opposite jaw and ligament movements are idle. There are no muscles to spread the lower jaws; they must be forced to separate and be stretched by the prey's bulk.

The fangs may remain folded into their protective sheaths or be employed while swallowing. Because they are mobile, longer, and independently manipulative (unlike other teeth), they are used for greater leverage and pulling power. They are especially effective when swallowing birds and very furry mammals.

Typical of more derived vertebrates, saliva (which is copiously produced during feeding) is not only a lubricant but also a medium for digestive enzymes. Once the prey is in the snake's throat, a series of undulations and muscular contractions force the bolus into the stomach. As its meal progresses inward, the snake moves slightly forward, straightening and stretching its neck to accommodate the mass. Gaping and yawning widely readjusts the jaws, fangs, and various other head parts.

The entire process may take a few minutes or more than an hour, depending on the size of the food. When swallowing a big meal, a snake will take breaks to rest and breathe.

Digestion

The digestive process is like that of all higher vertebrates. Digestive juices (mainly enzymes and acids) break down the components into absorbable amino acids, simple carbohydrates, and fatty acids. As might be expected with such a specialized animal, other forces

Above: This prairie rattlesnake, *Crotalus viridis viridis,* by the impact of its strike and the embedding of its fangs, has rolled the mouse off its feet and onto its side. In less than a second the snake will release its grip, and the mouse will run a short distance before it succumbs to the venom.

Opposite: A typical Texas gray morph northern blacktail rattlesnake, *Crotalus molossus molossus,* seeking refuge to digest the sizable pack rat, *Neotoma,* it recently ate. The distended mid-body skin discloses the meal.

are also at work. Venom has elements that are not only toxic but have effective digestive capabilities. In reality, venom starts breaking down the food inside the prey as soon as it is injected. As much as 30 percent of western diamondback, *Crotalus atrox,* venom has been found to consist of digestive proteases.

Gastric juices are extremely powerful, allowing the assimilation of not only the fleshy parts but bones as well. Pepsin breaks down protein, and hydrochloric acid dissolves the bone. All that is left after a trip through the gut is hair or feathers and occasionally teeth. How long the process takes is directly related to the ambient temperature. The quickest, most complete digestion happens when the snake remains within its optimum temperature range, usually between 80 and 85°F (27–29°C). The volume of the food dictates the snake's actions. If the prey is too small, it continues hunting to satisfy its needs. If the meal is adequate, digestion takes place with the snake coiled, hidden away in a warm, safe place.

Rattlesnakes digesting a meal may bask to maintain an optimum temperature, but mostly they remain secluded and almost sedentary. An oversized bolus and a lower than preferable temperature may require an inactive period of a few days to perhaps a week or more to complete the process. When finished, the serpent leaves its retreat and resumes foraging.

Remains of the digestive process, fecal material, are indiscriminately voided while on the move. Solid waste from the alimentary tract (feces mostly consisting of undigested hair and bone) is passed from the distal end of the large intestine through the cloaca.

Because snakes rely so heavily on temperature and are governed by seasonal changes, they must conserve energy and stored fat in every way possible in anticipation of inhospitable weather. Factoring in the effects of environmental hazards, it behooves them to move about as little as possible. Aside from migrating to and from denning sites, moving around during the mating season, procuring an adequate supply of food is the major requirement forcing them to prowl.

Unlike endotherms that must eat every few hours, a snake's overall metabolism is much lower, so it needs considerably less food to sustain itself and grow. By combining a lower metabolic rate with the larger meal size and the overall short period of activity, it has been calculated that the annual consumption of a medium-sized rattlesnake approximately equals a single meal for a large carnivore such as a coyote. The feeding rate may be as little as a half dozen adult rodents annually. A rattlesnake will remain healthy consuming as little as three times its body weight per year in a warmer region where the active season is longer.

Digestive Tract and Excretory System

The digestive tract contains the same complement of major organs as are found in other vertebrates, but they are modified to fit within the elongated body. Everything is attenuated, so much so that the alimentary canal is almost a straight tube. Only the small intestine is coiled.

The esophagus opens into a surprisingly short, chunky, cylindrical stomach. After curving around the compact pancreas, it becomes an extended, narrow, convoluted small intestine at the pyloric sphincter. Kidneys (part of the excretory system) and reproductive organs lie to the sides. In both cases they are staggered, the right being larger and more anterior. Extensive fatty tissues known as *fat bodies* are built up along the sides of the body cavity, supported by thin sheets of mesentery. The short, broad, large intestine opens to the outside just beyond the anal sphincter at the terminal end of the cloaca.

There is a large bi-lobed (but otherwise slender-shaped) liver and a gall bladder. A spleen, thyroid gland, and thymus (not part of the digestive tract) are also present.

The Santa Catalina Island rattlesnake, *Crotalus catalinensis*, is best known as the rattleless rattlesnake. It is frequently found in shrubs hunting birds.

No urinary bladder is necessary. The kidney reabsorbs most filtered fluids extracted from the blood by the kidneys. Additional water is absorbed in the cloacal area. The remaining uric acid, a chalky whitish or yellow-colored mass, is passed as a near solid. There typically is only a small flush of liquid urine, as most of the nitrogenous waste is in the relatively insoluble form of uric acid.

Circulatory System

After digestion, amino acids, glucose, and other dissolved nutrients are passed through the intestinal wall into the capillaries. The circulatory system transports them to the liver, where they are chemically altered into a form that can be metabolized. Some are stored as glycogen or animal starch, the most important source of readily available energy. The rest are carried throughout the body for use in the cells.

Blood supplies these nutrients as well as oxygen to the cells while carrying wastes from them. Also, blood implements exchange of gases in the lung. Blood is the primary vehicle regulating body temperature. Regulated by peripheral vascular nerves, blood warmed on the surface of the body is carried to the internal organs. Cooling is accomplished in a like manner and is aided by an elevated heart rate that more rapidly pumps excessively heated blood to the skin. Radiation from the skin effects the loss of heat to a cooler environment.

Heart

Unlike most terrestrial and arboreal snakes in which the heart is located less than one-fourth of the distance down the length of the body from the head (and thereby is better able to supply blood to the head when elevated), the rattlesnake's heart is set farther back, one-third to two-fifths the distance from the head. It is situated immediately anterior to the liver. This agrees quite closely with the heart's location in aquatic snakes.

The rattlesnake's heart has three chambers. There are two atria. The ventricle is almost divided into two chambers, but the separating wall (septum) is not completely connected. They are more properly called sections. A muscular ridge and complicated system of partitions (septa) permit the blood flow to remain essentially separate, with minimal mixing of the oxygenated and deoxygenated blood; some mixing does occur, however.

As with other land vertebrates, the rattlesnake heart supplies a double circulatory system. (In reptiles and adult amphibians, it is more appropriately called an *incomplete double circulatory system* because of the partially divided ventricle.) The pulmonary trunk division maintains oxygenation of blood by the lung, and the systemic division supplies oxygen-enriched blood to the rest of the body. Oxygenated blood from the lung is returned to the left atrium by the pulmonary vein and passed into the left section of the ventri-

cle. Although an elaborate system of internal partitions directs the majority of the blood through the aortic arches to the various arteries of the body, some mixing takes place.

Systemic veins bring deoxygenated blood through the sinus venosum to the right atrium, which empties into the right section of the ventricle. Because the section is too small to retain all the blood, some leaks into the left region, causing a partial mixing. However, most of the deoxygenated blood is pumped through the pulmonary artery to the lung.

Because the body is so elongated and lacks limbs, the arteries and veins are modified and reduced in number. Rattlesnakes have a single (left) carotid artery that is supplied by the right aortic arch, supplying oxygen-rich blood to the head. More primitive snakes have paired carotids arising from the left aortic arch, supplying a mix of deoxygenated and oxygenated blood.

The Lung

Rattlesnakes, like a variety of other snakes, have only one functional (right) lung that is serviced by a single pulmonary artery. Although proportionately larger than that of most snakes, the rattlesnake's lung is relatively small compared to those of most other vertebrates. This provides less gaseous exchange than is provided by the lungs of most other higher vertebrates, such as birds and mammals. The rattlesnake's lung is incompletely divided into two sections, the vascular and the saccular lung. The anterior-most portion, occasionally referred to as a separate entity, the tracheal lung, is partially combined with thin connecting tissues of the trachea, enabling a large area of direct access to incoming air.

In the area of the heart the tracheal lung changes into the main portion of the vascular lung. This vascular lung section is the primary respiratory chamber. Its lining is bright red from a profusion of capillaries, and it appears loose and spongy. A maximum surface area is provided for exchange of gases. Oxygen, from the air that has been breathed in, diffuses through the respiratory tissue into the capillaries and is carried by hemoglobin in the red blood cells to the body cells. Carbon dioxide, a waste of cellular metabolism, diffuses in the opposite direction and is expelled as the snake exhales.

A posterior-most section, the saccular lung, is primarily an air sac with a minimal ability for aerating the blood. It has a smooth surface with a decreased distribution of capillaries. Aside from storing air, augmenting intake through the trachea that may be partially blocked when the snake consumes large prey, the sac functions as an air bladder for swimming. When a rattlesnake is aroused, this section can be greatly inflated, providing air for hissing and part of the threat display as the appearance of increased bulk.

When a snake is under stress, its elevated heart rate, the relatively long distance the blood must travel, the increased mixture of oxygenated and deoxygenated blood, combined with a rather small respiratory exchange surface afforded by its single lung, all contribute to cause rapid fatigue. The circulatory system of most viperids appears to be a poor transporter of oxygen. When a rattlesnake is coiled ready to strike, the elevated head and neck place additional pressure on the cardiovascular system.

Although a few species have less difficulty than others, climbing—necessitating an upward tilting of the head and neck region—causes a severe drop in anterior blood pressure. This temporary lack of adequately oxygenated blood flow to the brain and cephalic area causes some loss of the senses and perception and may be a major reason why few of the larger rattlesnakes ever climb into bushes and shrubs.

Drinking Water

All animals need water to replace the tissue fluids lost during their daily activities. Although rattlesnakes differ in the quantity they require, it is believed the minimum annual intake must be equal to their body weight. Considering the demands of most wildlife, this is a very small amount indeed. At the very least, a human would require that proportion per month.

The snake's method of drinking is dependent on the source. At a stream, pond, or the like, the rattlesnake submerges its head with no concern for pits or nostrils. The opening and closing of the lower jaw in a pulsating motion sucks in water. A thirsty snake may drink in this fashion, without stopping, for as many as three or four minutes. After breathing, it continues until satiated.

Other rattlesnakes, prone to the opportunistic drinking of water captured in small depressions, "sip" the liquid. It is accomplished mostly by capillary action or by flattening and flooding the lower jaw. Dew provides an adequate amount of water by this process. Even more amazing is the ability of some snakes to gather dew and rainwater from condensation and mist on their own bodies. They tilt their heads downward and drink the liquid that reaches the angle of the jaw. To date, this last method has not been reported in rattlesnakes, but it has been seen in a closely related Costa Rican viper *(Bothrops asper)*.

Because a snake's tongue is mostly cylindrical, it does not lap up water, as do many vertebrates. However, I have observed a nearly dehydrated northern Pacific rattlesnake, *Crotalus viridis oreganus*, drinking from a very shallow puddle. The water was not deep

Submerging its lower jaw, a northern Pacific rattlesnake, *Crotalus viridis oreganus*, spends several minutes drinking at a temporary rain pool.

Because sidewinders, like this Colorado Desert sidewinder, *Crotalus cerastes laterorepens*, live in arid, mostly sandy areas where only a few inches of rain may fall a year, they have become highly adapted to retain the precious fluid. To avoid the lethal summer temperatures, they begin to crawl after the sun has set.

enough for the snake to submerge its lower jaw. Employing rapid tongue thrusts, it carried the liquid adhering to it (by capillary action) into its mouth. On several occasions I have observed thirsty pigmy rattlesnakes, *Sistrurus miliarius,* using another method to drink from equally shallow water sources. The snake turned its head perpendicular to the water supply and pressed its snout into it. The most anterior portion of the lower jaw (in contact with the surface) was alternately opened and closed slightly, apparently mostly by the pressure applied to the surface. There was some obvi-

coiled in a modified typical basking position, its body widely flattened laterally to permit a maximum amount of radiant energy to reach the skin, increasing the rate of heat absorption. A minor difference was that the coils were completely concentric and tightly juxtaposed. As rain pelted down, the snake remained motionless. This is unusual, as snakes routinely retreat from such an annoyance. After a thorough soaking, the snake stuck its snout between two of its coils and started to drink. The snake continued to drink for almost a half an hour from the water that had accumulated in the groove between the two coils (S. D. Aird and M. E. Aird, "Rain-Collecting Behavior in a Great Basin Rattlesnake, *Crotalus viridis lutosus*," *Bulletin of the Chicago Herpetological Society* 25:217 [1990]).

Sidewinders, *Crotalus cerastes,* live in the incredibly hot, arid, southwestern deserts, where rainfall is extremely unreliable and highly seasonal. It amounts to less than 12 inches (30 centimeters) per year. Most rainfall is absorbed in the ground or else it evaporates quickly. The sidewinder adapted to these circumstances and is in fact extremely abundant among stark habitats of apparently barren, windblown sand dunes. Certainly they drink when rain falls, but what about during the long dry spells?

Liquids are obtained, directly and indirectly, from food animals. Digestion enables fluids contained in the tissues and blood of the prey to be absorbed. During dry periods, metabolic water generated by cellular biochemical conversions is produced within the snake's tissues. This is done by the oxidation of stored fat from sizable "fat bodies" that lie laterally within the body cavity alongside the testes and ovaries. Metabolism of carbohydrates and proteins produces some water, but to a lesser degree. These stores are replenished by heavy feeding during optimum times. This is the same nourishment and water supply that maintains all snakes during hibernation. It is highly probable that other rattlesnakes use metabolic water as well.

Snakes have other physiological modifications to help reserve body fluids. Their digestive wastes contain little or no water, and urine is passed as semisolid uric acid, as discussed previously. They do not perspire or sweat, and their skin is less permeable than that of most other animals. Some water is lost through breathing. Desert snakes have even less permeable coats than those living in mesic (wet) areas. This is another adaptation to aridity, enabling them to be successful colonists in an otherwise hostile environment.

A small amount of fluid is dissipated with the shedding process, so most snakes seek drinking water at this time. If abundant water is available, many snakes may choose to soak just prior to shedding. Soaking helps loosen the outer skin layer, while preventing it from drying out. Whole body soaking in rattlesnakes, however, appears to be rare, mainly because in their preferred desert and upland habitats, standing water is rarely present.

The flourish of snake activity promoted by rainy periods (particularly if they are seasonal) demonstrates the importance of water. Almost everywhere, snake activity peaks during rainy weather.

ous tongue movement, but the action was difficult to observe. Again capillary action seemed to be the vehicle.

A Great Basin rattlesnake, *Crotalus viridis lutosus,* was observed using an exceptional behavior modification to gather rainwater. Because much of its habitat is subject to severe summer droughts, with brief localized showers that barely dampen the parched surface, this species has evolved its own temporary reservoir. Change in barometric pressure, signaling an oncoming summer thundershower, appears to have provoked the posture. The snake was

RATTLESNAKE RESPONSES TO WEATHER

In some districts the snakes used to assemble in hundreds or even thousands from all sides to sleep in the ancestral den, some of them, it is said, traveling distances of twenty or even thirty miles.

—R. L. Lydekker

Rattlesnakes living in climates in which winter conditions occur need to escape to a less hostile environment. Under such conditions all species seek refuge in holes and crevices beneath the frost line. Montane ones living in open, widely exposed rock slides or rocky areas simply move deeper within the fissures, away from the cold. Some species seek refuge individually in any place that provides suitable retreats, and others migrate during fall from foraging areas to congregate at denning sites.

Dens are almost always in rocky hillside outcroppings with a southern exposure. They can be rock ledges with numerous crevices permitting passage to a bewildering complex of underground passages or little more than a small opening between boulders leading to deep fissures. Some are talus and scree slopes composed of various granitic and sedimentary

Two canebrake rattlesnakes, *Crotalus horridus atricaudatus*, basking at the small entrance to their hibernating site. Unlike their closest relative, the timber rattlesnake, *Crotalus horridus horridus*, which mostly hibernates in fairly large, partially open rocky areas (within forests) with dozens or more others of its kind, canebrake rattlesnakes tend to hibernate solitarily. Because winters are less severe in southern climes, canebrake rattlesnakes usually hibernate for a shorter period of time and at shallower depths than their northern relatives. The majority prefer to hibernate in stumps and logs proximal to wetter areas, their typical summer haunts.

With the exception of colonies in the New Jersey Pine Barrens, timber rattlesnakes, *Crotalus horridus horridus (right),* mostly hibernate in rocky ledges with a southern exposure. This den *(above)* is in extreme northwestern Georgia.

rocks. The major requirements are accessibility to spaces below the frost line and suitable places for basking on the surface in the spring and fall.

Denning propensities are correlated with latitude and elevation for some wide-ranging species. Prairie rattlesnakes, *Crotalus viridis viridis,* that live in high-elevation areas at latitudes above approximately 38° N migrate from summer-foraging territories to communal dens. Some of the lower elevation, more southern examples of the same taxon hibernate individually in a suitable place, but this is not a strong trend. Also, members of the high-elevation, northern-latitude group hibernate for a longer period, occasionally two additional months.

Sites

Most eastern massasaugas, *Sistrurus catenatus catenatus,* Carolina pigmy rattlesnakes, *Sistrurus miliarius miliarius,* and certain populations of the timber rattlesnake, *Crotalus horridus horridus,* choose to hibernate in low wet areas and sphagnum bogs. Nearly all others prefer retreats that provide stable temperatures with some humidity. Open rocky areas (particularly talus slopes with a southern exposure), stumps, small caves, rotting logs, and the labyrinth left from decomposed tree root systems are ideal. Burrows excavated by prairie dogs, ground squirrels, kangaroo rats, badgers, foxes, burrowing owls, and gopher tortoises are also frequented.

It is ironic that in some places humans have altered the environment and embellished it by furnishing suitable hibernation sites. Abandoned mineshafts, foundations, wells, and poorly maintained or deserted railroad rights-of-way are a few examples. Large, open, rocky road- and power-line cuts are humanmade taluses. In parts of Mexico and the United States, rocks cleared from fields to provide land for farming are placed in piles or made into walls. Frequently, these furnish ideal retreats for small rattlesnakes.

Hibernation

Unlike mammals that lower their body temperatures by altering the metabolic cycle (inducing lethargy and a prolonged state of

An expansive, south-facing, rugged talus slope can be seen across this valley *(top left)*, in the Huachuca Mountains of southeastern Arizona. It is the habitat and den site of the banded rock rattlesnake, *Crotalus lepidus klauberi (bottom left)*. Nearby, in a less-specific habitat, mostly among larger rocks and boulders, northern blacktail rattlesnakes, *Crotalus molossus molossus (top right)*, have a similar existence. Below, in the forested valley, the Arizona ridgenose rattlesnakes, *Crotalus willardi willardi (bottom right)*, inhabit a somewhat moister environment. Occasional pockets of western twin-spotted rattlesnakes, *Crotalus pricei pricei*, live among talus and spree at the highest elevations of this mountain range.

In the extreme northwestern portion of its range, the timber rattlesnake, *Crotalus horridus horridus,* hibernates in fairly steep limestone ridges and outcrops *(above)*. This southern Wisconsin den is in a relatively open area, a few hundred feet above a meadow. Some herpetologists believe that the rattlesnakes found in the northwestern parts of its range warrant a new subspecies classification. Color morphs found in the region are the yellow morph *(right)* and the much less common gray morph *(below)*.

Three prairie rattlesnakes, *Crotalus viridis viridis,* are found basking outside the entrance of this hibernating site in southern New Mexico.

This huge rock slide *(above)* in Arizona's Chiricahua Mountains is an ideal habitat for the western twin-spotted rattlesnake, *Crotalus pricei pricei (below).* Nearly all of these little rattlesnakes spend their entire lives here. Deep crevices provide safe places to hibernate away from the normally long and extremely cold winters.

torpor), reptiles attain a comparable state strictly guided by the ambient temperature. They cannot regulate their body temperature metabolically. Both forms of natural torpor are called *hibernation,* but if the cooling period is induced artificially in captivity, it is called *brumation.*

During exceptionally cold winters, some rattlesnake dens may not provide adequate protection, causing a high mortality rate reported at more than 35 percent. Studies demonstrate rattlesnakes can withstand brief periods of slightly subfreezing temperatures and survive. Depending on the severity of winter, timber rattlesnakes, *Crotalus horridus horridus,* in the Appalachians remain dormant for 170 to 268 days, with 204 days as an average hibernation period. Other species may be forced to hibernate for longer periods.

Because temperatures in hibernacula (dens) are well below their preferred activity range, hibernating snakes become extremely lethargic but not completely immobile. Although they do not feed, forage, or mate, they will drink water and move about when temperatures permit (e.g., 55°F, 12.6°C). They will heap together, presumably to retain moisture and possibly to absorb some geothermal heat from an ideal warm spot within the retreat. An expansive, open area permits exposure to large volumes of air, providing an environment that is too unstable in maintaining temperature and humidity, so fairly confined spaces are preferred.

In some regions, during prolonged winter warm spells, rattlesnakes come to the surface and bask in the sun. There are reports of blacktail rattlesnakes, *Crotalus molossus,* moving about on bright sunny days while a thin covering of snow is on the ground. During hibernation, assimilating stored fat and body fluids provides all of their energy. Adults lose less than one-twentieth of their body mass over the winter, and juveniles may lose more than one-third of theirs.

Denning

Some snakes hibernate in large numbers. Western rattlesnakes, *Crotalus viridis,* in South Dakota have been reported in aggregations of more than a thousand. Others of the same species are not so gregarious, choosing places in which they overwinter with as few as a half dozen brethren. Although timber rattlesnakes frequently gather in groups of 30 to 60, dens harboring 150 to 200 have been recorded. Younger and smaller snakes inhabit some timber rattlesnake, *Crotalus horridus horridus,* dens almost exclusively. It is proposed that the crevices and entrances of these sites are too small for adult snakes.

A variety of reptiles and amphibians, as well as a host of different vertebrates and invertebrates, live together within winter retreats. Frequently, whipsnakes, *Masticophis,* and gopher snakes, *Pituophis catenifer,* overwinter with western rattlesnakes, *Crotalus viridis,* and western diamondbacks, *Crotalus atrox.* In the U.S. Southeast, eastern diamondbacks, *Crotalus adamanteus,* commonly share burrows made by gopher tortoises, *Gopherus polyphemus,* with as many as thirty-two species of invertebrates and an assortment of small vertebrates: the gopher tortoises; box turtles, *Terrapene carolina;* indigo snakes, *Drymarchon corais;* black racers, *Coluber constrictor;* eastern coachwhip snakes, *Masticophis flagellum;* gopher frogs, *Rana areolata;* or southern toads, *Bufo terrestris.*

In the U.S. Northeast, timber rattlesnakes, *Crotalus horridus horridus,* commonly den with one or several other species of snakes: northern copperheads, *Agkistrodon contortrix mokeson;* black rat snakes, *Elaphe obsoleta;* black racers, *Coluber constrictor;* milk snakes, *Lampropeltis triangulum;* red-bellied snakes, *Storeria occiptomaculata;* and garter snakes, *Thamnophis sirtalis.* In fact, there is an old folk tale claiming the rattlesnakes are led back to the dens by black rat snakes. This accounts for another vernacular name for the species, "pilot blacksnake." Evidence supports the idea that some Wyoming and South Dakota prairie rattlesnake dens have been used for thousands of years, and most likely even before prehistoric humans inhabited the area.

Relocating Dens

Occasionally, reaching dens necessitates a rattlesnake to travel great distances (sometimes more than 4 miles, or 6.5 kilometers) in autumn, long before the inclement weather arrives. No one has satis-

This rock outcrop *(opposite)* along a temporary runoff is the summer and winter home for mottled rock rattlesnakes, *Crotalus lepidus lepidus (above)*, in the mountains of Chihuahua, Mexico.

Lying among dried leaves in an ambush coil, a Durango rock rattlesnake, *Crotalus lepidus maculosus,* awaits a passing prey animal.

factorily explained what triggers the migratory behavior, but it appears to be a combination of changing temperature and shortening daylight period interacting with the snakes' inherent circadian rhythm, governing a fairly specific internal time cycle.

Recaptures of marked individuals at dens year after year prove that they come back each fall, reliably. Several hypotheses have been offered to explain how rattlesnakes find their way back to their dens. They are known to follow specific paths, which reinforces the most accepted proposal that they follow scent trails left by snakes dispersing in spring and by snakes that may have back-tracked earlier. It is interesting to note that some have been observed returning to dens on different and more direct paths. Minute traces of pheromones, deposited on the surface, are detected with the snake's extremely acute vomeronasal organs. These pheromones, and others deposited by black ratsnakes, likely are the basis for the pilot blacksnake folk tale. More research needs to be done with pheromones, specifically to see if they persist over an entire year.

The pheromone mechanism helps substantiate occasional anecdotal reports of snakes traveling year after year through specific rural backyards in spring and fall, each season in an opposite direction. N. B. Ford and J. R. Low, Jr. ("Sex Pheromone Source Location by Garter Snakes: A Mechanism for Detection of Direction in Non-Volatile Trails," *Journal of Chemical Ecology* 10:1193–99 [1984]) showed that male garter snakes, *Thamnophis,* detect and discern direction of movement of females by tongue flicking their trails on the ground and on objects they used to push against while crawling. Pheromones are released more strongly on the side of rocks and other objects the females push against. Regardless, it appears other stimuli must be employed as well. There may be visual cues defining the topography, celestial orientation, changes in slope, or other cues that remain unknown. One is that in some localities most dens are located among exposed higher areas, whereas summer retreats are in the lower surrounding valleys. It is possible they can see these high outcrops or simply follow some or all of the sensory cues while seeking a higher elevation.

Experiments to determine the cues rattlesnakes use in dens that are located at lower elevations than the summer range were conducted with radio-tagged prairie rattlesnakes, *Crotalus viridis viridis,* that had been relocated away from the den and tracked back to it. Although there is no positive evidence of what led them back, it appears most likely they used the sun to find the proper direction.

A recent hypothesis suggests their thermosensitive pits may be used to find the dens. Most northern dens are dense rocky hillside ledges with a southern exposure. In fall, daily sun movement through a limited arc above the horizon permits a lower, narrower band of sunlight to reach the rocks than would occur at other times. Surrounding vegetation and the sky provide a cooler region, whereas the heat retained and radiated from the rocks makes them a warm target for the heat-sensitive pits. However, facial pits have

Ground squirrel burrows *(above)* not only provide an available food source but are safe hibernation and aestivation sites for a variety of desert and grassland rattlesnakes. The Mojave rattlesnake, *Crotalus scutulatus scutulatus (left)*, commonly uses these sites.

Opposite: Rattlesnakes living in lowland habitats close to the equator likely never need to hibernate. Taxa such as this Venezuelan rattlesnake, *Crotalus durissus cumanensis*, may, however, need to escape from lengthy periods of drought by aestivating in temperature- and humidity-constant retreats for periods as long as a month.

been found to have a limited effective range (3 feet, or 1 meter), so this hypothesis appears unfounded.

There are data demonstrating that some individuals wander to different dens but return to the original ones in other years. This supports the pheromone-trailing principle or a combination of methods. Observers have noted that rattlesnakes, whether they are located in summer ranges or in dens, appear to be well oriented and virtually never lost. They seem to have an excellent sense of their surroundings.

Most young are born away from the den but large numbers are found there in fall and spring. Also, they have been observed to sometimes arrive at the dens later than the majority of adults. Because they have no experience or visual memory of topographic landmarks or of celestial cues, how do they find their way? Telemetric studies of adult and newborn timber rattlesnakes, *Crotalus horridus horridus*, in the New Jersey Pine Barrens, and in unrelated laboratory experiments, suggest that neonates follow adults to hibernating sites by vomeronasal or olfactory reception of pheromone odor trails. In addition, there could be a chain reaction with neonates trailing other neonates that are in turn trailing adults.

In early spring, rattlesnakes seek the warmth of the sun by bask-ing. They leave the confines of the immediate den for brief periods to bask around the entrance, returning to go underground when the temperature becomes too high or drops to an uncomfortably cool level at night. Although this strategy is generally short term, it may last for several days or weeks, depending on the temperature (particularly during the evening). A similar, but less pronounced, activity is undertaken in fall before entering hibernation. In northern climates, rapid changes in temperature during autumn promote an early return to the den and shorter basking periods.

Because sizable aggregations of semilethargic snakes can be found soaking up the sun rays at these times, they are vulnerable to predation. Humans are the major predator of rattlesnakes at their dens, where great numbers have been killed or collected, mainly in the spring and to a lesser extent in the fall. They have been trapped and shot, and in fact whole dens have been dynamited or cemented over in an attempt to eliminate a population.

Not all rattlesnakes live in temperate climates, so some never need to escape dangerously cold weather by hibernating. Many simply seek temporary shelter during cooler periods, returning to bask whenever the sun stimulates them.

While basking, they remain wary and are quick to retreat from predators. As might be expected, a majority of snakes from warmer and tropical regions have little need to hibernate. They tend to be more solitary, and they are less prone to aggregate.

Spring Migration

In spring, triggered by the lengthening period of daylight, warming nighttime temperatures, and the advent of spring rains, rattlesnakes begin their trek toward summer feeding haunts. Little is known about this period, but it is assumed that they disperse, mostly following the same paths they used in autumn. Again, pheromones are probably deposited during this vernal journey, marking the trails to be used later for their return.

Pregnant females do not travel as far as the others. At first they consume as much food as is available. Within a month they are forced to stop foraging and feed sparingly, if at all.

Pregnant prairie rattlesnakes, *Crotalus viridis viridis,* and timber rattlesnakes, *Crotalus horridus horridus,* are known to have secondary maternity dens (also called *birthing rookeries*) near over-wintering hibernacula, usually within 1,000 feet (305 meters). Although quite suitable as protective recesses during warmer months, they are inadequate as permanent dens during severe weather. Perhaps a dozen or more females gather in late spring or early summer after a brief foraging period. Some do not arrive until late summer. Pregnant timber rattlesnakes have been reported to remain at the rookery or in the nearby woods, rarely moving more than 30 feet (9 meters) in any direction for the duration of the pregnancy. Considerable time is spent basking in open areas to properly thermoregulate and provide favorable internal temperatures for the developing young. Their young are born here in late summer or early fall. Those females that remained nearby tend to give birth earlier than the others that had moved greater distances.

Aggregations of gestating female rattlesnakes are highly susceptible to commercial collectors, and an inordinate number are captured and taken from the population at this time. Summer snake hunting is thought to be the most important single factor in the decline of the timber rattlesnake, *Crotalus horridus horridus.*

Aestivation

Aestivation is similar to hibernation, but rather than a strategy for escaping from cold, it is a way of avoiding extreme heat and desiccation. Nearly all snakes are forced to aestivate during prolonged hot, dry intervals. This explains why so few of them are encountered through the hottest, arid summer months when there is little, if any, rain.

In the desert, the searing summer sun forces temperatures to well over 110°F (46°C) for prolonged periods. Because readings are always recorded in the shade, the actual surface may well exceed

Pack rat nests *(above)* are similar to ground squirrel burrows in offering temporary refuge for rattlesnakes such as this prairie rattlesnake, *Crotalus viridis viridis (opposite).*

160°F (71°C). Few reptiles can survive more than a few minutes in temperatures over 97°F (43°C). In most places, shelter barely a foot below the surface will remain cool and relatively moist throughout the hottest months. Many animals escape certain death from heat exhaustion and dehydration by retiring to these underground haunts.

The onset of heavy summer rains that periodically soak the ground stimulates the continuance of life-sustaining activities. During these periods snakes, as well as most prey animals, avoid the scorching desert sun by staying underground, surfacing at night when safe, desirable foraging temperatures prevail. Optimal periods may be of short duration, so they maximize their time by vigorously feeding to restore fat deposits consumed by daily activities.

Reaction to the Moon and Wind

Regardless of the season or temperature, many observers have noted a considerable decrease in snake activity on cloudless nights during a full moon. Conversely, activity peaks at a new moon. Nighttime wandering increases proportionately during the waning phase and lessens during waxing. Mammalian activity appears to follow a similar pattern in some regions.

One rational explanation is predation. Brightly illuminated nights afford less concealment for foraging animals, both mammalian and reptilian. Nocturnal predators, owls in particular, would have little trouble in spotting a moving kangaroo rat or a small rattlesnake. They would be an easy meal.

Another hypothesis is that this behavior may illustrate a cycle. However, we must first accept that snakes and prey animals are less likely to prowl on moonlit nights. Rattlesnakes may eat one or two sizable meals a month, and because perhaps one week is needed for digestion, they are immobile for much of the time. If a rattlesnake finds an adequate meal during peak prey movement (a darker moon period) and retreats to digest, it would not become hungry and seek another meal until the next semidark phase, approximately twelve to fourteen days later.

Wind seems to limit rattlesnake movement. There is a significant drop in snake activity during windy periods. One exception is the sidewinder, which has adapted to regions in which winds are a frequent occurrence. Nevertheless, when gusts blow debris and sand, they too remain in hiding. Rattlesnakes may be disoriented if the vomeronasal apparatus is negatively affected by the omnidirectional, stirring air movements, particularly when combined with sand particles.

Too little natural history fieldwork is being undertaken to explain the complexities of much animal behavior. Much of today's biological research is being done within the controlled confines of the laboratory. It is imperative that natural history data be amassed from within the animal's habitat while those habitats still exist.

Activity Cycles

Montane forms are most active during the daylight of the summer rainy season. Their aestivation cycle is guided by lack of water combined with extreme temperatures. The higher elevation and preponderance of canopy and dense vegetation tend to keep the periods of lethal daytime highs short. These rattlesnakes are frequently seen abroad immediately before and after the brief torrential downpours. It appears that the drastic change in barometric pressure before a thunderstorm stimulates their activity. The dense cloud cover and cooling effect of the rain are also stimulants of activity.

Rattlesnakes spend a great deal of their lives in hiding because of the effects of temperature on them. Aside from the process of digesting large meals and the necessity of avoiding daytime sun, much of their time is spent hibernating and aestivating. Hibernation may last for months at temperate latitudes or higher elevations and colder regions or be as short as a few weeks closer to the equator. Eastern massasaugas, *Sistrurus catenatus catenatus,* some prairie rattlesnakes, *Crotalus viridis viridis,* and timber rattlesnakes, *Crotalus horridus horridus,* as well as many higher elevation montane forms are inactive for as many as seven and a half months of the year. Rattlesnakes are most commonly seen abroad during daylight in spring, basking, moving to summer haunts, seeking mates, and foraging. Because many become crepuscular or nocturnal throughout the hotter months, encounters with humans are more infrequent.

The total time out and about for rattlesnakes living in desert environments may equal little more than thirty days a year. Eastern diamondbacks, *Crotalus adamanteus,* timber rattlesnakes, *Crotalus horridus horridus,* and canebrake rattlesnakes, *Crotalus horridus atricaudatus,* spend most of their active seasons (more than 80 percent) on the surface, sequestered among plants and surface litter.

In early autumn a western massasauga, *Sistrurus catenatus tergeminus,* in Parker County, Texas, begins its trek from a grassy foraging haunt to a nearby, long-abandoned barn foundation in which it will hibernate for the winter.

SEX, REPRODUCTION, AND GROWTH

Rattlesnakes don't come slithering out into the light of day. They come out coiled inside flimsy egg-shaped pouches from which they must escape. In some sense they are born. But once born, they have to hatch.

—D. C. Ipsen

Following a traditional evolutionary scale, reptiles form an important link between amphibians and birds. With the exception of some fishes, all caecilians, most salamanders, and some frogs, reptiles are the first animals to reproduce almost exclusively by internal fertilization. However, there are a few all-female populations of reptiles that are capable of reproducing without males. Approximately thirty-eight lizards (mostly of the genera *Cnemidophorus, Archaeolacerta,* and *Hemidactylus*) and three "primitive" burrowing blind snakes of the family Typhlopidae produce young by *parthenogenesis*. Parthenogenesis is an uncommon form of asexual reproduction in vertebrates that permits the ovum to develop into an embryo without the need for fertilization by a sperm. The offspring are genetically identical to the female and to each other, so in fact they are clones. The process is complicated by the presence of additional sexual reproduction in some of the forms. David Chiszar (personal communication, 1996) suggested that there is preliminary evidence (as yet unpublished) that certain snakes, including at least one rattlesnake, have reproduced asexually.

These San Lucan speckled rattlesnakes, *Crotalus mitchellii mitchellii,* are mating. They have been in contact for three hours. Normally mating rattlesnakes lie together, attached for several hours with little movement. As is commonly the case, the female (the one on the left) has decided the act is finished and is beginning to crawl away. The male's hemipenis is still inside her, and as she moves away, he gets dragged along with her until he releases her.

Procreation is paramount for the survival of any organism, and snakes (like most other vertebrates) have distinctive behavioral and physiological modifications that increase the percentages of successful mating. Both genders have reproductive cycles. These fertile periods, in which viable sperm and eggs are produced, are related to climatic conditions and the length of the activity season. The physical condition of the parents is also an important factor. The female must have a sizable reserve of fat bodies to form eggs large enough to ovulate and later to nourish the developing fetuses. She will feed little, if at all, during gestation. Egg production and gestation may consume as much as half the female's body weight, so it may take several seasons for her to return to adequate health to produce another brood. In cooler climates this nonreproduction interval may be as long as two or three or even four years.

Although most snakes lay leathery-shelled eggs, all rattlesnakes are viviparous—bearing live young. At birth, the baby rattlesnake is tightly coiled and encased in a fetal sac. The fetal sac is a thin membranous wrapping in close association with the mother's oviduct. The fetuses completely develop internally and are born alive.

Because rattlesnake species differ in size, it is consistent that the size of their young and number in a brood would vary as well. Smaller forms have fewer but proportionally larger young than do larger species. A twin-spotted rattlesnake, *Crotalus pricei,* may produce a litter of two to four that are 30 percent the length of an adult, whereas an eastern diamondback, *Crotalus adamanteus,* may have twenty or more young that are 20 to 27 percent the length of adults. It also follows that a smaller female will produce fewer young than a larger female of the same species. Mid-sized and wide-ranging species (e.g., western and timber rattlesnakes) average between six to ten young in a typical litter.

Time of Mating

The season in which rattlesnakes mate varies among species and habitats. Some species mate in the spring, a majority in the summer or fall, and some mate in both spring and fall. Females may become more receptive to males in late summer and fall, after they have had time to eat and build up fat stores before becoming pregnant.

Because males and females are brought together in large numbers at dens, it is a logical place to mate. Some do so in the spring preceding their summer dispersals, and others do so in the fall before hibernating. It is important to note that many species mate away from dens at different times, predominantly in the late summer or fall.

Before dispersing after emerging from hibernation, rattlesnakes bask as frequently as weather permits. Sunlight and gradual warming and changes in the snakes' circadian rhythm likely stimulate the pituitary gland and the hypothalamus to produce hormones. They prompt a shedding cycle, while arousing the gonads in both genders.

As she sheds, the female secretes seductive chemicals (sex pheromones) and possibly aromatic lipids produced from dorsal skin glands located between the scales. Additional chemicals may be produced in paired anal scent glands. As she moves about, minute amounts of sex pheromones (a group of compounds known as methylketones) are deposited.

Using his Jacobson's organ and tongue as a guide, the male intercepts the female sex pheromone trail and begins actively searching for her. In some species dens provide a balance of genders, as well as generous numbers. Here the male's search is short. In many cases they disperse early, however, so he may have to travel several miles to find a mate. Females have never been observed searching for males.

In northern climates, female prairie rattlesnakes, *Crotalus viridis viridis,* leave the den soon after emerging and begin foraging immediately. During the latter part of the summer, stimulated males have been observed traveling long distances (as many as 8 miles, or 13 kilometers) in incredibly straight lines, searching for females. Major obstacles (massive rocks, ponds, walls, and so on) preventing direct movement are circumvented. The trek continues, in an exact direction, on the other side of the obstruction. The direction of movement is followed almost exclusively until a strong female pheromone trail is intersected.

In theory, straight-line movement is purely functional. The chance of finding a mate increases dramatically by maintaining a straight-line course because the female leaves an erratic meandering path as she wanders about searching for food, whereas the straight-lining male is more likely to intercept her trail.

There are no guarantees a male will readily find a mate. In a study of prairie rattlesnakes, *Crotalus viridis viridis,* in Wyoming, nearly 50 percent of the males did not find a mate in one season. A male may find several females and mate with them all. The female is equally promiscuous. She too may have as many partners as are available, so long as hormones keep her receptive. This is well within the realm of their sexual prowess and promotes successful breeding. It is possible for a female to bear a brood of young fathered by several males, thus providing a mixture of genes within a brood. There is evidence that certain male reptiles (e.g., garter snakes, *Thamnophis*) deposit sperm plugs within the female that prevent additional mating. Supportive data suggesting sperm plugs occur in rattlesnakes are not known but likely may be found.

The male banded rock rattlesnake, *Crotalus lepidus klauberi* (on top), is rubbing his chin along the neck of a slightly different color-patterned female in an attempt to stimulate her to mate.

These mating canebrake rattlesnakes, *Crotalus horridus atricaudatus*, have been in coitus for nearly three hours. The female has reversed her position and is attempting to uncouple and crawl away.

Should mating not occur within a few weeks, the male may be nearly overcome by the hormone-induced need to reproduce and become aggressive. Refusing to feed, he will wander about, led by his genetically programmed, primal urging to follow volatile and substrate-borne pheromone scents. After a brief period, pheromone residues will dissipate, and the male's hormone flow will subside. Gradually the mating urge will lessen, and the rigors of survival, foraging, and feeding will resume. A mating period of seven weeks was noted in one population of prairie rattlesnakes, *Crotalus viridis viridis*.

Those rattlesnakes mating in late summer or fall appear to be stimulated by gradually falling temperatures, shortening of the daylight cycle, or the onset of rain combined with a rapid change in barometric pressure. It is uncertain what instigates active sperm production. Most likely, female hormones (related to vitellogenesis or yolk formation) induce the production of sex pheromones that stimulate the reproductive cycle in both genders.

Sperm from these matings are retained in a special structure within the oviduct of the overwintering female until ripened eggs are produced in her ovaries the next spring. This is one method of ensuring a successful reproductive cycle among snakes leading a solitary existence and in those that wander great distances. Long-term sperm retention has been reported in communally denning species, such as the timber rattlesnake, *Crotalus horridus horridus*, and prairie rattlesnake, *Crotalus viridis viridis*.

Combat Dance

Unlike some mammals and many birds, rattlesnakes (all snakes, for that matter) do not have elaborate male territorial rites. However, one uncommonly observed and interesting interaction that appears directly related to reproduction has been observed between males of the same species. This form of ritualistic fighting, called *combat dancing,* has been reported in many species of rattlesnakes. It has been observed among a variety of other snake genera as well. The majority of these events have been observed during late summer and fall.

Under certain unexplained circumstances, should two adult males happen on one another, a combat dance might ensue. A combination of sensory cues, visual and vomeronasal, seem to trigger the actions. Although there are variations among species, physical contact is always made.

The snakes quickly move toward each other, heads aloft, entwining necks while raising the fore portions of their bodies, almost vertically above the ground, often fully a third of their length. Each, with fleet darting movements, pushes and strains in an attempt to topple the other. Usually, both fall.

The bout is repeated, almost precisely, with comparable results. They engage vigorously several more times, duplicating their actions, following a highly ritualistic, instinctive behavioral pattern. The performance continues for half an hour or more. Eventually, one male will tire, be forced to the ground, give up, and move away. Defeated males refused to court females for at least a week. As one might expect, the victor is frequently the larger, more robust male, but not always.

Aside from one observation in sidewinders, *Crotalus cerastes,* fangs are not employed. Although there is no savage intent reported among rattlesnakes, combat in some of the larger, otherwise harmless (nonvenomous) snakes (e.g., indigo snakes, *Drymarchon*) has resulted in injury to one or both of the combatants. The outcome of these bouts is usually little more than chew marks, minor openings in the skin caused by biting. However, occasional overzealous confrontations have left one of the combatants with bleeding lacerations.

Some early observers of combating in the wild misinterpreted it as a courting dance. Little imagination is needed to see the similarity. But both participants have proven to be almost exclusively males. A captive female was reported assuming the vertical combat position in an excellent review of western diamondback combat by J. C. Gillingham, C. C. Carpenter, and J. B. Murphy ("Courtship, Male Combat, and Dominance in the Western Diamondback Rattlesnake, *Crotalus atrox," Journal of Herpetology* 17:265–70 [1983]). No one has confirmed whether these dances are territorial, a form of sexual stimulation, or competition over a particular female. Apparently, there is a strong sexual significance because, on many occasions, a female was observed in the vicinity. This is

A close-up of coital contact of the San Lucan speckled rattlesnakes, *Crotalus mitchellii mitchellii,* shown at the opening of this chapter. The female has her tail elevated.

believed to be the most recurrent situation in captive observations. Little, if any, other comparable contact or communication has ever been seen in other groups of animals in nature.

Reproduction

Male snakes have two copulatory organs known as *hemipenes*. Some consider this a misnomer, referring to one as a single organ and simply calling it a penis. Unlike a true penis, there is no enclosed internal seminal duct in the hemipenis to carry the sperm. Seminal fluid flows along a groove into the female's oviduct. Lying within the base of the tail adjacent to the vent, the two hemipenes are normally withdrawn or retracted and invisible until mating occurs. Like all the organs in a snake's attenuated body, the two elongated testes supplying the hemipenes are situated far forward within the body cavity. The left testis is slightly posterior, toward the vent. A long seminal duct carries the fluid from each testes to the hemipenes.

Ova (eggs) are produced in the female's ovaries. When the follicles burst, the ripened ova are released, passing freely a very short distance into the body cavity. A thin, lacy, funnel-shaped opening receives the ova into an oviduct. The paired oviducts are elongated and asymmetrically aligned, analogous to the male's testes. The eggs are arranged in a continuous chain, resembling a string of pearls in a tightly coiled section of the oviduct known as the *tuba.* Then they pass posteriorly into the uterus where they will be fertilized. After fertilization the embryos develop within the uterus.

Viable sperm can be stored or retained in the tightly coiled portion of the female's oviduct, in recesses known as *spermathecae.* Sperm can be retained for long periods, frequently for six to eight months, and on occasion for two years or more in the female. Sperm retention permits mating in the fall with fertilization occurring months later, in the spring. Births in successive years have been reported from females that have not been with males throughout the period. Sperm storage is an advantageous method of ensuring reproduction when there is no guarantee that pairing and mating will occur at the proper time, usually in early summer when development and gestation begin.

Once a receptive female is found, the male may remain in close contact with her for a few days. Some herpetologists refer to this as a guarding period. Throughout this time the accompanying suitor follows the female's every move, frequently touching and rubbing her. Although she remains quite passive during premating, the male tries his best to stimulate her. All in all, it seems to be a tender

Partially hidden among ground litter and mosses, this female dusky
pigmy rattlesnake, *Sistrurus miliarius barbouri,* gives birth to three
young. One remains within its sac. When the newborns crawl about for
the first time, the birthing fluids will evaporate from their skin.

Above: The swollen area toward the tail of this basking adult eastern diamondback, *Crotalus adamanteus*, discloses that she is pregnant. In a month (late August) she will bear a dozen or so very large young.

Opposite: This basking Coronado Island rattlesnake, *Crotalus viridis caliginis,* has a swollen posterior section, showing she is pregnant. Pregnant rattlesnakes bask frequently.

encounter, particularly for animals portrayed as having such lethal tools and irascible demeanors.

Approaching her from the rear, starting near the vent, he presses and rubs his chin along her back. His tongue darts in and out rapidly, gently touching her skin. He quickly becomes noticeably aroused, making short, thrusting, jerking movements combined with rapid tongue darting, while attempting to cause her to crawl. Responding, she begins to move but remains mostly inactive. As he moves, he gently presses his length along hers, attempting to elevate her tail with his. When she crawls, he follows, always in contact, sometimes riding her. Should she refuse his advances, he becomes more aggressive, prodding and pushing with increased fervor. Eventually, she elevates her tail slightly and begins waving it. Likely, she is releasing pheromones with this response because his tongue flicking and jerking movements increase in frequency and strength. He moves about more impulsively, his tail whipping spontaneously from side to side, maneuvering in an attempt to lift hers.

If receptive, when their vents are in contact she will elevate her tail and gape her cloaca, permitting him to enter her. The basal portion of the hemipenis (on the side most suitably aligned with the female's vent) is thrust into the open cloaca, often after several unsuccessful attempts. Once firm contact is made the rest of the hemipenis is everted. Eversion, intromission, and penile engorgement are accomplished by simultaneously filling the hemipenis with blood while contracting a special erector muscle.

Only one hemipenis is used at a time, while the other remains retracted. The everted hemipenis reveals a unique adaptation for ensuring successful copulation; it is covered with protuberances and spines that face backward toward its root. Once inside, the spines and bulbous shape firmly anchor the engorged organ. The pair of snakes are not separated until he voluntarily disgorges and retracts the hemipenis. While copulating they remain almost motionless; only infrequent twitching, mostly from the male, can be observed at the vents. Copulation may take minutes or hours, occasionally twenty-four hours or longer. It may be repeated over several days.

When mating is complete, they uncouple, sometimes with considerable difficulty. It is not uncommon for her to move away, dragging the still-attached male until the hemipenis is inverted and dislodged. Once detached, they may remain near each other for several days and mate again, or soon go their separate ways. It is possible that either or both will engage in additional mating.

Taxonomists find male snakes' hemipenes extremely helpful for differentiating species, genera, and even families of snakes. Size, shape, arrangement, and position of the spines, protuberances, and lobes are consistent within a subspecies or species but can differ greatly between species. Their size and other physical differences may be a major factor in preventing the crossbreeding or hybridizing of sympatric species.

Gestation and Birth

The pregnant female may attempt to feed for a brief time early in her pregnancy. Soon, other hormones, and the bulk of the developing embryos, will force her to stop foraging. She must find refuge for the duration of the summer. Females of populations that aggregate to hibernate mostly remain in suitable habitat nearby the den or gather in small numbers at brooding sites or birthing rookeries. Three months is a normal gestation period.

Maturing embryos receive sustenance and fluids from stored nutrients in the yolk mass and perhaps from a more direct fetal association, or primitive placenta. During this time, the female's thermoregulation is important to ensure normal growth of her embryos. She will move to and from warmer areas, basking for a time daily. Remaining highly secretive and sedentary, she travels short distances to find drinking water, mostly at night.

Each embryo develops encased in a transparent, membranous

Opposite: **The brightly patterned young Arizona black rattlesnake,** *Crotalus viridis cerberus,* **contrasts greatly with its male parent. The young snake will progressively darken as it grows, and after shedding eight to ten times, it will be as dark as its parents. The reason for this change is uncertain, but it most likely is related to cryptic coloration, habitat choice, and food preference.**

Below: **A newborn dusky pigmy rattlesnake,** *Sistrurus miliarius barbouri,* **another still in its sac, and three infertile egg masses passed during birthing.**

sac. Some scientists have described it as a "preplacenta." The developing snake is attached to the membrane by an umbilical stalk of tissue. Although some exchange of materials and gases is undertaken through the membrane, it is not nearly as sophisticated as a mammalian placenta.

When the fetuses are fully matured, the female finds a secluded area for parturition. Most captive births occur at night, which probably occurs in the majority of cases in nature. It would reduce the chance of predation. Rhythmic contractions move the fetuses toward the vent. The tail is elevated and the young are expelled individually (with a small gush of fluid) within their fetal sacs. They may rest a few minutes before breaking out of the sac. Crawling away from the drying residual tissues, they settle a short distance away in a suitable nook. Frequently they remain in contact with their sisters and brothers (sometimes entwined in a ball-like mass) for the first few days. A small section of umbilical stalk remains attached on the belly about two-thirds of the snake's body length back from the head. The scar remains for several months but is obliterated with a few sheds, within the first growing season.

Nearly all egg-laying snakes are born with a curious appendage, an "egg tooth." The egg tooth is very small, conical, sharply pointed, and calcified, at the front of the rostrum (the most anterior scale on the head). It is most prominent on oviparous snakes, where it successfully functions to slit the tough leathery shell, per-

mitting the hatching snake to escape. Though present on emerging newborn rattlesnakes, it is so diminutive, upturned, and unsharp that it is best considered vestigial. Its existence in rattlesnakes is a good indicator of their evolution from an egg-laying ancestry. The sac membrane is so thin, and is so greatly stretched from within, the snake needs to exert little pressure to break through. The egg tooth is lost about the time of the first shed, usually within the first week or two.

Maternal Protection

Little is known about baby rattlesnakes in nature during the few days immediately after birth. They may wander short distances to find suitable hiding places or stay secluded with the mother. Female prairie rattlesnakes, *Crotalus viridis viridis,* demonstrate a major change in temperament immediately after giving birth. Whereas they were confident in remaining motionless, relying on cryptic coloration before parturition, they became irascible and quick to confront intruders afterward.

Several scientists have observed some mothers staying close by the newborns for a brief time. After the first shed, youngsters scatter and the mother leaves as well. Most likely the mother's actions are stimulated by the odors produced in birthing that remain on the neonate until they shed. Three different female eastern diamondbacks, *Crotalus adamanteus,* and their newborn aggregations have been observed. Although there is no conclusive evidence of a maternal protection instinct, researchers hypothesize that short-term exhaustion keeps the mother in proximity to the neonates for several days (J. A. Butler and T. W. Hull, "Neonate Aggregations and Maternal Attendance to Young in the Eastern Diamondback Rattlesnake, *Crotalus adamanteus,*" *Copeia* 1995:196–98 [1995]). No observations of females protecting their offspring from potential predators have been made. Considerable additional research is needed to conclude that there is maternal protection, but it is certainly a possibility.

Another study showed newborn prairie rattlesnakes, *Crotalus viridis viridis,* remained aggregated for up to sixteen days. The young are reported to imprint on conspecifics by tongue flicking and pressing their faces against their mother's body, and researchers have observed mouth-gaping and head-shaking, presumably in order to transfer odors to the vomeronasal organ. This sensory imprinting enables the youngsters to follow the adults' trails to and from dens in the fall and spring.

When prairie rattlesnakes, *Crotalus viridis viridis,* are disturbed they produce an alarm scent. Neonate eastern diamondbacks, *Crotalus adamanteus,* show a similar reaction while they remain in contact with one another. Once baby rattlesnakes scatter from the birth site, they face the world, surviving—or not—on their own.

Growth

Neonate growth is dependent on the quantity of available food. If the supply is adequate, they may double their size within three or four months. Under excellent conditions, males of some species will mature during their second year and females in their third. Un-

The massive size of an exceptionally long (82-inch, 208-centimeter) western diamondback, *Crotalus atrox,* is displayed by a professional snake handler, Gordon Buchanon. This method, known as "tailing," is not recommended, because the sheer weight of its body could cause vertebral injury to the snake, which increases the holder's chance of being bitten. This snake lived under ideal conditions and was well fed (it was captive-raised from the time it was a juvenile), which permitted it to grow to this size and weigh in excess of 20 pounds (7.5 kilograms). Finding a giant like this one in the wild is very unlikely.

der the best of conditions the female may match the male, but in the wild that is uncommon. Most probably, females of some rattlesnake species reproduce in their third or fourth years. In northern timber rattlesnakes, *Crotalus horridus horridus,* however, a long-term study of marked females disclosed that most females do not begin to reproduce until their ninth or tenth years.

In cooler temperate climates and at higher elevations, healthy male rattlesnakes produce active sperm each year, but females are capable of only biennial egg production. The timber rattlesnake, *Crotalus horridus horridus,* in many northern regions requires three or four years to regain breeding potential. The three-month gestation period saps reserved nutrients, little of which can be restored before the declining autumn temperature forces them into hibernation. Mortality of postpartum females that have been unable to feed adequately after giving birth may be high during hibernation.

In general, newborns have enough remaining yolk that they can molt and enter hibernation with enough fat and stored glycogen to survive the winter without feeding. Neonates from warmer regions, or those born early (in the late summer), may have to feed to gain sufficient weight before settling in for the winter. No doubt, many baby rattlesnakes do not survive the first winter.

Sexual Dimorphism

Sexual dimorphism is most readily observed externally in rattlesnakes' tails. Males have proportionally longer, thicker, tails. Wider at the base, just distal to the cloaca, a male's tail accommodates the hemipenes. Males and females of some species show differences in overall body length, but the trait is not totally predictable, because growth rates are inconsistent. With the exception of sidewinders, *Crotalus cerastes,* where the females are longer, males of most species are 10 to 15 percent longer than females. In two subspecies, the canebrake rattlesnake, *Crotalus horridus*

Left: A newborn eastern diamondback, *Crotalus adamanteus,* falls victim to an adult eastern kingsnake, *Lampropeltis getula getula.* The kingsnake, here being bitten by the rattlesnake, is immune to the rattlesnake's venom.

Below: Because the rattlesnake is so small, the predator constricts it only partially, quickly and efficiently swallowing it alive. In this instance, again because the rattlesnake is so small, it is being eaten tail first.

A Carolina pigmy rattlesnake, **Sistrurus miliarius miliarius,** from Habersham City, Georgia, exhibits a reddish tinge, common to examples from that area.

atricaudatus, and the timber rattlesnake, *Crotalus horridus horridus,* the males are longer and bulkier than the females. This difference may be related to the side effects of testicular hormone production in that larger males may have an advantage in combat, or the overall body mass loss of the female's producing offspring may constrain her from growing as large.

Although sexual dichromatism (a difference in color attributable to one gender or the other) has been reported on rare occasions in other snake genera, it appears only partially substantiated in rattlesnakes. It was long thought that lighter colored (tan- or yellow-morph) timber rattlesnakes, *Crotalus horridus horridus,* were females, and the darker morphs (often nearly melanistic ones) were males. To date, this presumed correlation between color morph and gender is uncorroborated. There is one sexual dichromatic trait that is nearly always valid. As the male's tail is longer, the number of tail rings is consistently greater on males of those species with them (most diamondback forms—for example, *Crotalus atrox*).

Predation

Neonates are miniature replicas of adults, with completely operative fangs and venom. They are capable of killing prey at birth. Their lack of experience makes them most vulnerable to predation at this time, however. They naively roam about hunting suitably sized food while dispersing to find their own home range or to find their population's den. Small prey may be difficult to locate, so neonates may be driven to forage during daylight without the concealment of darkness and with less than adequate caution.

Predators that would never attempt to confront an adult rattlesnake find babies an easy meal. Ravens, crows, roadrunners, large wading birds, raccoons, opossums, skunks, foxes, coyotes, weasels, whipsnakes, kingsnakes, and racers all take a heavy toll. The tinier forms are killed by small predatory birds, such as jays, shrikes, and kingfishers. Bullfrogs and other larger anurans have been known to eat small rattlesnakes. Although snakes grow quickly and those who make it to their second year fare proportionately better, coyotes, eagles, hawks, owls, javelinas, feral pigs, badgers, indigo snakes, and kingsnakes find them readily acceptable meals. Hungry adult rattlesnakes are occasionally cannibalistic and will devour an unfortunate neonate. Ants of the genus *Formica* are reported as possible predators of small rattlesnakes. Three prairie rattlesnakes were found dead while they were being consumed, just as another one was being attacked by ants and near death. Although not reported to date, it is highly likely that the vexatious and extremely aggressive red imported fire ant, *Solenopsis invicta,* is a rattlesnake predator.

Many rattlesnakes are killed by cars as they cross roads. Inadequate hiding places during temperature extremes (a hot dry summer or freezing winter), drastic weather conditions, and an insufficient supply of small prey are other life-threatening natural obstacles. Chances of living through the first year are slim. Juvenile mortality is high; as few as 20 percent of newborns may reach their second spring.

Adulthood brings a greater chance for survival. In fact, a rattlesnake that endures into its fourth year has a very good probability of living to be ten years or older. Timber rattlesnakes, *Crotalus horridus horridus,* have been found to live twenty-five years in the wild, but a more normal life span appears to be between fifteen and twenty years. Other species have reached beyond the quarter of a century mark in captivity.

The granddaddy of all rattlesnake longevity so far reported is a canebrake rattlesnake, *Crotalus horridus atricaudatus,* that lived just over thirty-six and a half years in a college biology laboratory. It survived on a diet of small mammals, fed only three or four times a year.

Adults are large formidable predators. They have learned to acclimate to varying conditions, have a fairly established home territory, and have a wider selection of food animals available to them. Humans become an adult rattlesnake's greatest enemy, as only a few other animals (e.g., large hoofed stock, hogs, badgers, and alligators) will chance confronting one. During the mating season, adult males spend a greater amount of time moving about, searching for receptive females, so they are at a decided disadvantage. This is most likely why the proportion of males killed by cars or by local residents is so high during the mating season, often in mid-summer.

Viviparity and venom-injecting capabilities are advantageous for ensuring the survival of an individual, but innumerable natural factors keep the numbers of all rattlesnakes in line with the environment's capacity to sustain a population. The forces of nature, therefore, keep the chance of being overrun with rattlesnakes most unlikely.

This photograph was taken a few months before Snifty, a twelve-year-old captive dusky pigmy rattlesnake, *Sistrurus miliarius barbouri*, died of natural causes. It is the record length for the subspecies (32.5 inches, 82.5 centimenters) and likely the record weight (23.2 ounces or 721.5 grams). A greater length has mistakenly been reported elsewhere for this individual snake.

HOW RATTLESNAKES MOVE

A crawling snake suggests a stream of water flowing along a winding bed.
—C. H. Pope

Snakes are pretty much all ribs. They have more ribs than any other vertebrate, ranging from 160 to 400 pairs. In contrast, frogs have no true ribs, horses have seventeen pairs, and humans have twelve pairs. Rattlesnakes are at the lower end of the range for snakes. In snakes, the number of ribs almost matches the number of ventral scales, because the ribs are individually connected to them by an elaborate musculature. This is an important adaptation for locomotion. Except for the atlas and axis (vertebrae that attach to the skull) and the tail vertebrae, a pair of the long, thin, movable, saber-shaped ribs are attached to an equal number of vertebrae. Like all snakes, rattlesnakes do not have a sternum. The ribs curve around the body, providing support while giving the body its cylindrical shape. The ribs do not attach ventrally, and the undersurface is somewhat flexible, allowing distention of the body to facilitate the intake of large food animals.

Each vertebra articulates with its neighbor by ball and socket joints, the cup (socket) being at the anterior end. Two lateral processes with matching cavities permit considerable articulation while limiting complete movement. Besides protecting the spinal cord, the joints inhibit potentially dangerous overrotation. In addition, two longer processes add protection and strength. One process lies ventrally, toward the body cavity, and the neural spine opposes it dorsally. The

S-shaped tracks in the loose sand clearly demonstrate the preferred method of locomotion of this Sonoran Desert sidewinder, *Crotalus cerastes cercobombus*. At full speed the snake appears to glide over the otherwise untrackable surface.

123

Directional light delineates the form of this skeleton of a young prairie rattlesnake, *Crotalus viridis viridis.* The skull and each of the vertebrae and ribs have been carefully prepared and attached, simulating their position within the live snake. The rattle was added to better represent the rattlesnake. In nature, the rattle along with the uncalcified body parts likely would have disintegrated or been eaten by one or more of a myriad of nature's recyclers.

effective range of movement between each pair of vertebrae is approximately 25 inches vertically and 25 inches from side to side.

The vertebrae of rattlesnakes are larger and denser than those of most snakes, affording greater strength and support. This is particularly beneficial in delivering precise and powerful strikes. Larger vertebrae with longer processes (especially the neural spine) provide more surface area for muscle attachment. The need for strength is most obvious in the defensive position, where as much as a third of the body may be elevated in an S-shaped coil for an extended period. All forms of the neotropical rattlesnake, *Crotalus durissus,* have prominent neural spines, giving them a conspicuous, almost serrated-appearing vertebral ridge along the back. They also are known for having the most dramatic, elevated defensive coil.

Climbing Ability

Rattlesnakes move freely among rocks and other solid substrates that offer adequate surface traction, but many species appear unable or unwilling to climb onto more precarious perches, such as tree and shrub limbs. As for most vertebrates, the labyrinth of the inner ear, in concert with the eyes, controls balance. This partially governs a snake's ability to climb. One hypothesis to explain a rattlesnake's reluctance to climb among branches and limbs is its lack of constrictor muscle bundles and its proportionately greater

body weight than many thinner snake species. This may allow too much pressure to be applied to points of contact, which, in turn, can constrict the flow of blood.

There seems to be some correlation in size and climbing propensity. Many of the smaller, montane races live in steep talus slopes and move among the rocks. This species can enter small bushes readily. Dusky pigmy rattlesnakes, *Sistrurus miliarius barbouri,* will wait a foot or more off the ground on clumps of cord grass or low shrubs in ambush for unwary lizards or frogs. As would be expected, larger, more heavy-bodied species do not balance well on objects such as small branches. Some rattlesnakes are more adept at climbing than others. Blacktail, *Crotalus molossus,* and timber rattlesnakes, *Crotalus horridus horridus,* have been spotted several feet above the ground in bushes or on tree limbs, either searching for prey (birds) or basking. I once almost walked (chest-high) into a basking timber rattlesnake on a cool autumn morning in northern Georgia. The snake was in a dense, massive stand of mountain laurel and had climbed into the branches to reach the warming sun's rays. Mojave rattlesnakes, *Crotalus scutulatus scutulatus,* and western diamondbacks, *Crotalus atrox,* have been found up on cholla and other branching cacti. Charles Bogert, former curator of herpetology at the American Museum of Natural History, related that the Santa Catalina Island rattlesnake, *Crotalus catalinensis,* is frequently found in shrubs hunting birds, a major food source for the species.

Left: The Mojave Desert sidewinder, *Crotalus cerastes cerastes*, uses unique sidewinding movements that allow it to rapidly glide over soft sand, escaping pursuers that tend to be slowed or bogged down by their own weight.

Below: A complex, coordinated use of vertebra, ribs, and muscles enables a Mojave rattlesnake, *Crotalus scutulatus scutulatus*, to support a suspended length of "neck" as it moves. The same physical attributes supply the powerful thrust of a strike.

Below: A western diamondback, *Crotalus atrox*, basking a few feet above the ground on a clump of cholla cactus and dry desert shrubbery.

Above: This red diamond rattlesnake, *Crotalus ruber ruber*, unlike most other large, heavy-bodied rattlesnakes that rarely climb, has moved into a shrub, likely following the scent trail of a small rodent or bird. Rattlesnakes climb into trees, shrubs, and cacti to escape enemies and quickly rising floodwater, to hunt birds, or simply to find a suitable basking site among dense ground cover.

This complements the observation that this taxon's fangs are proportionately longer than those of any other rattlesnake, an adaptation for piercing the fluffy feathers of a bird's body.

In captivity, most species will climb while searching for an escape route, to look for food, or to get closer to a radiant heat source. They prefer expansive areas of solid support and spend nearly all their time on the ground.

Swimming

All rattlesnakes are excellent swimmers, mostly floating atop the surface with their heads held aloft. Rattlesnakes rarely dive, even when attempting to escape. Using an undulating motion, they can move rapidly in a chosen direction. At first their rattle is carried out of the water, but it quickly becomes waterlogged and sinks below the surface.

Only a few snakes are adapted to, and known to be capable of tolerating, prolonged contact with salt or brackish water. Sea snakes (a highly venomous, totally aquatic group of fifty or so species of

Above: The undulating waves of this swimming canebrake rattlesnake, *Crotalus horridus atricaudatus,* demonstrate serpentine movement. Because it has been swimming for some distance, its rattle has become slightly waterlogged.

Right: A southeastern Arizona color morph of a northern blacktail rattlesnake, *Crotalus molossus molossus,* climbs amid a pile of rocks.

the families Hydrophilidae and Laticaudidae) inhabit warm Pacific Ocean waters. It is surprising then that rattlesnakes have been observed swimming in this type of environment, far from land. An eastern diamondback, *Crotalus adamanteus,* was observed swimming in salt water 22 miles (35 kilometers) offshore. Others have been seen swimming among the Florida Keys and Georgia Barrier Islands. They and western diamondbacks, *Crotalus atrox,* are recorded among tidal wrack and in salt marsh habitats along the Gulf Coast. Red diamond rattlesnakes, *Crotalus ruber,* and southern Pacific rattlesnakes, *Crotalus viridis helleri,* are known to swim short distances in the Pacific Ocean. Many species, including insular forms, live in grasses and rocky areas along beaches.

Methods of Movement

No doubt being legless has many disadvantages, but snakes have formidable advantages as well. An ability to enter realms that would be inaccessible without a slender, cylindrical body unencumbered with appendages is an obvious plus. This is readily apparent when a snake glides into a tunnel barely larger than its circumference in pursuit of a small mammal. Other predators would be impeded, having to stop and dig a wider access, while the rodent would likely beat a hasty retreat through another opening. Anyone who has chased a snake knows the body shape is equally effective when it is the prey.

Recent experiments have discredited the idea that leglessness evolved as a method of conserving energy. More energy is expended through undulating than through walking. An adaptation to pursue subterranean prey is one possible answer for limblessness. Incidentally, it is believed that snakes did not evolve from legless burrowing lizards but that both groups independently became limbless.

Not being able to walk using a varying gate to step over and around objects appears to be a great disadvantage when traveling through diverse terrain. Here too snakes have adapted quite well. Rattlesnakes, using the four forms of movement (serpentine, sidewinder, caterpillar, and accordion) used by a variety of other snakes, have little trouble in getting from one place to another. Each method is a complex action of vertebrae, muscles, ventral scales, and tactile perception in precise unison. A snake's musculature is extremely intricate, with different muscles and muscle groups being coordinated to produce different forms of motion.

Serpentine Locomotion

The most common and primitive form of locomotion in all snakes is undulating or serpentine motion, properly known as *lateral undulation*. Surface irregularities (e.g., stones, pebbles, grass, stems) are needed as bases for most expeditious maneuvering.

A desert-grassland massasauga, *Sistrurus catenatus edwardsii,* travels using serpentine movement.

Other forms of locomotion produce a more exacting directional movement but are more heavily dependent on specific static points of contact.

Sidewinding

Sidewinders, *Crotalus cerastes,* have a modified undulation adapted for crossing the soft, hot, barren sand they inhabit. By using only a small area at the lower side of one coil for purchase, the forward coil is lifted and thrown ahead. Barely clearing the sand, the advancing coil seeks a similar contact point. The "step" gained by this section of coil triggers a similar thrusting wave from the rear coil. It is not unlike a person climbing stairs—one step supports the weight and stabilizes the body for the progression of the other.

At full speed, a sidewinder glides over loose sand at a velocity of approximately 2 miles (3.2 kilometers) per hour, although it appears to be moving considerably faster. This is not only an excellent method of escape but is useful to prevent overheating because so little of the snake touches the hot sand. The tracks disclose the diagonal direction achieved and illustrate why its common name is sidewinder. The desert-grassland massasauga, *Sistrurus catenatus edwardsii,* the Baja California rattlesnake, *Crotalus enyo,* and other desert snakes use a variation of this method occasionally, but not nearly as effectively as the sidewinder.

Caterpillar Locomotion

A third way rattlesnakes move is called *caterpillar,* or *rectilinear, motion.* Stretched almost straight out, they proceed on their ventral scales appearing as though they are moving on a continuous row of invisible feet. As discussed earlier, ventral scales are wide (nearly the width of the snake's belly) and have a loose, sharp edge toward the rear. Continuing waves of contracting muscles control these loosely attached scales. Forward movement is not one continuing ripple running from the head through the tail but rather is a series of short ones moving a section at a time.

It was once believed that snakes "walked" on their ribs. Not so! Paired long muscles attached to the ribs move the ventral scales. The scales' posterior edges provide "footing." When no more rapid method is needed, most heavy-bodied rattlesnakes use this slow, deliberate form of movement. This mode of travel is commonly found in snakes crossing roads at night or crawling during cooler periods. No specific reason has been offered, but it probably conserves energy and (because of their large size) makes them less prone to be spotted or attacked by predators. No doubt, rectilinear crawling provides excellent stealth advantages when approaching prey. This is the most effective way of crossing surfaces lacking adequate irregularities for serpentine motion. All rattlesnakes can travel this way.

Three long muscle cords running along and connecting the vertebrae produce the smooth gliding motion. Working together with several small muscles attached to vertebral processes, others attached to ribs, and still others attached to the skin and scales, rattlesnakes are capable of rapid undulatory movement.

By applying a series of muscular contractions and relaxations, the snake tosses its body into a series of horizontal waves. Once an anchoring object has been found, force is exerted against it with the back of a coil. The wave continues, using that point, while reaching and exerting similar pressure more forward on the next prominence. The undulating action yields directional movement, but it is somewhat random because it relies on unpredictable surface irregularities. Without these points, little advancement is made.

A snake, attempting a quick escape on a smooth, hard-topped road, will writhe frantically, frustrated, until some purchase is attained. Over natural terrain, serpentine movement produces rapid progress. But because the snake is actually moving against each point of contact, an optical illusion is created. The perception is of much greater speed than is actually realized. Serpentine motion is also the method used when a rattlesnake is swimming in open water.

Accordion Locomotion

Rarely used by rattlesnakes, which nearly always prefer to use one of the methods described previously, concertina or accordion-like movement is still worth mentioning. When a rattlesnake needs to pass through a highly confining, smoothly lined tunnel, too narrow or too steeply inclined to permit serpentine movement, it may use this method. Lateral loops are pressed against the walls near the head region, and the rest of the body is pulled forward until there is no space. Similar loops toward the rear of the snake are pressed against the walls, and the anterior section is pushed forward. Using these muscular expansions and contractions in unison, forward movement is produced. A rattlesnake strike is little more than a modification of this type of movement. The strength and speed of muscle contraction in the neck region produces the velocity of the thrust.

A highly modified form of accordion locomotion is employed by arboreal boas and pythons to facilitate climbing vertical, limbless branches. The snake tightly entwines the branch toward its tail, forming an anchor, and pushes its head section onward. Another coil is entwined at the head section, and the remaining body behind is pulled forward. The procedure continues until the snake reaches its goal. This push–pull method is almost identical to the vertical rope climb familiar to those who have undergone military

Stretched nearly as straight as a rope, a large western diamondback rattlesnake, *Crotalus atrox*, moves across open ground by caterpillar locomotion.

During the rainy season, the Baja California rattlesnake, *Crotalus enyo enyo*, is commonly found at night crossing the few paved roads on the northern part of that peninsula.

training. Rattlesnakes are incapable of this modified accordion locomotion because they lack the proper musculature and body control.

There is no doubt that rattlesnakes have evolved as well adapted and sophisticated predators. Fangs, teeth, and a modified expandable jaw structure (for swallowing) help eliminate a need for appendages. The lack of arms and hands for grasping and digging is outweighed by their ability to follow prey through openings no bigger than the snake. Slow, straight-line crawling and mixed undulatory modes of movement effectively enable a rattlesnake to travel from place to place while performing its day-to-day activities.

FANGS: THE BUSINESS END
OF A RATTLESNAKE

**There are People in Europe, especially England, that tremble at the name
of a Rattlesnake, imagining that the country of Carolina is so full of them
that there is no going into the Woods without Danger of Life; but this is an
Error as ill-grounded as the most part of the Reports spread abroad as to
the disadvantage of this New World.**

—G. Millegan

A rattlesnake's head may appear all beauty and symmetry, but internally it
is all business. The head developed its spear-like shape to accommodate
the venom-injecting apparatus. However, this is not considered a major characteristic of venomous snakes, because many harmless snakes have similarly
shaped heads while totally lacking venom. Also, many extremely venomous
snakes in other families (Elapidae, Hydrophiidae, Laticaudidae) have a much
simpler venom-injecting apparatus that does not necessitate a pronounced
widening of the head. This elaborate mechanism is a relatively recent adaptation in the family Viperidae.

Dentition

Fangs are special, modified teeth. It is important
to realize that all snake teeth are not fangs. Like
most of the early evolved and primitive snakes,
a majority of living taxa have solid (aglyphous)
teeth and no venom apparatus. A pair of long,
highly movable, canaliculate (hypodermic
needle–like) teeth affixed to the front of the

The strike of a western
diamondback, *Crotalus atrox,*
is frozen in a series of
1/20,000-second stroboscopic
flashes. The entire process
(which happens in less than a
second) clearly shows the elaborate steps in delivering a protective strike.

maxillae and connected to venom glands are called *solenoglyphous fangs.* They are the most recent and advanced dentitional adaptation in snakes and are found almost exclusively in Viperidae.

The viper's adaptation of front movable fangs permits the fangs to be folded back into a soft, white or pinkish sheath of oral membrane within the roof of the mouth when the mouth is closed. During a strike the fangs are erected into an almost perpendicular position. While swallowing prey, the fangs are frequently retracted or folded into their sheaths in the roof of the mouth.

A third modification, a pair of short, mostly stationary, and canaliculate teeth, affixed to the front of the maxillae and accompanied by a venom apparatus, are called *proteroglyphous fangs.* They are found in the Elapidae (cobras, mambas, coralsnakes, and others) and the Hydrophiidae and Laticaudidae (seasnakes). Unlike viperids, proteroglyphs have many additional unmodified teeth on the upper maxillary bones along with the fangs.

A widely accepted view suggests that rear-fanged snakes with a pair of enlarged, stationary, grooved (opisthoglyphous) teeth attached at the rear of the mouth are a transition from nonvenomous snakes. Frequently referred to as *rear-fanged snakes,* their dentition is found in many colubrid genera believed to be closely linked to Viperidae. In these rear-fanged colubrids the elongate maxillae contain a larger complement of teeth, rather than a single fang.

Although quite possibly there are others, two African colubrid snakes, the boomslang, *Dispholidus typus,* and the birdsnake, *Thelotornis capensis,* are known to be the most dangerous snakes in the rear-fanged group. Examples of these snakes have the dubious distinction of fatally biting two of the world's most acclaimed herpetologists. The former killed Karl P. Schmidt in 1957 and the latter Robert Mertens in 1975. At the time, neither snake was believed to produce highly toxic venom, so the victims responded to the bites with little more than first aid. As a macabre aside, both of these scientists maintained detailed diaries of their reactions to the bites.

The punctures of ophisthoglyphs are produced by a less sophisticated chewing motion rather than by a stabbing injection. Considerable research is being undertaken to isolate venomous properties in the saliva of these snakes. Some are known to produce venom in

Right: A plaster and wire model on display at the Columbus Zoo in Ohio shows a rattlesnake with its fangs partially erected.

Left: The prepared skull of an eastern diamondback, *Crotalus adamanteus,* has been photographed with its mouth partially opened and fangs erected to show its structure. This 6-foot (1.8-meter) specimen was a longtime captive, which is the primary reason it had two pairs of functional fangs when it died. During its sedentary life, it was fed killed rats. It did not strike but merely swallowed them. Because the fangs were not used, they were not shed at a normal rate. The replacements continued to grow and would have forced the others from their sockets in short order. Other, shorter fangs in stages of growth can be seen on one side. These replacement fangs normally would be embedded in a skin sheath in the living snake.

paired glands (Duvernoy's glands) situated immediately above the teeth in the upper jaw. The venom and saliva flows along a groove in the tooth into the wound. Venom of rear-fanged snakes appears to have adapted for killing amphibians and lizards and is usually less toxic to mammals than is the venom of viperids.

Most snakes have six rows containing as many as fifty or more short, sharp recurving teeth that are used to help hold and swallow prey. Two rows lie along the outside of the lower jaw (dentaries), two coincide along the upper jaw (maxillaries), and a parallel pair is found toward the center of the roof of the mouth (palatines and pterygoids). Although vipers have the normal six rows of teeth, only fangs are found on the heavily modified, shortened maxillaries. With one exception, vipers in the genus *Atractaspis,* the placement of long, hollow, needle-sharp fangs at the front of the mouth on these movable bones is found only in viperids.

Actractaspis is a peculiar African burrowing species that has received much attention by biologists. For a long time it was considered

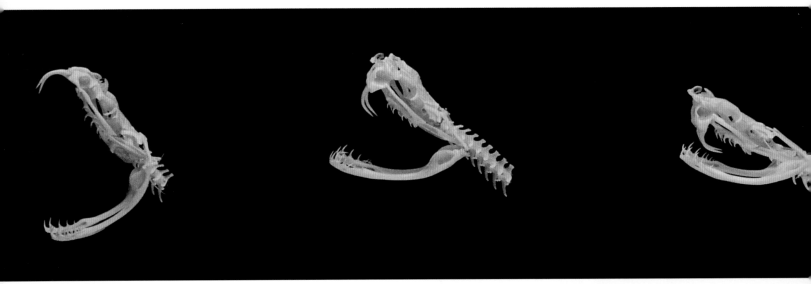

part of the family Viperidae because it has a pair of very long erectile, canaliculate fangs. But it is now classified as one of the three genera along with *Aparallactus* and *Macrolaps* in the family Atractaspididae. Taxonomists working with these forms claim their movable fang mechanism evolved differently, without any direct relationship to viperids, and is the product of convergent evolution. *Atractaspis* is commonly called the stiletto snake because of its unique biting ability. With its mouth closed, its frontal, retracted fang tips protrude from beneath the upper labials. This allows it to bite by twisting its head and lower jaw, pulling the exposed fang backward, hooking the prey and injecting venom, without opening its mouth. No doubt this is an extremely efficient method of killing small rodents within underground tunnels.

Rattlesnake's Strike

When partially into a strike, the rattlesnake's mouth is agape with the fangs erected on the same plane as the thrust of the strike. The stabbing effect, coupled with a partial closing of the mouth, all but ensures fang penetration when contact is made with skin.

The process is quick and complex. Contractions of strong pterygoid muscles pull the long pterygoid bones, which in turn articulate with the maxillae, rotating it and erecting the fangs. Complementary muscles reverse the movements and retract them. It has long been debated whether the process is a reflex action. Because rattlesnakes frequently will erect one fang and then, in turn, the other during a yawn (demonstrating independent muscular control), the striking and fang-erecting process is regarded as voluntary.

Rattlesnakes exhibit two distinct striking postures, one for procuring food and the other as a defense mechanism. In both cases, aside from some specific feeding actions during which the

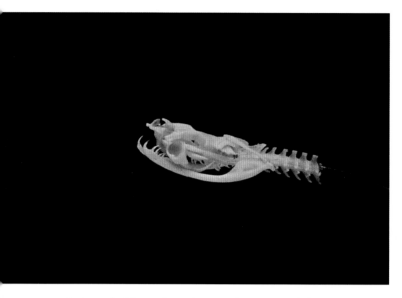

Left: A series of skulls show the sequence of mouth opening and fang erecting during the strike of a prairie rattlesnake, *Crotalus viridis viridis.* At the point of impact, the thrust drives the fully erect, sharply pointed fangs into the prey's body with an inflexible stabbing motion.

Opposite (below): A close-up of the active and reserve (bedded) fangs of a western diamondback, *Crotalus atrox.*

snake has a holding grip on its prey, fangs are withdrawn immediately after penetration.

When striking prey the snake thrusts downward with a decided kinking and twist in the neck. This action applies greater pressure and impact, embedding the fangs more deeply. Toward this end, the head is forced into a downward position as well. Most strikes to prey are delivered from an ambush or resting position as the neck is laterally coiled in preparation. Prey strikes are directed at animals usually moving perpendicularly or diagonally to the snake's head and penetrate into the main body area. When a rodent approaches a rattlesnake head-on, the snake will frequently back away, avoiding contact and refusing to strike. This may be at least partially because of its poor depth perception caused by incomplete binocular vision. Another theory is proposed by Jim Murphy (personal communication, 1996): The purpose could be "to increase the chance of placing the strike in the shoulder region. I have watched many captive rattlers wait until the mouse is in the right position (laterally) before striking."

A defensive strike is usually delivered from an aroused position, with the head cocked atop the long S-shaped coil. Because most offenders are larger than the snake, the strike is more lateral or upward. Also, it is delivered at a greater distance, when the provoker enters striking range. Contact is made with the snake's neck extended, resulting in a shallower fang penetration.

Fangs

The fang is likened to a hypodermic needle both in design and function. A hollow canal runs nearly its length, connecting the venom supply within the gum to the tooth. Venom travels through the fang's canal from a duct at its base and out the orifice immediately adjacent to (and in front of) the exceedingly sharp, pointed tip. The surface and canal are made smooth and shiny by enamel. Its long, thin, scimitar shape is sturdy, but it can be broken. They are easily the longest teeth. Fangs of a big eastern diamondback, *Crotalus adamanteus,* can be 1 inch (2.5 centimeters) in length.

Because fangs are the rattlesnake's primary source of food procurement, an array of smaller fangs (in progressive stages of development) remains at the ready. They are adjacent to and to the rear of each active fang, within the soft tissue of the sheath. A broken fang is replaced by the next in line within a few weeks. Like all the teeth of other snakes, fangs are periodically shed and replaced, approximately every six to ten weeks during the active season. They are shed from alternate sockets, guaranteeing that the snake is never fangless. Occasionally the full-sized replacement is aligned adjacent to its predecessor, giving the snake two fangs on the same side for a brief period.

Traced from their connection at the root of the fangs, elongated venom ducts run toward the posterior, deep in the musculature along the jaw. They widen appreciably into long triangular-shaped sacks, immediately posterior to the eyes. The venom follows a continuous path to the root of the fang. Here, within the fang sheath, epithelial tissue loosely connects the duct with the fang. During a normal predatory strike a tendon forces the fang against the duct opening, affording a stable, adequate seal. When muscles attached to the glands contract, a dose of venom (a viscous, usually amber-colored liquid) is forced through the fangs into the wound. The snake controls the contraction, size of the dose, and amount dispensed by either fang. The measure injected is proportionate to the size of the prey. Regardless, a bite never completely depletes the venom supply. Also, a strike at prey often brings forth a larger quantity than does one in defense. This conserves the precious fluid and may offer a partial answer about why such a high percentage of the reported defensive bites on humans are "dry" (no venom injected).

By forcing the fangs over the lip of a beaker and simultaneously massaging the venom glands, venom of an eastern diamondback rattlesnake, *Crotalus adamanteus,* is extracted into a funnel and collected in an enclosed beaker submerged in ice. Here a drop of venom can be seen at the tip of each fang.

Another dry-bite hypothesis suggests that in a defensive strike the angle of penetration (lacking the normal arched neck position in a predatory strike) disrupts the normal position of the jaws and fangs, thereby possibly physically disrupting the venom flow.

The size of the snake and its age and health are factors determining the amount and toxicity of venom injected. Climatic conditions, season, time of day, number of strikes, depth of penetration, location of the bite, and whether one or two fangs penetrate are also important variables.

In rattlesnakes, envenomation is the preeminent method of acquiring food. Injected toxin is a highly specialized means of immobilizing and digesting prey. Defense by striking is secondary, another last-ditch technique of survival.

Venom

There are two kinds of snake venoms: those that primarily affect the blood by preventing coagulation while also destroying the vessels (hemotoxic or cytotoxic venoms); and those acting on the nervous system causing paralysis, heart and respiratory malfunctions, as well as impaired senses (neurotoxic venoms). This explanation is somewhat of an oversimplification because it is now known that varying amounts of both properties are found in all rattlesnake venoms. However, the two-venom classification is an uncomplicated way to help explain how venoms function in general. The proportion of these two venom qualities not only varies between species and subspecies but also is even correlated with a myriad of environmental factors governing the same forms inhabiting differing habitats. Also, the toxicity of venom is somewhat specific to the snake's preferred prey. One study found major changes in the toxicity and digestive properties of the venoms of northern Pacific rattlesnakes, *Crotalus viridis oreganus,* and southern Pacific rattlesnakes, *Crotalus viridis helleri,* as the snakes matured. Young predominately ate lizards, whereas adults preferred small mammals, and the venoms, therefore, were proportionately stronger.

Although any in-depth discussion of venoms is beyond the scope

Right: The arm of a woman bitten by an eastern diamondback, *Crotalus adamanteus,* has an elongated scar, the remnant of a fasciotomy, the surgical removal of damaged tissue. Fortunately, this disfiguring treatment is rarely used today in countries in which proper medical attention is readily available. The scars at the base of her thumb disclose the site of the bite.

Below: The effects of a bite of a banded rock rattlesnake, *Crotalus lepidus klauberi,* to the right hand ten days after successful antivenom treatment was administered. The hand and arm are still considerably swollen, small blisters are present on the forearm, the thumbnail is discolored, and the fang puncture is evident at the base of the first finger.

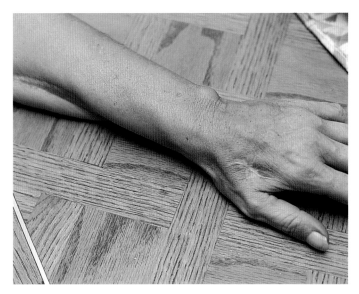

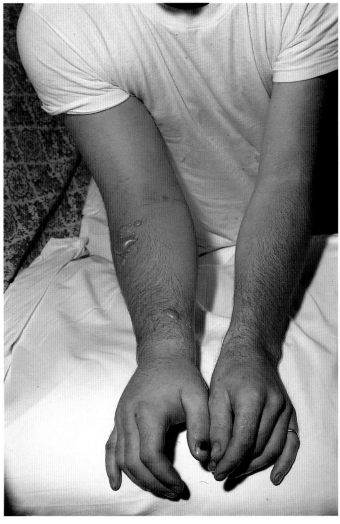

of this book, and beyond the comprehension of all but the most devoted biochemists and pharmacologists, some basic explanation is in order.

Composed of a variety of chemical compounds (primarily proteins, proteolytic enzymes, and low molecular weight polypeptides), snake venoms are some of the most complex and dangerous natural poisons in the animal world. More than twenty-five enzymes have been isolated from reptile venoms. Many of these proteins are little more than modified saliva enzymes. Breaking down proteins into simple molecules expedites digestion and is an initial part of assimilation.

Injected venom is rapidly dispersed throughout the victim, causing digestion from within the prey to commence, even as the carcass is being swallowed. Many scientists feel this is the major reason the venom-injecting system evolved. It is particularly expeditious because the food animal is not masticated or physically broken apart while being eaten. As deadly as rattlesnake venom can be, it is ineffective if it does not enter tissues; if swallowed, the host's digestive enzymes destroy it.

Envenomation (the injection of foreign proteins) causes a violent response in the body of the prey. Using the victim's circulatory system or its lymphatic vessels, the toxin is rapidly absorbed and carried throughout the body to the organs that will be affected. In various combinations, these proteins produce devastating effects on connective tissues, organs, blood, and blood components. Many components actively attack the lymphatic and nervous systems and the genetic code carrying nucleic acids, RNA and DNA.

Phospholipase A (a group of similar enzymes) is the most common element in animal venoms. It is found in snake venoms along with a plethora of other tongue-twisting components. Phosphodiesterase, hyaluronidase, ribonuclease, deoxyribonuclease, exonuclease, nucleotide pyrophosphatase, oxidase, exopeptidase, and adenosine triphosphatase are a few, with a variety of proteases and L-arginine-ester hydrolyases more specific to rattlesnakes. Simply put, together these venom enzymes form a deadly family.

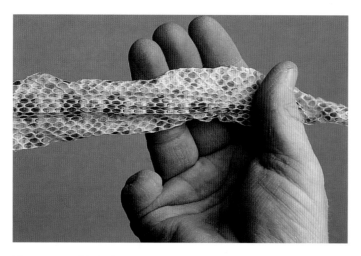

The amputated little finger on this hand demonstrates the results of a bite by a dusky pigmy rattlesnake, *Sistrurus miliarius barbouri.* The shed skin of a southern Pacific rattlesnake, *Crotalus viridis helleri,* shows some of the dark pigment (pattern) remaining in the outer skin layer.

Specific rattlesnake venom may contain more than one form of phospholipase A. They are important catalysts in breaking down lipids to form saturated and unsaturated fatty acids, and they interfere with motor functions while altering muscle contractility. Hyaluronidase destroys intercellular material, enabling venom to spread rapidly in the tissues, while phosphodiesterase induces a rapid fall in arterial blood pressure.

A complex polypeptide, crotoxin, has been isolated in the South American members of the neotropical rattlesnake group *Crotalus durissus.* There has been confusion, discussion, and debate about its makeup through the past four decades. However, one thing is clear: Crotoxin is the principal reason this rattlesnake's venom is so highly neurotoxic and deadly. The venom of some populations of this group contains concentrations of crotamine, a component that has been demonstrated to cause paralysis of the lower extremities. Another ingredient, convulsin, causes convulsions and acute hypertension. It also interferes with respiration.

Human Body's Reaction to Envenomation

A rattlesnake bite is a very serious (and expensive) matter and must always be considered a medical emergency. Failure to respond is dangerous and stupid. A severe eastern diamondback, *Crotalus adamanteus,* envenomation in 1992 was successfully treated with a cost of more than $162,000. Nearly $7,000 of the cost went for antivenom and the rest for hospital and physician fees. This excludes the cost of one and a half years of rehabilitation.

The victim, a 112-pound (42-kilogram) woman, related the following information to me about the envenomation. The bite oc-

curred as a wild-caught, 4.5-foot (1.37-meter) female eastern diamondback was being weighed and measured as part of a capture–recapture field study in Florida. The victim received three fangs (one obviously nearing replacement) on the dorsal aspect of her left hand between the thumb and first finger. At least one and possibly two fangs injected venom directly into the vein. Within three minutes paramedics arrived, inserted a standard I.V., and began transporting her to the hospital. Against the victim's vehement objections to what she knew was an incorrect treatment, they applied ice to the hand and elevated the limb above the plane of the heart. Within ten minutes she was at the hospital. As the medical staff questioned her about the bite (twenty-five minutes after the initial envenomation), she lost consciousness. Within the first hour her blood pressure dropped to 40/0. Her heart stopped twice, necessitating fibrillation to be revived. She received forty-two vials of antivenom and spent sixteen days in the intensive care unit. During this critical period, amputation of the hand was considered because of necrosis, severe muscle deterioration, and the concern of gangrene. Instead, a partial fasiotomy of the entire length of the ventral aspect of her forearm was performed. After an additional seven days in the hospital, another fourteen days of intensive rehabilitation were needed to restore her walking, speech, and language cohesiveness. Six years later, she suffers memory loss, difficulty in minor mathematical calculations, severe scarring at the wound site, and pain.

The intense pain, itching, swelling, and discoloration that begins at the site of the bite spreads to adjacent areas. The reaction is intensified by the body's normal immune system with the production of histamine and bradykinin. Frequently, an unpleasant tingling sensation, like a mild electrical shock, spreads over the lips, tongue, and face. Destruction of the lymphatic vessels causes fluids to pool in the tissue spaces, resulting in excruciating pain. The breakdown of cell membrane control of permeability disrupts the containment of cellular fluids, causing massive edema, swelling the bitten body part to extreme size. Areas around the bite may suffer acute necrosis and must be removed and skin grafts performed. It is not uncommon for victims of bites on fingers or toes to have them amputated. Partial paralysis, lack of tactile sensitivity, and abnormal thermal sensitivity of extremities may be long-term or permanent disabilities.

The permeability of capillaries is destroyed, liberating plasma and small quantities of blood into the already overtaxed tissues. Localized throbbing joins the overall misery. Although uncommon, pulmonary edema with hemorrhaging within major organs occurs, releasing blood into the respiratory, urinary, and alimentary tracts, causing destruction while producing bloody excreta. Additional bleeding may occur from the nails, gums, and lips. In one-tenth of the cases, a sharp drop in arterial pressure further disrupts all normal functions. Severe headaches, nausea, and abdominal cramping precede cardiac and circulatory failure. Rattlesnake envenomation is a horrible, painful experience. It may be fatal.

The South American rattlesnake, *Crotalus durissus terrificus,* has one of the most potent rattlesnake venoms. It, like others in the *durissus* group, has a very high percentage of neurotoxins in its venom. Many people in remote areas of South America are killed each year because proper treatment and antivenom are not available to them.

The severity of these symptoms is lessened in rattlesnake venoms that produce neurotoxic responses (e.g., South American subspecies of *Crotalus durissus*). Instead, some of these cases demonstrate a variety of reactions in locomotor, auditory, and gastrointestinal functions. In addition, mental incoherence, slurred speech, partial blindness, chills, cutaneous numbness and tingling, vertigo, massive headaches, and difficulty in swallowing may be symptomatic.

Since 1975, venom of the Mojave rattlesnake, *Crotalus scutulatus scutulatus,* has been known to have a neurotoxic fraction affecting the phrenic nerve and diaphragm muscle in laboratory animals. It is called Mojave toxin. In 1978 researchers discovered two distinct groups of this venom in the Mojave rattlesnake. One (type A) has highly neurotoxic and lethal qualities, and the other (type B) has fewer of these qualities and is less lethal. Additional research has revealed Mojave toxin is present in other rattlesnake species—

e.g., midget faded rattlesnake *(Crotalus viridis concolor)*, rock rattle-snake *(Crotalus lepidus)*, tiger rattlesnake *(Crotalus tigris)*, and speck-led rattlesnake *(Crotalus mitchellii)*. Preliminary DNA analysis suggests that the Coronado Island rattlesnake, *Crotalus viridis caliginis*, has it as well. Most likely, future venom analysis will disclose additional rattlesnakes with this dangerous toxin.

Incidence of Envenomation

Although the threat of rattlesnake bite to animals and humans is highly overrated, bites to humans number in the hundreds annually throughout the Americas. In general, the original description of an incident is fortified, expanded, and sensationalized as it is related from one party to the next. This inflated misinformation feeds unwarranted fear to undereducated adults and susceptible children. Also, a rattlesnake bite appears much worse than it may be, because there is so much visible damage. The increased awareness of ecology and predator–prey relationships have been instrumental in educating some sectors of the public, but many others remain misguided. There are thousands of interactions between humans and rattlesnakes annually, with a significant number resulting in bites. However, very few are fatal. Fewer than a dozen deaths a year is typical in the United States.

Venomous snakebites are classified as "legitimate" when they are purely accidental in nature, by an unseen snake. Those caused by a person purposefully interacting with a snake (e.g., handling, feeding, capturing, photographing, killing) are labeled "illegitimate." A great many bites are thus illegitimate, and a high percentage of those occur while the victim was handling snakes under the influence of alcohol or other drugs. It logically follows that leaving venomous snakes alone greatly reduces one's risk of danger.

Many persons suffering illegitimate bites foolishly spend precious time waiting to judge the severity of their bites before going to a medical facility. This occurs most commonly when the animals are being kept illegally and the keeper fears reprisals. Some seek emergency room treatment for the intense pain with an injection of a painkiller. Accepting the temporary relief, they refuse additional treatment. This routine puts the patient at extreme risk and has produced unnecessarily grave results—amputation and death.

A realistic incidence of rattlesnake bites is difficult to ascertain because many records are unavailable. In Latin American countries a high percentage are unreported, and no U.S. federal agency solicits a count of those that are not fatal. Although the statistics for all venomous snakebites worldwide are staggering, fatalities from rattlesnake bites in the United States are so low (compared with those from other injuries) that it is not considered a serious medical problem.

During the 1950s and early 1960s, Dr. Henry Parrish polled thousands of American hospitals and physicians about snakebite in the United States. The results of his studies, as well as those of others, were published in book form in 1980 *(Poisonous Snakebites in the United States,* New York: Vantage Press). Although somewhat dated, many of Parrish's conclusions remain valid today. Even though human population densities have fluctuated, the proportion of bites per capita today is probably in line with the earlier statistics. Some victims of dry bites do not seek treatment, so the actual number of snakebites is higher than reported.

To simplify matters, Parrish chose 1959 as a typical year: 6,680 persons were treated for snakebites and 14 died. Using 1960 census population figures (excluding Hawaii and Alaska, because neither has indigenous venomous snakes), he calculated that less than 1 person in 10 million died of snakebite annually in the United States.

Compared with bites and stings of other venomous animals, snakebites came in second, causing 33 percent of all venom-related deaths. Hymenopteran insects (bees, wasps, hornets, yellowjackets, and ants) accounted for 40 percent, and spiders and scorpions for 18 percent, of the deaths. The latter two percentages may even be conservative, because deaths from acute insect allergy occurring during hot weather can easily be misrepresented as heart attack or heat stroke. A single sting of a bee to a hypersensitive person, for example, which may go undetected, can cause death too quickly for treatment, frequently within fifteen to thirty minutes. Occasional snakebite-related deaths may actually be a result of allergic reactions, not unlike those initiated by insects and arachnids.

Because Parrish's findings included all U.S. venomous snakes (rattlesnakes, as well as copperheads, cottonmouths, and coral snakes), it is difficult to extrapolate the rattlesnake data separately. However, combining his statistics with those of others, we find that rattlesnakes are responsible for a majority of the bites in the U.S. western states. Copperheads are far and away the greater villains in the U.S. southeastern and south-central states but cause virtually no deaths. Most rattlesnake bites are from smaller species and newborn snakes. The larger *Crotalus* species are to blame for the most severe envenomations and 75 percent of the annual fatalities attributed to snakebites. Remember, annually fewer than a dozen deaths in the United States are attributable to rattlesnakes.

Eight years' worth of data compiled more recently for a study of snakebites in Arizona revealed some interesting information:

Of the individuals bitten, 80% were male and 20% female. The age range was 2 to 81 years with 67% of the age group 11–40. More than 90% were bitten during the warmer months of April through October with peaks in May (15%), August (18%), and September (23%). More than half occurred at home either outside (by unsighted rattlesnakes) or inside (by captive rattlesnakes). Only two victims (1.3%) were bitten while hiking in the mountains. The upper extremity was involved two thirds of the time (over half being finger bites), and the lower extremity in one third.

Two-thirds of all the bites were inflicted by snakes 8 to 20 inches in length. Western diamondbacks and Mojave rattlesnakes give birth during August and these newborns are 8 to 12 inches in length. They appear again in the spring as 18 inch snakes. Although their numbers are reduced by predators and prey availability, they make up a large proportion of the rattle-

A complete polyvalent antivenom kit is produced by Wyeth Labs in the United States as an antidote for most rattlesnake and other pitviper venoms. The ampule to the right is more specifically for the venom of neotropical rattlesnakes, *Crotalus durissus*, which has a much higher percentage of neurotoxic elements. This is produced at the famous Butantan Venom Institute, São Paulo, Brazil.

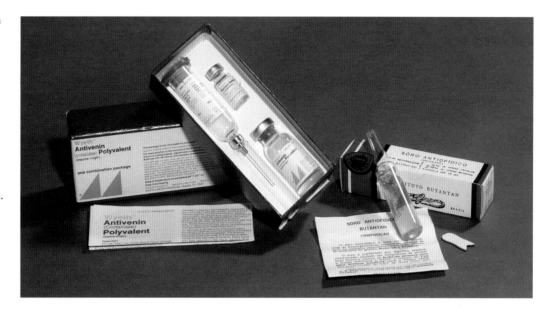

snake population at certain times of the year. This may explain their frequent involvement. (D. L. Hardy, "Epidemiology of Rattlesnake Envenomation in Tucson, Arizona, 1973–1980: A Preliminary Report," *Tucson Herpetological Society Newsletter* 1:33–36 [1988])

Treatment of Rattlesnake Envenomation

The leading factor inhibiting survival is the lapsed time between the bite and treatment. If specific antivenom therapy is administered within the first hour or two, the chances for recovery are better than 99 percent. Most deaths occur between six and forty-eight hours after the bite. The location of the wound and physical condition of the victim are other important factors.

The field of emergency medicine has spawned physicians and paramedics who are trained to perform the approved, necessary medical procedures. Over the years, several procedures were considered proper for treating snakebites. As medicine progressed and changed, so did the treatment. (Because I am not a physician, I can only report the procedures and treatments that are currently accepted and recommended by the most knowledgeable snakebite authorities.)

The victim should be under observation or treatment in a medical facility (preferably a hospital) for a period of eight hours or more to ensure proper measures are taken. First aid should be administered even if no symptoms of envenomation appear. It is important that diagnosed dry bites (lacking injection of venom) not be overlooked, because secondary infection is probable. Infectious bacteria are commonly found in snakes' mouths and venom glands. The wound is conducive to the growth of gangrene. If left untreated, severe complications may arise, necessitating amputation

The Great Basin rattlesnake, *Crotalus viridis lutosus,* is the most distinctly patterned of the *viridis* group.

(and occasionally resulting in death). The wound should be thoroughly cleaned, with deep punctures being treated with a broad-spectrum antibiotic. A tetanus booster should be given if the victim has not been actively immunized.

Sudden, emotional response is expected of all involved, but this must not cloud the clinical picture. Fainting, profuse sweating, cold clammy skin, weak pulse, and rapid shallow breathing are frequently produced by fright. Punctures made by fangs are not sufficient reason to induce drastic medical procedures. Usually, localized swelling and pain appear within the first half-hour of the bite. Immediate swelling at the site of the bite is an almost certain sign rattlesnake venom has been injected. In general, the severity of a bite can be determined if swelling has spread extensively, for example if the swelling of a bite on a finger spreads well above the elbow in two hours or less. Overall signs of shock increase, and extensive changes in the blood are readily apparent.

Because the body's reaction to antivenom can be dramatic, antivenom injection is not recommended until the patient arrives at a medical facility where monitoring and complete emergency attention are available. An intravenous route is the preferred method of administration. Antivenom will most likely later induce serum sickness, so it is prudent to establish the severity of the bite before beginning treatment. Allergic manifestations from serum sickness may require steroid injections for some time afterward.

Emergency medical technicians in regions with potential rattlesnake emergencies should be properly trained for such an event. Any institution keeping rattlesnakes should maintain an adequate supply of polyvalent antivenom (minimum of ten ampules). Nearby medical facilities should be well aware of the possibility of a bite and prepared to treat it as an emergency. This includes stocking additional supplies of antivenom. All precautions should be undertaken to prevent a bite, and the institution's staff should be fully trained in advance to react in case of an emergency.

If you are bitten by a rattlesnake, *do not*

- make any incisions
- apply suction with the mouth
- apply pressure or squeezing at the site of the bite
- use tourniquets or other constrictive devices
- use ice or ice-water immersion (cryotherapy)
- inject antivenom
- use a stun gun or electroshock

If you are bitten by a rattlesnake, *do*

- use an extractor immediately
- proceed to the nearest medical facility as quickly as possible
- remain as calm as possible
- reduce physical activity and exertion as much as is practical

Right: The contents of an extractor kit.

Below: The Poison Control Center in Tucson, Arizona, receives hundreds of calls weekly about a variety of venomous bites and stings, as well as other types of envenomations and poisonings. Their quick response has saved hundreds of lives and prevented the unnecessary or unwarranted treatment of thousands of others.

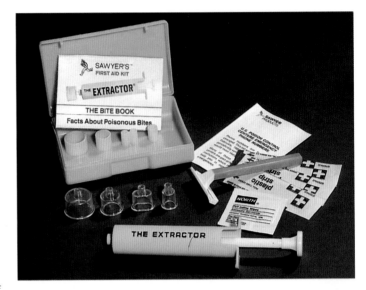

- immobilize the bitten extremity with a splint while attempting to keep it below the level of the heart
- remove tight-fitting garments and constricting jewelry, such as rings
- try to identify the snake accurately, noting a reasonable approximation of its size

In 1985 an unorthodox snakebite treatment, electroshock, was reported by a missionary doctor, Ronald Guderian, in the lowlands of Ecuador. After five 1-second, high-voltage (20-kilovolt) shocks were applied (via an insulated wire connected to the spark plug of a running outboard motor) at the site of the puncture wound, the effects of the venom were reportedly nullified. The doctor claimed no fatalities among thirty-four natives treated, whereas the effects of envenomation were apparent in seven others who refused the shock treatment. Later, two of the untreated victims needed amputation.

Dr. Guderian continues to use this procedure because antivenom is too costly. He considers electroshock the most inexpensive, convenient, "last-chance" therapy available. As of 1994, he claimed that more than 300 snakebite cases have been successfully treated with electroshock.

He has modified a stun gun to approximately half its power and is currently employing it as therapy in some instances. Although not approved by the U.S. Food and Drug Administration, a modified stun gun (called The Snake Doctor) has been marketed in the United States by an Oklahoma company. It is now widely used to treat bites at rattlesnake roundups (discussed in the next chapter).

This procedure received sensational attention in newspapers and magazines. However, medical professionals specializing in venom research are extremely skeptical of the claims. They have offered two reasons for the apparent success of the treatment. First, it is possible that the bites were inflicted by nonpoisonous snakes or were dry bites. Second, because envenomation is common among native peoples, they may have built up antibody protection from previous encounters. Crotalid antibodies have been found in certain peoples in other parts of Ecuador. Laboratory studies to date have failed to show positive results or effectiveness of electroshock treatment for snakebite in experimental animals.

A variety of snakebite kits have been available commercially for nearly a century. Because they employ some of the detrimental procedures listed previously, and the suction devices supplied with

An excellent reason for not wearing sandals in rattlesnake country is shown in this photo of a western diamondback, *Crotalus atrox,* striking a prosthetic foot.

most of them are poorly designed and incapable of producing adequate suction, none is recommended as a useful form of treatment. If a first aid measure is necessary, an inexpensive, substantial suction syringe kit (called The Extractor) can be purchased at better sporting and outdoor recreation stores. No cutting is required. Properly applying The Extractor suction syringe at the site of the wound (within one to three minutes of the bite) has effectively extracted some venom.

Poison Control Centers

Help in diagnosing and evaluating the severity of a rattlesnake bite is available through a network of poison control centers throughout the United States. Even though western diamondbacks, *Crotalus atrox,* and Mojave rattlesnakes, *Crotalus scutulatus scutulatus,* range widely throughout the Southwest and inflict most of the bites, Arizona has more rattlesnake species than any other state. So it is no surprise that the Arizona Poison Control Center at the University of Arizona Medical Center in Tucson fields more venomous snake consultation calls (from within Arizona and from many other U.S. states) than any other facility.

With a telephone call, the attending medical staff can discuss all aspects of the problem, from clinical procedures to locating adequate supplies of specific antivenom. Access to poison control centers is particularly important because many physicians are inadequately trained in the current mode of treatment. Nearly any type of venomous snake may be found (legally or illegally) in many private collections throughout the United States. Although polyvalent pitviper antivenom is in ample reserve throughout most of the United States (in hospitals or in cities with zoos that maintain large venomous reptile collections), some hospitals do not maintain a supply or have only a few updated ampules on hand.

Fear of a Rattlesnake Bite

The incidence and repercussions of snakebite are greatly exaggerated and should not interfere with time spent exploring the natural world. Being aware that the possibility of being bitten exists, knowing which species inhabit the area, and being observant and careful are all common-sense preventative measures. The most logical precautions are to dress in suitably protective clothing and to watch where you step and where you place your hands. Mid-ankle or higher leather boots and full-length pants made of a tightly woven, coarse material afford protection. Wearing shorts and athletic shoes or sandals when traipsing through rocky, grassy areas or through knee-high palmetto thickets is inviting disaster.

Remember that the majority of bites occur to people who are handling, catching, or trying to kill venomous snakes. Avoiding an interaction drastically decreases the chance of a serious consequence. Findley Russell, one of the world's foremost authorities on snakebite, has said about being bitten by a venomous snake, "If you haven't done anything except get to a hospital, you haven't done anything wrong."

RATTLESNAKE ROUNDUPS

Rattlesnakes . . . and bison lived together in western Oklahoma for thousands of years, and it was not the snakes that nearly exterminated the buffalo.

—Richard Lardie

During the past half century in the United States, enterprising people have managed to combine the fascination for and unwarranted fear of rattlesnakes with commerce and exhibitionism. Rattlesnake roundups are highly visible commercial events promoted as a method of controlling rattlesnake populations (ostensibly to prevent the deaths of cattle and people). Civic associations organize and manage these events, which are sometimes called rattlesnake rodeos. Some of the profits are donated to regional charities or given as scholarships. In their simplest form, rattlesnake roundups are events for which rattlesnakes are caught and brought to a site where they are displayed and sold. The snakes are bought by the foot, and the purchaser will slaughter them for a variety of by-products. Contests are held, with cash prizes and trophies for the longest, heaviest, and greatest number of snakes caught, to generate more collecting and participation.

Year-long publicity attracts thousands of tourists, and hundreds of thousands of dollars may accrue to small towns that often have little else to offer tourists. Snake collectors receive sizable amounts of cash for their snakes,

A snake hunter in southern Georgia carefully listens for distinctive sounds of rattlesnake movement or rattling through a long flexible plastic tube that has been forced into the burrow of a gopher tortoise, *Gopherus polyphemus*. Freshly disturbed sand or snake tracks at the entrance disclose that an animal has been using the burrow recently.

At most Georgia and Alabama roundups eastern diamondbacks, *Crotalus adamanteus,* are piled on top of each other in chicken wire pens. This bird's eye view was taken before dozens more were added.

making roundups a profitable venture for everyone—except the rattlesnakes.

The first roundup was held in 1934 at Okeene, Oklahoma. The grandfather of rattlesnake roundups is held annually (and has been since 1958) in Sweetwater, Texas, on the second weekend of March. The Jaycees, sponsors of the four-day event, report that 35,000 visitors come to enjoy "The World's Biggest Rattlesnake Roundup!" Outstripping many county fairs in organization and array of amusements, it is easily the slickest of all roundups.

Jaycees and Kiwanis are responsible for more than a dozen roundups held in other southern cities. The other large, heavily attended spring perennials, along with Sweetwater and Okeene, are at Big Spring, San Angelo, Freer, and Taylor (Texas); Waurika and Waynoka (Oklahoma); Opp (Alabama); and Claxton, Fitzgerald, and Whigham (Georgia). At various times roundups have been held in South Dakota, New Mexico, Kansas, California, West Virginia, Florida, Arkansas, and Mississippi. In Pennsylvania, although small by comparison, no less than a dozen roundups are held each year. In total, about thirty rattlesnake roundups are promoted annually in the United States. An estimated 5,000 rattlesnakes are captured and killed for and during roundups each year.

Recent changes in Kansas wildlife laws that have increased the number of rattlesnakes allowed to be taken from four to thirty have encouraged roundups there. Roundups are being attempted or proposed in Louisiana and southern New Mexico. As one might expect, they are being met with vigorous opposition from conservationists, herpetologists, and animal rights groups, but they appear to be thriving nevertheless. The established roundups are being challenged by environmental and animal rights groups. From a disjointed handful of protesters a few years ago, the protesters and pickets have grown into an organized movement, numbering in the hundreds today. The media are beginning to disclose the carnage involved that their attention unwittingly promotes. With increased pressure from the public, attitudes will change, it is hoped, before the environmental damage is irreparable.

Sweetwater Roundup

At Sweetwater, as well as the other roundup sites in Texas and Oklahoma, the western diamondback, *Crotalus atrox,* is the main attraction. The number killed each year is mind boggling—so much so that amounts of snakes are recorded by the pound, not by the number of individuals. The annual catch varies, but the sponsors boast that no less than a ton has been brought in each year. In 1985 a whopping 13,500 pounds (5,035 kilograms) were claimed. Unlike in the early days, few really large snakes (over 5 feet, or 1.5 meters, in length) have been caught in recent years. The majority are in their second or third year (between 3 and 4 feet, or 1 meter) and weigh 2 pounds (less than 1 kilogram) each. One dealer offers a standing $1,000 bonus for any rattlesnake longer than 8 feet (2.4 meters).

Left: As part of the measuring and weighing, a handler holds each eastern diamondback, *Crotalus adamanteus,* against a post marked as a ruler.

Below: A staged hunt provides a photo opportunity for dignitaries. In this case a variety of Georgia beauty contest winners pose with a large eastern diamondback, *Crotalus adamanteus.*

Opposite: A focus of the roundup parade is the Rattlesnake Queen's float. As she waves at the throngs, a massive stuffed eastern diamondback, *Crotalus adamanteus,* sits at her feet.

The contest rules are ambiguous and notably flexible. Nowhere is a time period set for collecting, so many snakes are caught during the previous summer and fall and stockpiled by the collector. To continue with the professed ideal of controlling the size of their populations, rattlesnakes are supposed to be captured on specific private ranches, although this restriction is not always followed. The hype surrounding the roundups leads citizens to believe that rattlesnakes are proliferating and pose a serious risk to humans and cattle in the area. In reality, many of the snakes are trucked in from all over Texas and from the surrounding states. Older collectors now admit having to hunt much wider areas and for longer periods to catch quantities of snakes. Attempts have been made to purchase and import rattlesnakes from other states, most specifically from Arizona. For example, the western diamondback, *Crotalus atrox,* although not native to Kansas, is the most common snake at Kansas roundups, and thus it is obvious that this species is being brought in from other states.

"Gassing" the Dens

The largest numbers of rattlesnakes are caught from their dens during winter and early spring while they are hibernating, by means of a method known as "gassing." A long, flexible plastic hose is forced into the deepest fissures of the den. The hunter twists the hose about and listens for rattling or movement. If the response is appropriate, a hiss or rattle, gasoline is poured through the hose. The gassed snakes react to escape the fumes by abandoning their haunt. Volatile fertilizers, as well as other noxious and environmentally unsafe chemicals, are used occasionally instead of gasoline.

This form of underground fumigation can produce startling results. Frequently, a number of rattlesnakes flee from the pestilent vapors. Their fate, along with the fate of a bevy of frogs, toads, lizards, tortoises, nonvenomous snakes, and other small animals, is all but sealed. A study on the effects of gassing on burrowing animals proved that this technique has "severe and obvious short term effects on the vertebrate species" (J. A. Campbell, D. R. Formanowicz, and E. D. Brodie, Jr., *The Effects of Gasoline Fumes on Selected Reptiles and Amphibians,* Austin: Texas Parks and Wildlife Department, 1989). Known commensals in burrows include amphibians, reptiles, moles, shrews, prairie dogs, foxes, skunks, and a broad spectrum of other animals. It is ironic that rattlesnakes have proved to be the most resistant to the gasoline fumes.

What happens to those animals that have become disoriented and unable to escape? Most likely, they are overcome and they suffocate. Others may suffer permanent, debilitating damage. The fumes, much heavier than air, lie trapped in recesses, making the sites uninhabitable for an unknown period, possibly as long as a year. With their retreats poisoned and limited denning sites available, many forms of wildlife face exposure during the remaining winter. The majority of captured rattlesnakes, after being gassed,

show lingering adverse physical effects and die from the fumes or improper care within a few months.

Gassing has been outlawed in some states, so many roundups do not permit its use. The practice is difficult to monitor, however, and few state wildlife organizations (e.g., Department of Fish and Game, Department of Natural Resources) enforce the law. Also, many older hunters find gassing the simplest way to capture snakes with a minimum of effort. The practice will doubtless continue as long as roundups continue.

When gassed snakes exit the den, they are grabbed with special snake tongs or are noosed. Because the snake is held tightly by a 2-inch or shorter constricted section, nothing supports the weight of the rest of its dangling body as it writhes and thrashes about, attempting to escape. Larger snakes suffer serious spinal and internal injuries, many of which will eventually prove fatal. The snakes are kept (sometimes for several months) in containers with luckless brethren that have been caught the past summer or fall. A 50-gallon drum will hold a 15-inch-deep layer of a dozen or more western diamondbacks, *Crotalus atrox*. Stored in outbuildings, they are not fed, rarely offered drinking water, and not protected from inclement weather. Many will die of suffocation or dehydration. The rest will be butchered eventually anyway, so collectors accept this treatment as a matter of course.

Main Event

At Sweetwater there is a Miss Snake Charmer beauty contest. Aside from meeting the requirements of a pleasing physical appearance, contestants must be able to milk a rattlesnake. At best, this is an interesting attribute to include in a personal résumé.

In the name of education, "experts" milk venom, behead, and rip the skin from the doomed snakes. They lecture on the various dangers imposed by rattlesnakes. A country dance, flea market, and gun show add to the carnival atmosphere. For three days, an hourly bus provides transportation to a nearby den where would-be collectors and tourists are shown how "real" snake hunters do it. The rattlesnakes that these hunters will learn to catch have been seeded (released there previously).

A somewhat dubious recognition given to persons bitten while collecting or handling rattlesnakes (at some of the roundups) is enshrinement into the Order of the White Fang. As many as thirty people have been so honored in a single year. A majority of handlers receive the award by participating in the sacking or quick-bagging contest. In this competition, a pile of rattlesnakes is released in a pen or pickup truck bed and pairs of contestants work against the clock. One pins, grabs, and throws the rattlesnakes into a bag being held by the other. The fiercest competitors waste no time in pinning, and instead resort to "free-handing." Because bites are common, this practice all but guarantees enshrinement.

Perhaps the most macabre part of the roundup is the preparation of the meal—rattlesnake meat. As part of the entertainment, the snakes are beheaded, skinned, chopped into sections (while still writhing and jerking), breaded, and deep-fried. Attendees wait in long lines to gobble thousands of pounds of rattlesnake meat at $2 or more per serving. Gourmets can have it as barbecue, in chili, or on pizza. Other roundups offer rattlesnake burgers. A rattlesnake-meat-eating contest is a popular activity. The meat is not inspected and can be unsafe. *Salmonella* bacteria have been found in improperly prepared snake meat. Most likely, the bacteria flourish while the snakes are being improperly maintained prior to the event. Also, gassed snakes absorb some of the toxic chemicals and pass them on to the consumer through their flesh.

Validity of Venom Extraction

The roundup sponsors report that venom is extracted and sold for scientific research. Legitimate venom research facilities, however, want to buy quality venom collected from healthy snakes under sterile conditions. Roundup snakes are so poorly maintained that their venom is sometimes laden with impurities such as blood and pus. The majority of research-quality venom is provided by private institutions.

Claxton Roundup

The Claxton roundup in Georgia appears more humane on the face of it. There is little cruelty or foolish showmanship. Each part of the event is well organized and carefully orchestrated (albeit somewhat ironically) by the Evans County Wildlife Club. The whole local community is involved, producing a multifaceted fair and pageant. It is run as a business, but the outcome for the snakes is the same: death. Here the victim is the eastern diamondback, *Crotalus adamanteus*.

The weekend festivities of the Claxton Roundup 1992, for example, began with a parade of floats carrying an astounding array of queens and princesses, from Miss Georgia and Miss Gum Spirits of Turpentine to Little Miss Sweet Vidalia Onion. The previous year's Rattlesnake Roundup Queen shared a float with an imposing stuffed eastern diamondback. Sheriff and fire department vehicles, their sirens and horns blasting, led the half-mile-long procession down Main Street. The Marines and Army supplied bands and platoons of marchers. The Coast Guard was represented by a rescue helicopter fly-over. A dozen restored cars and customized big-wheeled vehicles carried still more princesses, as well as a mixed group of smiling, waving local politicians. Several thousand onlookers crowded the narrow, flag-decorated sidewalks. There was a holiday atmosphere. It was a gala hometown happening. A VIP rattlesnake hunt (a staged capture at a gopher tortoise burrow) provided an advantageous photo opportunity for the politically astute. A cross section of queens and princesses were in attendance. They were somewhat out of place in their formal attire, more befitting a prom than circling a gopher tortoise hole in the pinewoods. This captive audience of visitors and press provided the perfect setting and opportunity to rationalize and explain the event.

Dan Strickland, president of the Evans County Wildlife Club and spokesperson for the event, addressed those present: "We are conservationists. If we wanted to eliminate the rattlers, we would hunt every day, not just a few days in the spring. Like deer hunting, we are managing their numbers, while saving the lives of our children."

There is no similarity between culling herds of large grazing animals and killing snakes, however. Deer can do incredible damage to crops. During lean times, deer run the risk of starvation that may precipitate disease, endangering their entire population. In contrast, the exploited rattlesnake is a slow-growing, late-maturing reptile whose demographic traits do not allow rapid replacement or quick recovery when harvested at excessive rates.

After being weighed, measured, milked of venom, and handled several times, the eastern diamondback rattlesnakes, *Crotalus adamanteus,* are dumped into pens. The gaping rattlesnake is attempting to regurgitate what proved to be a mass of semidigested, putrefying ground meat and sawdust that the snake had been force-fed to increase its weight. Another is writhing and rolling in the throes of death.

Members of the media were assured that the sponsors do not condone gassing. Rather, the sponsors claim rattlesnakes found in burrows are dug up and captured. Miss Georgia asked what happens to the gopher tortoise whose home is destroyed. She was told, "He simply digs another tunnel." The fact that the resident tortoise is left exposed to weather and predation and that a sizable excavation takes years to accomplish was never explained.

The Claxton Tobacco Warehouse, a cavernous metal structure, housed the business end of the venture. There was a $2 admission charge. Two-thirds of the building was filled with craft booths. Unlike at other roundups, rattlesnakes receive a temporary reprieve here. No rattlesnake decapitation was shown, and no meat was served.

As expected, booths selling an assortment of rattlesnake-skin items did a brisk business. Only a few objects made from western diamondbacks, *Crotalus atrox,* were represented; the bulk were made from eastern diamondbacks, *Crotalus adamanteus,* and canebrake rattlesnakes, *Crotalus horridus atricaudatus.* Some items made of the skin of harmless snakes could be found as well. Possession of indigenous harmless snakes or by-products is illegal in Georgia. Keeping any local harmless variety is grounds for prosecution. To protect their constituents, powerful state bureaucrats have managed to ensure the continuation of roundups by making it legal to possess any and all of Georgia's venomous snakes.

The back end of the building was cordoned off with cattle gates covered in wire mesh. Bleachers closely followed the crescent shape of the fence. A few feet inside, eight waist-high, 3-foot-by-8-foot mesh pens fanned along it. As many as 2,000 spectators sat crammed against the perimeter. Another 3,000 wandered about the flea market. A total of 25,000 attended by closing time, late the next afternoon.

The hunters backed their vehicles to the rear door and carried their boxes full of rattlesnakes to the center of the check-in area. Many of the boxes were coffin sized, requiring several persons to bear the total weight. Four to six persons were sometimes needed to carry in the boxes. Each snake was hooked from its box, held by the tail, and stretched to the floor. The approximate size was called out and recorded. In 1992 they paid $6 per foot. Other roundups vary from $4 to $8 dollars, depending on supply and demand.

Very large specimens, presented by people who were vying for awards for the biggest or the heaviest, were weighed in a lard can and stretched out along a ruler for a more legitimate measurement. The current leader replaced its predecessor in a special mesh enclosure near the onlookers. The former king was unceremoniously dethroned and pitched in with the others.

After weighing the snakes were slid, like giant hockey pucks, a few feet across the cement floor to a waiting club member. The handler prodded, hooked, and dragged them 3 or 4 yards farther and flipped them into one of the holding pens. By 2:00 P.M., the weighing officially ended.

This kind of handling is extremely stressful for the snakes. They demonstrated agitation and discomfort by furiously rattling, coiling, and striking at anything close. The fangs of some were briefly hung up and broken off in the mesh. Many snakes were bitten by others in the crowded pens. For the most part, nothing comes of these bites because rattlesnakes are at least partially immune to their own venom. However, strikes to the head can be fatal.

Intimidated by waving hands and general movement, the snakes attempted to back away, piling several high in corners. Some pens had a foot-deep layer of entwined bodies, with more being dumped on top. Those unlucky enough to have been stockpiled for weeks or months before the roundup, withered and emaciated from not feeding or drinking during the long storage, were crushed. They were simply too weak to move away, so they suffocated.

A few inordinately large, bulky snakes, as a result of being thoroughly riled, regurgitated gray, saliva-coated, putrefying masses. A close inspection disclosed the repugnant, amorphous shapes were a mixture of wet sawdust and some kind of ground meat. This was evidence of an attempt to increase the snake's weight by force-feeding the mixture in order to win the prize for the heaviest snake.

Milking Venom

A main attraction was the extraction and preparation of venom. At Claxton, the owner of an extraction company made every effort to present the process in a professional manner under partially sanitary conditions. A glass funnel (fixed to drain into a beaker that is placed on crushed ice) was used as a collecting device. The milker and his assistant hooked ten or so diamondbacks from the most distant pen into a large plastic trash can. This was carried to a small table a few feet behind the milking apparatus.

Each snake was hooked from the can, pinned, and carried to the apparatus. The head was held with the accepted three-finger grip, while its midsection was pressed under the milker's arm. Its fangs were forced over the funnel's lip, unsheathing them, and the venom glands were squeezed and massaged. About two cubic centimeters of viscous, amber-colored venom (an average yield) flowed down the funnel. In two hours the beaker was one-third filled. The snakes were placed in another can, carried and dumped into to an awaiting pen at the opposite side. This ensured that they would be milked only once that day.

On with the Show

One of the Wildlife Club members periodically pinned a large diamondback and carried it to the audience, where questions were fielded and photographs could be made. Disdain on the faces of the audience members revealed the entire event upholds the established abhorrence for rattlesnakes.

As a continuing part of the public relations, VIPs were guided inside a closed-off area where each was photographed with a rattlesnake. Some demonstrated bravado and were willing to grasp the snake's mid-body while a handler tightly held its head. Unlike snakes in some roundups, these snakes had not undergone the fatal process of having their mouths sewn or wired shut to render them harmless for picture taking.

At the end of the roundup, the catch was loaded into boxes and driven to Waldo, Florida, for processing. In a week or two they were either frozen or decapitated and skinned. The owner of the largest rattlesnake-skin processing plant in Florida has claimed, "95 to 98 percent of the rattlesnake skins this shop uses are from road kill, from snakes killed by hunters, and from people killing them in their yards" (quoted by C. Lowe, in "The Tale of the Rattler," *Florida Living* [August 1996]: 12–25). If this were true, simple arithmetic

Each rattlesnake is "milked" as part of the entertainment. A drop of venom can be seen.

(considering the 420 snakes from the 1992 roundup in Claxton to be 5 percent of the snakes they purchase) indicates they could be processing more than 50,000 skins annually.

Obviously, something is wrong with the numbers. It is mandatory that all snakes processed in the state of Florida be reported to the Florida Game and Freshwater Fish Commission. Recently mandated tallies and statistics show that 13,213 eastern diamondbacks, *Crotalus adamanteus,* and 2,461 timber rattlesnakes, *Crotalus horridus horridus,* and canebrake rattlesnakes, *Crotalus horridus atricaudatus,* were killed by Florida processing plants in the one-year period from July 1, 1990, through June 30, 1991. The three Georgia roundups alone amassed nearly 1,500 rattlesnakes for the "skin trade" in the same year.

Entertainment and Sideshows

Other roundups offer variations on the accepted rattlesnake-roundup theme, with different ancillary events. Some have family-oriented diversions such as thrill rides and games. Most have musical entertainment. Gospel singers, country and western groups, and cloggers are common, and rock bands are finding their place as well. Western roundups tend to include more dangerous and grisly snake events to attract an audience, like "quick-bagging," "free-handing," and live skinning. At one Oklahoma roundup $5 will buy the "thrill" of chopping off the head of a live rattlesnake.

A daredevil snake show, with all the flair and hoopla of a carnival sideshow, is an integral part of several of them. Surrounding a pen filled with an assortment of worn-out, emaciated, traumatized rattlesnakes, the audience is talked through the performance by a barker. Spewing an amazing amount of misinformation, while constantly reinforcing the danger, the host performs an assortment of free-handing tricks and demonstrations designed to dazzle and thrill. Bites are a fairly common occurrence at some western roundups but are rare in the East.

Effects of Gassing

Although the sponsors of Alabama and Georgia roundups say they do not condone gassing, it is being done, seemingly as routinely as always. But the effects are even more critical in this region of the United States than in the western states. An apparent consensus among active collectors and herpetologists is that eastern diamondbacks, *Crotalus adamanteus,* are diminishing in numbers at a staggering rate. If something is not done soon, they will join the passenger pigeon and the Carolina parakeet in extinction.

Unlike in West Texas and Oklahoma, expansive habitat no longer exists for eastern diamondbacks in the U.S. Southeast. Vast areas of pinewoods have been altered or obliterated by housing and industrial developments, agriculture, logging, and tree farming. Associated pollution has contaminated waterways, further upsetting the food chain. The addition of hundreds of roads crisscrossing what remains of this special environment has left few remaining habitable, isolated pockets of natural habitat. These changes have made the larger snakes more vulnerable and much more accessible to snake hunters.

In many parts of the U.S. southeastern coastal plain, gopher tortoise burrows are a key element in the rattlesnake's environment. They are the preferred hibernacula for adult eastern diamondbacks, *Crotalus adamanteus,* where most are caught for roundups. Aside from furnishing a home for threatened gopher tortoises and indigo snakes, these burrows also shelter rare gopher frogs and dozens of other animals. Larger burrows, with tunnels that are 15 to 20 feet (4.6 to 6.1 meters) long—some as long as 30 feet (9 meters) have been found—are the most suitable refuges. A tortoise may live in the same burrow most of its life, seventy-five years or more. Gopher tortoises start excavating when they are small and expand their burrows as they grow. Both gassing and digging out snakes devastate the burrows, leaving the occupants homeless or dead.

Opposite: **A large, restrained eastern diamondback,** *Crotalus adamanteus,* **is brought to the attendees as part of the "education process" at roundups.**

Placing western diamondbacks, *Crotalus atrox*, and prairie rattlesnakes, *Crotalus viridis viridis*, on and around a woman seated on the ground is part of the "Pit of Danger" tent.

More Fuel for the Fire

As if gassing were not enough, another sadistic wrinkle is added by some of the older, more experienced collectors. Large fish hooks are sewn through holes drilled in the end of the plastic pipe. Snakes that do not respond readily to fumigation are gaffed and yanked out of their holes. Externally the injuries can appear to be little more than gashes and rips in the skin, but the internal damage can be considerable.

It is paradoxical that sponsors promote roundups as a method of eradicating dangerous snakes, and yet, if the snakes were destroyed, they would not be able to maintain an annual cash flow.

In this demonstration, a dozen or so rattlesnakes are placed in the sleeping bag with this couple. The paying audience appears less than enthusiastic about the feat.

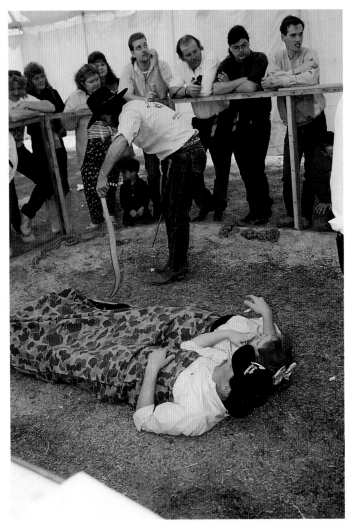

THE REAL VALUE OF RATTLESNAKES

The fat of the rattlesnake is very sovereign for frozen limbs, bruises, lameness by falls, aches, and sprains. The heart of the Rattlesnake, dried and pulverized, and drunk with wine or beer is an approved remedy against the biting and venom of the rattlesnake.
        —John Josselyn

Some important research is being done with rattlesnake venom, and Native Americans have used various parts of rattlesnakes ceremonially and medicinally for centuries. However, the majority collected for roundups and by commercial collectors are killed to make money for hucksters and entrepreneurs. The public is seduced and persuaded to believe rattlesnakes are expendable because they are perceived to be dangerous, because they are seen as nothing more than an accident waiting to happen. Other people are manipulated into believing rattlesnakes are an exploitable, renewable natural resource with little additional value. Their true economic significance lies in their continued existence and their natural role in the ecosystem rather than in their extermination, however.

Part of the Food Chain

Rattlesnakes are important predators. They are a meaningful link in the food chains that maintain the delicate control and balance of all living things. Because their primary food is small mammals, they exert a major influence in keeping the number of destructive rodents in check.

A Mexican woman explains the medicinal value of dried rattlesnakes, while attempting to sell the fresh skins of two Mexican blacktail rattlesnakes, *Crotalus molossus nigrescens.* Dozens of skinned, eviscerated carcasses of the same species are drying on the rack behind her.

Drying carcasses of Mexican blacktail rattlesnakes, *Crotalus molossus nigrescens (above)*, are for sale at one of a series of roadside stands near Huizache, San Luis Potosi, Mexico. The boxes of gelatin capsules *(right)* containing ground, dried rattlesnake can be purchased at many ethnic and alternative medicine stores throughout the world.

Opposite: Sliced in two by the wheels of a speeding car that had purposely veered to hit it, this adult eastern diamondback, *Crotalus adamanteus,* shows faint twitches of life. Although this snake had managed to survive four or five years in the nearby Everglades hammock, the few minutes it took to try crossing Alligator Alley exposed it to a violent end caused by its greatest enemy: humans.

Using mathematic progression it is possible to calculate the annual potential offspring from a single pair of mice or rats. Employing a gestation period of twenty-one days, an average litter size of seven, and maturation at six weeks, under favorable conditions the original parents can potentially produce thousands of young in one year. Although it varies from region to region, assuming an adult rattlesnake consumes between twelve and twenty-four adult and newborn rodents each year, the probable number of future mice and rats it would eliminate could number in the thousands.

Pernicious rabbits, ground squirrels, prairie dogs, gophers, and chipmunks are also kept from over-reproducing, saving millions of dollars in crop damage. Although mostly unnoticed, rattlesnake predation is important in stabilizing many natural environments.

Uses of Venom

Dried rattlesnake venom has had many uses over the centuries. Drying retains its potency. Some early Native American peoples used it on their arrow tips to embellish their effectiveness. Frequently it was mixed with other venoms and poisonous substances to increase the toxicity. It is quite possible that ethnobiologists may uncover beneficial medical uses and chemical properties of pitviper venom that are now known only to some natives of Latin America.

Taxonomists and evolutionary biologists employ the chemical properties of intricate venom components to better understand evolutionary relationships of taxa. As molecular biological techniques and tests become less costly, an even greater understanding will emerge.

Biochemists have made astounding discoveries about venoms that may prove advantageous in improving humanity's quest for extended life and for finding cures for assorted terminal maladies. As tools in the study of blood components, data have been uncovered about two physiological processes, the release of kinin and the clotting mechanism.

A nerve growth-promoting factor has been segregated in the venom of some rattlesnake species. This has opened new doors and accelerated research into the complexities of diseases that produce permanent nerve damage, such as multiple sclerosis and Alzheimer's disease.

Folk Medicine

For hundreds of years, certain Native Mexicans have believed dried rattlesnake flesh holds miraculous medicinal qualities. They accept it as a cure for a myriad of problems, including various skin conditions, diabetes, arthritis, and cancer. Sun dried, pounded, and ground into a fine powder, the flesh can be purchased neatly boxed as pills or powder in *boticas* (herb shops) and pharmacies. Venders

at roadside stands in the Mexican state of San Luis Potosi display and sell complete desiccated rattlesnake carcasses.

This folk medicine has found a place among Hispanics in larger U.S. cities, where its use has become a serious medical problem. Much of the dry flesh is contaminated with powerful strains of *Salmonella* bacteria. *Salmonella arizona* is the most commonly found species. These gram-negative bacilli are a perplexing group that is constantly evolving.

Usually, salmonella produces little more than a gastrointestinal bout that lasts a few days. However, to persons afflicted with serious maladies that precipitate low immune systems, ingesting it could put them at significant risk. Several such patients in El Paso and Los Angeles have suffered dire consequences from salmonellosis. Six deaths have been recorded in two years. These patients were hospitalized and treated for advanced life-threatening diseases, and salmonella may not have been the single lethal agent.

Many people in the Asian community buy rattlesnake organs for their purported medicinal value. Nearly half are exported to the Far East, and the rest are consumed in the United States. Many in the Chinese and Thai community believe venomous snake gall bladders are aphrodisiacs, and they are willing to pay a premium for them. The gall bladders are cut out and sold at $1 a piece. Because they are minute, a pound fetches $7,000 to $8,000.

While photographing rattlesnakes in Mexico for this book, I found a Mexican blacktail rattlesnake, *Crotalus molossus nigrescens*, lying at the base of a tree. From a distance it appeared to be alive, but farmers planting seedlings nearby had killed it a few hours before. Aside from a machete gash on the skull, there was only a small slit through which the gall bladder had been removed. It was obvious that the farmer was highly adept and knowledgeable about the organ's location and had done this extraction many times before.

In some cultures snakes are boiled alive, and the broth is consumed as an elixir to cure a variety of maladies. Others are cut and bled live, and the blood is drunk as a tonic to prolong life.

Food Source

During the 1950s and 1960s thousands of small cans of eastern diamondback rattlesnake meat were sold by Ross Allen's Reptile Institute in Ocala, Florida. This was never a serious food staple, but rather it was mostly a curiosity, a memento of visiting the facility, or a conversational offering at cocktail parties. A similar product (likely western diamondback meat) is produced today in Texas and Oklahoma. The early variety sold for $1.00 to $2.50 per can, and a currently concocted Denver variety is sold by gourmet shops for $12 to $15 a can.

Unfortunately, rattlesnake meat is served at specialty restaurants. On a more exclusive basis, it is often served at gatherings of secret societies whose members are dedicated gourmands. This sort of society, satirized in the movie *The Freshman*, is difficult to fathom. Very wealthy, somewhat eccentric persons have periodic feasts of extravagantly prepared exotic foods. The fare varies, but basic items include monkey, sea lion, tiger, eagle, hummingbird, a variety of insects and arachnids, rattlesnakes, and a legion of other unusual, sometimes rare, animals. No canned goods here, as it is imperative that all items be fresh, never frozen.

Rattlesnake Oil

Rattlesnake oil has long been depicted as a cure-all. During the formative days of the U.S. West, it was sold by itinerant medicine men from the backs of wagons. Actively bought by the gullible for its magical powers, it was promised to relieve rheumatism, gout, deafness, toothaches, tumors, the croup, as well as almost any other malady afflicting human or beast. This is the origin of the brusque and degrading expression "snake oil salesman." These preposterous claims carried over to modern times. Hucksters still can be found in rural regions selling "Genuine Rattlesnake Oil." One Dominican professional baseball pitcher attributes the success and strength of

This can of "gourmet" rattlesnake meat is a by-product of rattlesnake roundups and is available from specialty shops.

his arm to a daily application of snake oil. Although real snake oil can be purchased, much of the modern version is nothing more than a mixture of oil of wintergreen, olive oil, and a solvent.

Rattlesnake oil had a strong influence in the United States, but it can be traced back much earlier, to the Nahuatl women of central Mexico. The Nahuatl believed rattlesnake oil, applied to their hair, stimulated opulent healthy growth. Also, the hair was supposed to attain the length of the snake from which it was extracted. Great care had to be taken with its use, the legend continued, for if rain fell on the treated hair, it would twist about like a snake and strangle the woman.

The genuine product is made by heating or broiling the fat bodies removed from the rattlesnake carcass until they melt into a dripping, clear, light-colored yellow oil. The oil is skimmed, as one might remove bacon grease from a frying pan. Rattlesnake oil is a less significant by-product of rattlesnake roundups.

Tourist Attraction

During the 1940s, 1950s, and 1960s, before airplane travel became acceptable and widely affordable, a majority of Americans toured by automobile on their vacations. In the winter, northerners, eager to escape the cold, were especially enamored with Florida's warm climate and expansive beaches; they flocked there by the hundreds of thousands. Prior to the interstate highway system, a typical leisurely trip to Miami would take four or five days from New York, for example, with stops at a series of favored attractions along the way. One of the most famous side trips along the north–south route was to Ross Allen's Reptile Institute at Silver Springs, Florida. Glass-bottomed boats offered a fabulous view of the underwater world, while immaculately groomed, flower-filled gardens provided a beautiful taste of the Sunshine State. But there was little doubt—the allure for the kids was the reptile show!

On a regularly scheduled basis, Allen—a former movie actor—would jump into a shallow pond and "wrestle" an alligator. It was just as they had seen him do in many motion pictures and on newsreels. Although this was surely an attraction, it was fairly

Four rattlesnake oil bottles ranging from the "patent-medicine" era through the mid-twentieth century. *From left:* Worner's Rattler Oil, Phoenix, Arizona (ca. 1870); Clark Stanley's Snake Oil Liniment (ca. 1880); Blackhawk's Rattlesnake Oil (ca. 1930); and Ross Allen Pure Snake Oil (ca. 1950).

Table displays of a variety of items made from rattlesnake parts and skins for sale at rattlesnake roundups.

commonplace nearer the Everglades, where dozens of Seminoles put on similar shows. However, the major draw was the snakes, more specifically big eastern diamondback rattlesnakes, *Crotalus adamanteus*. Rarely fewer than a hundred, including dozens of heavy-bodied, nearly 6-foot (1.8-meter) giants that were still fairly common at that time, were always on display in a series of enclosed pits.

Throughout the day Allen, and occasionally his wife Celeste, would handle and give talks about snakes. The rattlesnake talk was easily the most exciting presentation. As they spoke, they walked in the pit among the rattlesnakes. The snakes responded with a cacophony of furious rattling and by striking at the Allens's knee-high, "snakebite-proof" leather boots. Venom was "milked" to fill the demands of pharmaceutical laboratories in a special sanitary area as part of the show. Although he started milking venom in the late 1930s, the demand for polyvalent antivenom, useful against Asian crotalids that were quite commonly encountered by American troops overseas during World War II, made his venom lab the most productive in the world. He boasted about being able to milk two or three rattlesnakes a minute, but his personal record was 150 cottonmouths in less than an hour. A truly amazing feat!

With the many thousands of venomous snakes he handled, he claims to have been bitten six times, once each by a cottonmouth and copperhead, and twice each by a western and an eastern diamondback. The only nearly fatal bite was from a large eastern diamondback that sunk both fangs into the base of his thumb and into an artery. Gangrene forced the removal of a portion of the thumb. It was a similar, but fatal, eastern diamondback bite in 1992 to one of the snake handlers at the facility that is the reason venomous snakes are no longer handled there.

Away from public view, hundreds of snakes were killed, skinned, and cooked. The institute's curio and mail order shop sold thousands of cans of rattlesnake and alligator meat annually, along with an array of products nearly identical to those found at current rattlesnake roundups. It is important to note that the massive commercial, industrial, and agricultural development of Florida was just beginning, and rattlesnakes (and alligators) were considered pests or plentiful, renewable resources.

It was easy to see why Allen became a folk hero and the most famous "rattlesnake man" of his era. He was handsome, a championship swimmer, very active and respected among the Boy Scouts (he was an Eagle Scout), and a great showman. Allen's Reptile Institute flourished to become the major attraction in northern Florida and a stop few tourists bypassed. Thousands of postcards of Allen "milking" a diamondback or wrestling an alligator were sent as greetings or brought back as mementos of Florida.

Once, while wrangling rattlesnakes for the original version of the motion picture *The Yearling*, Allen told the director that a close-up of an eastern diamondback striking the hand of Gregory Peck was not realistic enough, as an artificial arm was being substituted. Allen said it needed a real arm, and he would take a real bite. The director thought he was insane but offered him $500 for the stunt anyway. That was a lot of money in the early 1940s. After Allen milked the snake several times to extract as much venom as he could, the scene was filmed. He suffered only a minor reaction.

The addition of Wilfred Neil (a somewhat flamboyant and controversial yet brilliant scientist) in 1949 added a new dimension to Allen's facility, namely scientific validity. He and Allen produced a series of papers on reptiles and amphibians at the institute and those they encountered as they traveled throughout the Caribbean and Central America.

During the same time span, as well as currently, dozens of similar attractions have been started at various locations throughout the United States, but none has had the longevity or has been as famous or as consistently well attended as Ross Allen's Reptile Institute. Showing his great disdain for such attractions—most kept their animals under inhumane conditions—Carl Kauffeld, famed curator of reptiles at the Staten Island Zoo, always referred to them as "miserable roadside snake exhibits."

Ross Allen's Reptile Institute no longer exists. It was purchased by a corporate conglomerate and fell victim to the need for more contemporary entertainment. Now the sprawling natural environment and labyrinth of crystal clear canals is simply called Silver Springs. It is visited for the magnificent gardens, summer music concerts, petting zoo, glass-bottomed boat rides, and river safari boat and jeep safari rides through "natural" areas containing penned wildlife from around the world.

Fate of Rattlesnakes Bought at Roundups

Jaycees and other sponsors of rattlesnake roundups proudly volunteer that little of the snake is "wasted." Nearly everything is sold, they explain. A dozen or so large commercial skin factories in Texas, Oklahoma, and Florida buy most of the snakes at roundups. One Oklahoma dealer has been in business for more than twenty years and employs fifty people in his eleven U.S. facilities. He claims to buy, manufacture, and supply more than 80 percent of the rattlesnake skins and by-products in the United States. He says that his wholesale business grosses more than $1 million in annual sales.

Skins are tanned for belts, guitar straps, gun holsters, hat bands, watch bands, briefcases, wallets, and purses. Rattlesnake-covered vests, jackets, chaps, pants, and baseball hats have also become fashionable with a certain clientele. Walking canes, pool cues, and custom-crafted writing pens covered with rattlesnake skins are available. One company offers sunbathing bikinis. They are strictly for show, because water submersion would have disastrous results on the already unstable material.

Because of the current demand and proliferation of limited-edition trading cards—they were called bubble gum cards when I was a youngster—publishers have resorted to extremes to garner a piece of the market. A North Carolina manufacturer, specializing in auto racing cards, has really stretched the envelope in an attempt to be unique. He produced a small run (749 cards of each of eight NASCAR drivers = 5,992 cards) called Diamondback Authentic. A diamond-shape cutout reveals a piece of tanned snake skin affixed beneath it. One thousand feet (305 meters) of eastern and western diamondback skin was used. Zealous collectors and dealers paid as much as $300 for the cards.

Western-style boots have become fashionable, particularly those embellished with unusual skins. Rattlesnake skin has joined a host of imported reptile leathers as the in material. Row on row of boots, mostly covered with western and eastern diamondback and canebrake rattlesnake skins, can be found in Western stores and boutiques. Gaudy street signs lure shoppers with "We have rattler boots!" No doubt, the patterns are attractive, but the raised texture of the scales appears to be the major enticement. Unlike more appropriate, properly tanned mammal hides, the reptile scales provide an extremely poor wearing surface. Although many are prepared with a secret "velvet chrome tanning process," they abrade

Collectable memorabilia from a formerly major tourist attraction in Florida, Ross Allen's Reptile Institute, of Silver Springs, near Ocala.

and flake from a minor rub or bump. One may only hope those spending $500 and more for a pair of rattlesnake boots will demand more suitable footwear, forcing the chic trend to be short lived.

Many of the snakes are freeze-dried and stuffed into threatening striking coils with mouths agape. Globules of resin are affixed to erect fangs, simulating venom droplets, in a totally unnatural presentation. There are two recorded cases of persons being envenomated by residual venom in the fangs of stuffed, freeze-dried rattlesnakes.

Heads are embedded in clear plastic for paperweights, belt buckles, or book ends. Some are sawed in half and glued to large snake-skin-covered belt buckles. A truly macabre item is a container of pool-cue chalk stuffed into the gaping mouth of a severed freeze-dried rattlesnake head. In addition, heads and rattles are available as souvenirs, key chains, and earrings. Fangs, jaw bones, vertebrae, and rattles are combined with various beads in necklaces. Fully formed, unborn rattlesnakes are cut from pregnant females, mummified, varnished, coiled, and sold as miniatures called "little rascals." The most ludicrous item (reserved for the person who has everything) is an adult rattlesnake, entombed in a transparent plastic toilet seat.

The bulk of these snake products are not sold at roundups but at flea markets, curio shops, boutiques, and western stores. They are in great demand in northeastern cities. Alarming quantities are being carried by mail order and by specialty shops at shopping malls across North America. Prices vary, but they tend to be fairly high-end items. Gift shops at several western airports and nearly all roadside western souvenir shops display and sell a variety of these articles.

Many peddlers at rattlesnake roundups attempt to cut out the wholesaler, offering to buy rattlesnakes directly from collectors year round. They do their own tanning and assemble the various curios. The meat is thrown away, and venom is not extracted. Generally, the quality of work and tanning (many using glycerin or antifreeze) is so poor that the products quickly disintegrate. The heads are so badly shriveled and misshapen, they are little more than grotesque mummies. Even the highest quality tanned rattlesnake skins are short lived, impossible even to be graded as seconds. Although the skin serves the snakes well, it makes inferior-wearing leather, as mentioned previously.

Roundups cannot fulfill the demand for rattlesnakes. Throughout the year, professional snake hunters collect and sell additional thousands of them to established dealers and intermediaries. There is no other way the estimated astounding number—a half million rattlesnakes per year—could be killed and processed.

RATTLESNAKES IN LORE AND RELIGION

The rattlesnake in one form or another has been common to all of the United States; however, he grows larger in the West and Southwest, and somehow the talk about him in those regions seems bigger than elsewhere. Perhaps the sunshine accounts for this.

—J. Frank Dobie

Ophiolatreia, the worship of snakes, has been practiced for thousands of years in nearly all major societies. Many of the world's great museums harbor arrays of ophidian artifacts used in pagan rituals. It is interesting that a preponderance of these artifacts depict venomous species, demonstrating their revered status in early civilizations.

To ancient Egyptians and Greeks, snakes were symbols of good, but to most others they were demons, messengers of evil. Christianity's hatred of snakes is mainly derived from commonly accepted passages of the Bible. The most widely known is the tale of the serpent that inhabited the Garden of Eden, who was responsible for persuading Eve to commit the Original Sin.

Greek mythology accounts for dozens of stories. Medusa's head had a mass of writhing serpents for hair, denoting divine wisdom. Some Greek cities and places bear names derived from snakes. In early writings the island of Cypress was called Ophiusa for the serpents that presumably thrived there. The god of medicine (*Askepios* to the Greeks, *Aesculapius* to the Romans) was said to have acquired his knowledge of healing and his wisdom from snakes. The medical profession's emblem today is a staff entwined with serpents.

At a snake-handling service of a small, fundamentalist Christian church in the southeastern United States, the church's minister holds aloft a timber rattlesnake, *Crotalus horridus horridus,* and stares into its eyes.

In the Americas, Mayan, Aztec, and Toltec temples are adorned with snake deities of all types, but rattlesnake carvings are prevalent. Quetzalcoatl, one of the most important early Mexican deities, is most frequently depicted as a plumed serpent with rattles. In 1636 Bernal Diaz del Castillo marched through Mexico with Cortez. His account, riddled with extravagant and dubious observations, noted the following about the great temple at Terraguco, the town of the serpents:

Moreover, in that accursed house they kept vipers and venomous snakes, who had something at their tails which sounded like morris-bells, and these are the worst of vipers. They were kept in cradles and barrels, and in earthen vessels, upon feathers, and there they laid their eggs, and nursed up their snakelings, and they were fed with the bodies of the sacrificed, and with dogs' meat. (B. Diaz del Castillo, *The True History of the Conquest of Mexico . . . Written in the Year 1668* [Reprint], New York: A. D. H. Smith, 1800)

North American natives maintained an aura of superstition about rattlesnakes, perhaps second only to their veneration of the wolf. They venerated and feared them. This fit well with their basic theology of animism (assigning supernatural powers to natural creatures and objects). Some peoples may have worshiped rattlesnakes, but general reverence and respect were likely the more pervasive attitudes. On the darker side, Edward Curtis, famous photographer of Native Americans, reported having heard of newborn babies being sacrificed to a exceedingly large rattlesnake in elaborate worship ceremonies among the New Mexican Tewa.

In his journals, the early American naturalist William Bartram mentioned that eastern Native Americans avoided snakes rather than killing them "lest the spirit of the reptile should excite its kindred to revenge" (quoted by A. J. Barton in "Replacement Fangs in Newborn Timber Rattlesnakes," *Copeia* 1950:235–36 [1950]). This trepidation appeared to be accepted among various native peoples. Offering tobacco, a common display of friendship and method of appeasing offensive actions, was noted in numerous accounts when confrontations with rattlesnakes arose. Native Americans believed tobacco to be a major rattlesnake repellent. They spread tobacco about or burned it at camps, attached it in small pieces to their ankles, and smoked it heavily before going to sleep.

Other explorers recounted that several native peoples call rattlesnakes "grandfather." J. Carver made reference to a Menominee who carried a rattlesnake with him always, "treating it as a deity, and calling it his great father." Cherokee Indians assumed the rattlesnake to be "chief of the snake tribe" and an ornament of the thunder god (J. Carver, *Travels through the Interior Parts of North America, in the Years 1766, 1767, and 1768,* London: author, 1778).

Many Native Americans maintain a protective attitude toward rattlesnakes, because they believe there is a close relationship between the snakes and the weather. The quickness of the rattlesnake's strike is likened to lightning, and the rattle represents thunder and the sound of falling rain.

Rain Ceremonies

Some ethnologists believe that other native peoples may have used snakes in rain rituals at an earlier time, but for the Hopi of the northern Arizona plateau it is an integral part of their heritage. The Hopi are a religious people who have a self-sustaining agricultural lifestyle. They raise sheep and goats, grow corn, wheat, beans, sunflowers, and peppers, and oversee fruit orchards. Their need for, and reliance on, rain is apparent.

Witnesses have graphically described the nine-day ceremonies that are enacted at various pueblos during the last two weeks of August to stimulate late summer rains. Photography of this highly dignified religious rite was banned in 1915, so only a few lesser quality images were ever made.

For several days members of the Antelope and Snake Societies, religious groups within the community, perform sacred acts and dances in an effort to contact their gods. Unlike the gods of most groups, their deities are believed to live inside the earth, in the underground. Each society meets in respective *Kivas,* 8-foot-deep (2.4-meter-deep) in-ground rooms that are about 14 by 20 feet (4.3 by 6.1 meters) in size, with roofs constructed of logs and earth. The only entrance is a hole at the center of the roof.

Much about the highly secret preparation ceremonies remains unknown, but we know the Antelope priests, the main participants in the dances, have nothing to do with the snakes. They make prayer sticks and prepare an elaborate altar of colored sand with various symbols of rain. Priests, with the aid of younger tribal members, present a drama depicting the ancient myth of the Corn Maiden and Snake Youth (the basis for the ceremony) and have a Corn Dance and Antelope Race.

Each day snakes are caught, brought into the snake Kiva, and kept in well-guarded earthen jars. Prayers are offered and many ceremonial smokes are partaken. On the sixth and seventh days the snakes are carefully washed in a purification ritual. After washing, the snakes are released on the floor of the Kiva to dry. Young boys with "snake whips," wooden sticks with two eagle feathers at the end, herd them. Many Native Americans believe that eagles have special powers. Because eagles actively prey on rattlesnakes, they accept that rattlesnakes fear eagles and will not strike at their feathers. (It is not true.)

The climax of the festivities is the public snake dance at sundown on the ninth day. The snake priests are naked to the waist, and their bodies and faces are painted mostly black, with white outlining their mouths and splotched about their bodies. They appear surrealistic and sinister. The elaborate blue costumes, conjured up by the priests over the years, have brightly colored fringed belts with a fox tail attached at the back. Silver and turquoise necklaces dangle around their necks. Small eagle feathers adorn their long black hair. Turtle shell rattles, tied to each knee, add an infectious

At a moment of empowerment, a canebrake rattlesnake, *Crotalus horridus atricaudatus*, is defiantly held high above the head of a church elder. Other participants in the service chant, pray, sing, and dance in response.

rhythm as the snake priests perform a quick circular dance with snakes firmly held between their teeth. More often than not these are a local race of the western rattlesnake *(Crotalus viridis)* that is called the Hopi rattlesnake *(Crotalus viridis nuntius)*, but whipsnakes *(Masticophis)* and bullsnakes *(Pituophis)* are used also.

The dancer holds the snake's head within 6 inches of the his own mouth, and the bulk of the snake's body is left dangling. If the snake is exceptionally large, the dancer will support its body with the other hand. The rattlesnakes are held by the short section of the neck because the Hopi believe that they cannot strike unless they are coiled. Hopi never pick up a rattlesnake that has assumed a defensive posture but use eagle-feather snake whips to uncoil it first.

After the chief leads a final prayer, the festivities end with the snake priests grabbing handfuls of snakes and running out into the desert. There the snakes are released as messengers to the gods.

Above: A visiting minister from West Virginia fervently preaches amid the nearly deafening music while followers "take up serpents."

Opposite: Members of the congregation pray and chant as an elder weeps in exultation at "conquering the power" of a dark phase timber rattlesnake, *Crotalus horridus horridus.*

Why are the snake priests not known to have ever been envenomated? Klauber reported on two rattlesnakes used in the ceremonies that had been captured and sent to him by Charles Bogert. In both specimens, the fangs, reserve fangs, and underlying tooth-producing tissue had been skillfully cut out, rendering the snakes nonvenomous. Klauber concluded: "Thorough and repeated venom removal (milking), immediately following the catching of the snakes and during the ceremonies in the Kiva . . . [is] the probable source of the Indians' immunity from serious accident. I am more than ever convinced that if fang removal is a comparatively recent development, say within 30 years or so, it was antedated by a system of milking" (L. M. Klauber, *Rattlesnakes: Their Life Histories and Influence on Mankind,* Berkeley: University of California Press, 1956, p. 1126).

Serpent-Handling Sects

One of the most remarkable forms of modern-day religion, "serpent handling," can be found not in developing countries or as tools of

the occult but in the United States. This is not "snake worship," however; snakes are not considered deities, not benefactors, but rather the epitome of evil. Adhering closely to the scriptures, certain churches (predominantly independent fundamentalist Christian denominations) use rattlesnakes, as well as copperheads and cottonmouths, in their services.

Snake handling is considered a test of personal faith and Christian obedience; the premise is borrowed directly from the Bible. According to the Gospel of Mark (16:17–18), the words spoken by Jesus after the resurrection were, "And these signs shall follow them that believe: in my name shall they cast out devils; they shall speak with new tongues; they shall take up serpents; and if they drink any deadly thing, it shall not hurt them; they shall lay hands on the sick, and they shall recover."

Snake-handling services were founded during the summer of 1906 in Grasshopper Valley, Tennessee, by George Went Hensley, and have managed to survive a roller-coaster existence. Cases are tested periodically in the courts, with advocates holding as an infringement of rights to religious freedom the prohibition of such

Above: An elder prays with the help and rapt attention of the attendants.

Right: A young male participant is actively supported by another at the moment of annointment.

Opposite: Intensity, reaction, and handling styles may differ, but there is no discrimination in age and gender among the adult congregation.

ceremonies, but currently only two states, West Virginia and Georgia, do *not* outlaw the meetings. Hensley, considered the grand prophet of American snake-handling sects, died at the age of seventy from the bite of an eastern diamondback, *Crotalus adamanteus,* received at an illegal service in Florida.

Originally appealing to poor southerners, mostly white, as an opportunity for salvation and a deeply emotional escape from the harsh realities of poverty, snake-handling sects peaked at the end of World War II. There was one short-lived group in southern California. Although considerably lessened now, a small, secretive, dedicated following maintains the beliefs throughout the rural South, not far from the birthplace of snake handling, in Appalachia.

Many persons engaged in the rites are terrified of snakes. Their absolute belief in God (most frequently in the form of the Holy Ghost) allows them to use the snakes as a way of overcoming the devil. Their intensity and faith cannot be denied. In no other American religion do the worshipers actually confront death. Before racial desegregation, African Americans were accepted into and became active in some southern snake-handling churches, particularly in Florida. This may have been influenced by the influx of Jamaicans, Haitians, and other Caribbean peoples with histories of occult religions.

A visitor at a snake-handling church might witness these kinds of events: The congregation typically meets on a Saturday evening in a small, one-room, frame church. Accompanied by guitar, piano, and drum music, the minister leads the faithful in inspired hymns. Soon the room is flooded with rhythmically moving bodies. Partici-

pants move to a large unobstructed area at the front of the room, where they sway, dance, stamp their feet, and clap hands while singing and volunteering praises to the Lord: "Hallelujah!," "Praise Jesus!," "God is Real!," "Amen!" Others counter by raising Bibles, many openly testifying their faith. Some brandish tambourines.

The preacher expounds on evil, on the devil's influences (alcohol, smoking, and promiscuity). His compelling, sensational, fire-and-brimstone delivery solicits vociferous praises to Jesus. The sermon intensifies as he proclaims every word in the Bible is true. The pace quickens; several more communicants move to the front, where they are "getting the spirit" (anointing), "talking in tongues" (glossolalia), crying, shouting, praying. The air is heavy with terrific energy, undeniable devotion, and honest faith.

Dancing about singly or with others, many demonstrate quick, violent, spastic motions. Worshipers thrust their hands upward while tossing their heads backward, praising the Lord. Oppressive heat emanates from the mass of reeling bodies; all are sweating.

A tiny elderly woman in a simple cotton dress falls to the floor, writhing uncontrollably, still chanting and uttering unrecognizable words. This ecstatic seizure attracts others who pray over her. Contagiously, others are overcome, and the frenzy continues for more than half an hour.

A parishioner occasionally gives a contemptuous kick at one of several flat wooden boxes that lie to one side, almost unnoticed. They contain the snakes. The buzzing of the aroused rattlesnakes cannot be heard through the overpowering music and incantations.

Eventually the preacher throws open a box, reaches in among

the knot of serpents, and quickly pulls out a timber rattlesnake, *Crotalus horridus horridus,* with a sweeping motion. Grasping it at mid-body while cradling its rear section, he holds the snake aloft. The rattle, a barely visible blur, confirms that the snake is awake and riled. Participants react with the foreseen response, still more delirium. Grabbing the first snake is considered a supreme test of faith, because the first touch to the aroused snake is most likely to elicit a bite.

The minister passes the snake to a nearby dancing worshiper who holds it overhead, and takes out two more magnificent timber rattlesnakes. Draping one around his neck and shoulders, he holds a 4-foot-long, velvety black one. Soon a dozen others are handling rattlesnakes and copperheads, while chanting, swooning, swirling, and continuing the jerking motions. The music is thunderous, overpowering. One woman in a trance-like state, her head pitching from side to side while rolling back and forth, has a half-dozen snakes stretched between and around her hands. She is at a moment of extreme ecstasy. She is fully anointed, receiving a blessing from the Holy Ghost for her devotion. A deacon, wearing a copperhead wrapped around his head like a turban, slowly raises a 4-foot timber rattlesnake. While permitting its head to brush against his mouth, he allows another to crawl inside his shirt. After thirty minutes of near hysteria, the ceremony reaches a crescendo.

The music subsides, the snakes are returned to the boxes, and the minister continues his impassioned sermon; people volunteer their faith while continuing their reeling motions at a slower pace. Within minutes the tempo of the music builds, and the congregation quickly becomes embroiled in renewed celebration. Snakes again are taken from their boxes and passed among the invigorated, nearly delirious assemblage. After fifteen minutes or so the frenzy subsides and the snakes are again returned to the boxes.

The minister calls those in need of healing to come forward. Using his palms he grasps the head of a sufferer, and she immediately falls limp into a trance. Staring deeply into her eyes he commands her to have faith in God's power; only with total faith can a miracle happen. She writhes uncontrollably, shaking (almost vibrating), while babbling and sobbing. A group gathers, pressing in, praying and continuing the rhythmical swaying. An obese man pushes toward the preacher crying for help to cure his diabetes. Hands are laid on him and on other beseechers. The service continues for several more minutes. Slowly it subsides as the participants tire, many near exhaustion. The service ends much more abruptly than it started, with emotional kissing and hugging.

Several phenomena are revealed here that are difficult to explain. Actually, many seem to defy rational explanations. Certainly, handlers are bitten, but only occasionally with serious consequences or death. Some preachers claim to have received hundreds of bites. The number of missing fingers and mangled, atrophied hands of longtime practitioners attests to the danger. Hensley is said to have survived 146 bites (the 147th killed him). Considering the method and amount of free-handling, however, the number of these incidents (particularly fatal ones) is extremely low. It has been estimated that seventy-five or so cultists have died since snake-handling sects got started nearly ninety years ago. There is an account of handling snakes at the funeral of one individual who was bitten and of burying the rattlesnakes (alive) in his coffin. (Because he had succumbed to snakebite, they believed that he had not conquered the devil and he was therefore buried with him.)

It is important to interject that believers follow a strict interpretation of the Bible, denouncing any form of medicine as a lack of faith in God's ability to cure the sick. Of course this includes any medical aid for snakebites. A coal miner bitten at a service vehemently refused medical attention, saying, "I'm lettin' the Lord do my doctorin'." He survived.

Evaluating Snake Handling

A variety of media representatives have examined the snakes used in many of the rituals, verifying that they had not been physically tampered with. The rattlesnakes' fangs and venom apparatus were intact. Also, the snakes are usually in excellent health, many having been recently captured. There is no proof that they are milked. In any case, milking would not completely deplete a snake's venom supply.

Although timber rattlesnakes, *Crotalus horridus horridus,* used in the majority of Appalachian services envenomate a sizable yearly number of people other than worshipers, this species is considered to be rather mild tempered and not particularly prone to strike. As with copperheads, *Agkistrodon contortrix,* the potency of timber rattlesnakes' venom varies and is usually not fatal to healthy adult humans. This does not explain, however, the low number of fatalities among older, potentially more susceptible, worshipers. Many are in their seventies. Children are not bitten because they are not permitted to handle snakes at services.

On the other hand, eastern diamondback rattlesnakes, *Crotalus adamanteus,* and cottonmouths, *Agkistrodon piscivorous,* employed in some illegal ceremonies in South Carolina and Florida, are irascible and disposed to strike at the least provocation. They are extremely dangerous snakes. Their venom is injected in large quantities, and it is not uncommon even for properly treated persons to die. One deacon was bitten on the temple by an eastern diamondback and died ten hours later. (This is the same species that killed George Went Hensley.)

Herpetologists are at a loss to explain why flagrant mishandling does not result in a much greater number of bites. There are little empirical data, and research is complicated because of the unorthodox nature of the rites. It is difficult or impossible to reproduce the fervor and intensity of the religious experience under controlled conditions.

One particularly baffling observation is the way some rattlesnakes react when held aloft by their midsection: they go limp

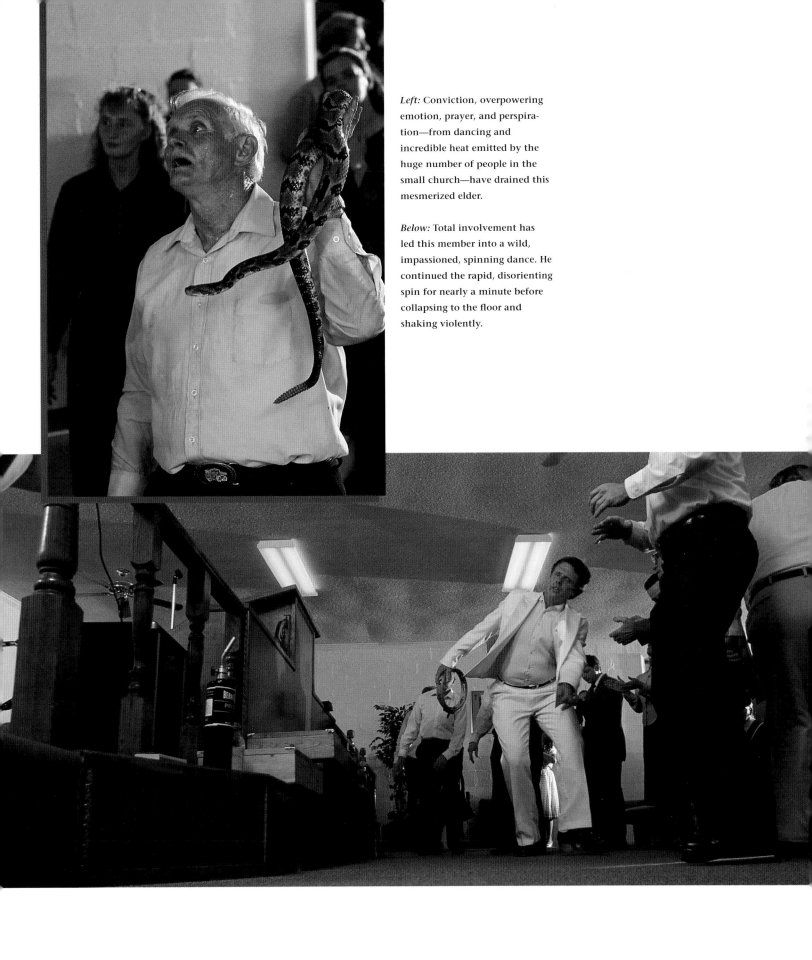

Left: Conviction, overpowering emotion, prayer, and perspiration—from dancing and incredible heat emitted by the huge number of people in the small church—have drained this mesmerized elder.

Below: Total involvement has led this member into a wild, impassioned, spinning dance. He continued the rapid, disorienting spin for nearly a minute before collapsing to the floor and shaking violently.

and stop rattling. W. H. (Marty) Martin, an expert on the biology of *Crotalus horridus horridus,* relates that, for some reason, timber rattlesnakes are much more prone than other rattlesnake species to go limp when held this way. Several species of snakes are known to enter a catatonic state as a defense mechanism when subjected to excessive physical abuse. The most notable is the death-feigning behavior of the harmless eastern hognose snake, *Heterodon platirhinos.* When prodded, the snake simply rolls over onto its back and plays dead until the threat has abated. This specific behavior has not been noted in rattlesnakes. Most rattlesnakes react pugnaciously if threatened, striking out at anything coming into range, and attempting to crawl away as soon as the opportunity arises. This is also typical when they become annoyed or disoriented. Occasionally, rattlesnakes that have been restrained or taunted unmercifully will hide their heads beneath coils and cease rattling.

Some scientists hypothesize that the jerking motion and dance befuddles the snakes or somehow induces the catatonic state. Still others feel the hand's warmth soothes them, or the continual passing from one worshiper to another disorients and disturbs their normal reflexes. All of these suggestions are unproven.

It is also difficult to explain how those who receive severe bites during such services survive without medical attention. Doubtless an occasional victim receives a dry bite, not infrequent even under normal conditions. But what about those who have been envenomated? Possibly the body reacts to combat and neutralize the venom. But why is there only minor necrosis (the expected normal destruction and permanent damage to the skin and underlying tissue) at the location of many of the bites? Martin (personal communication, 1992) noted the following about *Crotalus horridus:*

> Timber rattlesnake venom seems to cause more blood platelet destruction and blood-clotting problems, accompanied by severe swelling and pain, than it does tissue destruction. Also, in biting defensively it will often give a "nip," not a full-fledged, hard-driving, fang-plunging bite. It often seems reluctant to give a hard bite, preferring rather, to give a soft, pricking, stab.

The intense spiritualness and pervasive supernatural aura produced by the emotionally consumed participants introduce a unique variable. Although many people do not accept that the state of emotional holiness can interfere with normal physical reaction to a rattlesnake bite, this theory requires much more study. An aroused endocrine–immune response or other physiological preparedness to stress deserves serious consideration, and a form of holistic medicine cannot be ruled out. No doubt these North American snake-handling sects see rattlesnakes as very special, distinctive, exceptional. The interpretation of rattlesnakes as potent and mystical deities, and their inclusion in widely practiced Native American religious rituals, appears to have been rediscovered by modern snake-handling sects.

Opposite: The intense stare of an elder demonstates his unwavering commitment to overpowering the snake's representative powers.

Below: A pen is used to unsheath the fangs of a timber rattlesnake, *Crotalus horridus horridus,* showing that the snake has not been defanged and retains its ability to inject venom.

RATTLESNAKES AS SYMBOLS: THE GOOD, THE BAD, AND THE UGLY

There's a beautiful snake with a rattle
That is meant for defense, not for battle.
But the fear it begets
Will caution your pets;
If the dog doesn't warn you, the cat'll.
—Martha (Mickey) Bogert

Artists have always sought new methods of expressing their creative vision. There is little wonder, then, that the fascination surrounding rattlesnakes makes them likely subjects of artistic interpretation. Aside from the endless dried, tanned, and stuffed goods produced from rattlesnake roundups, rattlesnake skin and other body parts have been used in serious art. The texture and color of the skin lends itself to collage. Rattles, fangs, vertebrae, and skulls embellish sculpture. This is not a recent direction taken by pop artists but was an integral part of nineteenth-century Western Americana.

Woodcarvers and sculptors produce a variety of rattlesnake likenesses. Their work ranges from symbolic interpretations to extremely realistic recreations. They are as simple as primitive whittling or as elaborate as skillfully carved, intricate copies. Some are cleverly

Part of the author's collection of rattlesnake-related ephemera. It ranges from shirts to movie stills and postage stamps. None of the items are made of rattlesnakes collected commercially or at roundups.

designed with moving interlocking pieces. Others are direct, life-sized reproductions, made from castings of real snakes. The latter may be painted or airbrushed to faithfully represent the original snake. The Seri of western Mexico, known for their beautiful iron-wood carvings of animals, make rattlesnakes on occasion.

One of Frederic Remington's most famous bronze castings is titled, "The Rattlesnake." This 1905 sculpture depicts a cowboy astride a frightened, rearing horse that has encountered an aroused rattlesnake along the trail. Remington's knowledge of horses and his ability to capture the moment have made this a most celebrated piece.

Jewelry makers often use a snake motif or snake parts in their creations. Earrings, pins, bracelets, and barrettes, in the form of realistic and impressionist rattlesnakes, are available in many boutiques. The bulk are the costume variety, but many are carefully enameled or inlaid. Solid gold and silver ones, frequently embellished with gemstones, can be bought from quality jewelers.

Rattlesnake designs are also fashionable as bolos for western string ties. They range from inexpensive stamped metal to hand-crafted fine silver. A dozen or so variations of oversized western-style belt buckles are also produced. Nickel-silver appears to be the metal of choice, but cast brass and bronze are becoming increasingly common. The designs, ranging from realistic to impressionistic, are limited only by the creativity of the maker.

Native American Arts

Because rattlesnakes are deeply rooted in Native American culture and religion, it is reasonable that they should be part of their art as well. Although not common, very early rattlesnake likenesses have been found. This scarcity appears to be caused by the superstition, fear, and reverence linked to the many mystical powers early Native Americans credit to these snakes. Most commonly the snakes are avengers of actions such as the death of another rattlesnake, the neglect of religious obligations, or the affront to the gods (mostly gods of weather). Pervasive avoidance, a taboo, is so great that even today few Native American artisans produce any rattlesnake representations. The reason for this may never be known, because many Native peoples are so highly protective of their customs, rites, and rituals, but most likely these fears are based on ancient religious beliefs wherein rattlesnakes represent evil.

For centuries the Zuni have produced a series of animal fetishes that are intended as the embodiment of powerful beasts. Although they may be carried individually, usually they are part of a set, each providing a unique force. Kept in a secret place within special clay jars and venerated, they provide help in confronting the daily problems of life. They are always considered holy and extremely powerful entities and are maintained with assigned ritualism. "Feedings" (offerings) are provided through a hole in the jar, and they are cleansed (washed) periodically.

Frederic Remington's famous bronze sculpture, "The Rattlesnake."

Left: Solid silver and solid gold pendants cast from rattles of eastern diamondbacks, *Crotalus adamanteus,* resemble the real ones surrounding them.

Below: A selection of metallic rattlesnake-motif belt buckles.

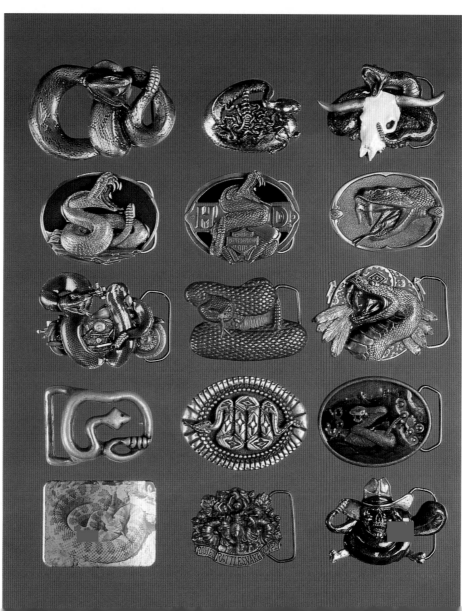

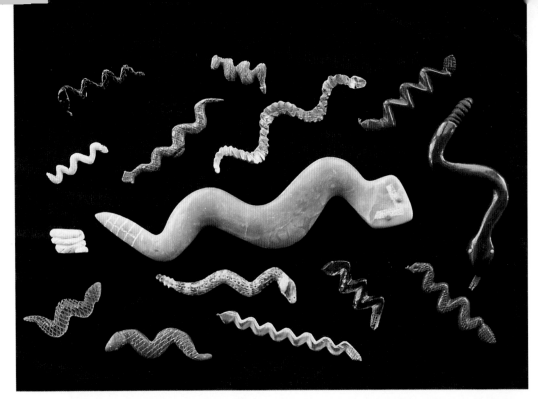

Left: A group of Zuni rattlesnake fetishes mostly carved from stone and shell and adorned with turquoise.

Middle: A Mexican painted terra cotta rattlesnake (artist and period unknown).

Below: A sandstone, Hohokam Indian incense burner (3.0 inches by 3.7 inches; 7.7 centimeters by 9.5 centimeters ; ca. A.D. 900–1200).

Each fetish is a powerful talisman, embracing a specific ideal or need. Fetishes are carried to help protect and embellish humans' senses and abilities, for good luck, to suppress evil, to increase fertility, to ward off disease, and to control the weather. Some are tools of the priests and are thought to be medically beneficial. There is a specific set for curing snakebite. Most commonly they provide good luck on a hunt. A mountain lion fetish promotes a fruitful deer hunt, and a coyote induces success with smaller game.

The rattlesnake symbolizes a powerful predatory animal. It is quiet, strong, and capable of killing anything. Its fetish provides the bearer with stealth, speed, precision, and agility when hunting an extremely dangerous animal such as a bear or mountain lion. The Zuni, as well as other

Native Americans, depict the rattlesnake as being closely related to lightning and sometimes interchangeable with it.

Fetishes are carved from an array of natural objects and minerals, including shell, antler, bone, and a variety of stones. Many are inlaid with turquoise. Feathers, shells, pieces of turquoise, or small carved arrowheads may be tied to their backs with a thin buckskin thong. They have become so collectable that many appear not to have true fetish qualities. Rather, they are modern, mostly decorative symbols carved by industrious artisans for the tourist trade. Personal fear, reverence, and need may be so intense that faith in the power of a specific charm is all that is needed to make it a genuine fetish. In the purest sense, a Zuni fetish is a symbol on which the owner focuses to maintain the age-old sagacity of the tribal elders.

Navaho necklaces made of rattlesnake vertebrae, interspaced with chunks of turquoise and occasionally pieces of deer bone and antler, have been produced. Likely, they are a form of talisman.

Another Native American art form, hand-woven baskets, are

Above: A highly valued miniature Papago basket with a rattlesnake motif, approximately 1.5 inches (3.8 centimeters) in diameter.

Right: A magnificent woolen *tapete,* dyed with cochineal and rock lichen, by the famous Oaxacan weaver Issac Vasquez (41 inches by 47 inches; 104 centimeters by 119 centimeters; ca. 1972). The stylized Mayan plumed serpent (rattlesnake) pierced by an arrow is likely derived from a depiction in the pre-Hispanic Borgia Codex. It symbolizes drought and famine.

A Hopi snake dancer katchina created by Chester Polyestewa (14 inches; 36 centimeters high). It is carved of cottonwood root and decorated in the traditional style.

Above: Detail of a Hopi katchina showing the rattlesnake in the mouth of the snake dancer.

Left: A pair of Hopi katchinas (chaser and snake dancer) by Roy Fredricks (19 inches; 48 centimeters high). These are carved in the modern style.

Left: Another variation of a cottonwood Hopi snake dancer in the modern style by Tchawas (13.5 inches; 34.3 centimeters).

Opposite, left: A Hopi snake dancer katchina by Henry Shelton of Orabi, Arizona (19 inches; 48 centimers high). It is carved of cottonwood in the modern style, and a carved rattlesnake is afixed to the base.

Opposite, right: A stylized, nonauthentic snake dancer by Irene McBride of Shiprock, New Mexico (15 inches; 38 centimeters high).

prized collectibles. A variety of amphibians and reptiles (mostly frogs and lizards) are within the accepted designs. Although occasional rattlesnake patterns adorn Papago baskets, they are uncommon or rare elsewhere. Mexican and Latin American weavers produce magnificent *tapetes* (rugs and tapestries), some with rattlesnake likenesses. Of these, variations of the feathered serpent, Quetzalcoatl, are depicted most often. Their beauty and craftsmanship have elevated them above the merely utilitarian. They are commonly displayed as wall hangings.

The Katchina clan is a very active Hopi religious faction. Males are indoctrinated at the age of 10. Hopi believe everything in the world has two parts: a tangible visible presence and a spirit essence. Members of the group wear stylized masks and dress in costumes representing the spirits of a myriad of ancient and modern religious

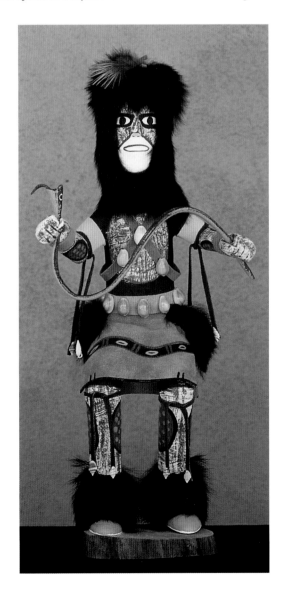

Left: A carved Navajo snake dancer and chaser by S.T.P. (14 inches; 36 centimeters).

Below: The small Hopi rattlesnake, *Crotalus viridis nuntius,* is best known as the rattlesnake used by the Hopi in their rain dance ceremony.

figures. They appear in seasonal tribal dances and ceremonies. Outfits worn range from very simplistic to outrageous and bizarre. Other peoples, mostly Navajo and Zuni, share many of the ideals and have evolved their own Katchina-like deities.

Doll-like replicas of the gods, Katchinas (called *tihu* by the Hopi), are carved from cottonwood root, elaborately painted, detailed, and decorated, and given as tokens by the Katchina participants to infants and females. They are not children's playthings, but important effigies, believed to bear some of the spirit of the Katchina. They are hung about the home to remind and educate youngsters about tribal beliefs and customs. Katchinas have been produced for centuries. Because of their deep religious significance, tribal elders frown on having them leave the confines of the pueblo.

Although not true Katchinas (they are society personages), snake dancers *(Chusona)* are occasionally produced. They demand very high prices from collectors because they are so uncommon. Recently, modern, more realistic looking versions are being produced. Unlike traditional Katchinas that are staid and inanimate, these are lifelike, highly detailed, and shown in action. As in life, these snake dancers are not portrayed with masks but wear distinctive black and white face painting.

A few dioramas of snake dances are known. The complete tableau, including more than a dozen meticulously carved and

La gente tiene hambre. La gente tiene frío.
Los ricos han robado la tierra.
Los ricos han robado la libertad.
La gente exige justicia. De otra manera. Revolución.

painted snake priests and antelope dancers, is captured within an authentic dance scene. These dioramas are considered highly religious symbols. A magnificent one is located at an Indian trader's store in Arizona, but the artist was superstitious and fearful of reprisal and thus he refused to permit it to be photographed. The diorama is complete with buildings and an entrance to a Kiva.

Still another form of rattlesnake art has become a popular collectible in recent years: biological illustration. Produced by some of America's best biological illustrators, these outstanding drawings, paintings, lithographs, and etchings are actively collected. Mostly done to illustrate scientific papers and books, recent ones are highly detailed, faithful renderings of the animal. Every feature is meticulously replicated with the finest techniques, producing a nearly perfect two dimensional representation. Earlier versions (from the seventeenth, eighteenth, and nineteenth centuries) are more impressionistic and frequently misleading but are valued by collectors.

Advertising and Symbology

Creative advertising types find the "danger and ferocity" of rattlesnakes a strong attractant for potential purchasers. The draw is so great that the products need not be in any way related to snakes. An illustration of a rattlesnake wrapped menacingly around a western boot, mouth agape and fangs poised, was widely used as an ad for the boot's manufacturer. Unfortunately, the snake was being stepped on and about to be beheaded by an ominous hunting knife. Consternation from wildlife advocates brought tremendous negative publicity to the depicted cruelty, and the ad ceased to run. However, a poster and a postcard are still available from the company. The original intent—to attract attention—was successful beyond the company's wildest expectations. There are eleven other ads depicting a variety of other animals in similar soon-to-be-killed predicaments.

A Texas company markets Rattlesnake Beer. The logo, prominently displayed on the bottle and carton, is of a striking rattlesnake with the slogan "Drink It If You Dare." "America's Beer" is also prominently displayed in the brand's packaging. There is nothing special about the beverage, produced by an anonymous brewery, but it is a sought-after souvenir of some beer-drinking visitors to the U.S. Southwest. Another beer, Diamondback, is brewed for the owner of a major-league baseball team of the same name and sold only in Arizona; Red Rattler is a carbonated beverage with a different kind of "bite"—caffeine, and a lot of it. It is sold mostly in Texas; this bright red, novel tasting soda pop is popular with long-haul truck drivers. It is selling so well that it is being test marketed in other states and is expected to have much wider distribution in the near future.

Rattlers brand is a tough, quality line of outdoors clothing (including snakebite-proof chaps) made in southern Georgia in the heart of eastern diamondback habitat. A striking eastern diamondback adorns the trademark that embellishes the label as well as the packaging.

A major Japanese camera and binocular manufacturer used a photograph of a western rattlesnake, *Crotalus viridis,* in an ad with the tag line "How to get close without getting rattled." It fell a little short of the goal, however, because the snake's rattle was not in the frame and the image was of poor quality.

The rattlesnake's association with danger and its perceived dominant position among the animal world have made it a logical eye-catching symbol. Many more subtle, underlying attributes have been suggested as rationales of its success as a symbol. Some of these include the following: rattlesnakes lie in wait, always at the ready; their fangs are hidden until action is needed; having no eyelids, they are constantly awake and aware; they rattle to warn of their possible response; and when aroused, they fight with viciousness and tenacity.

An obvious example of this is the aroused rattlesnake depicted on a variety of American Revolutionary War *Don't Tread on Me* flags. A few confederate states took on the slogan and reintroduced their variation of the flags during the Civil War. Although there is no confirmation, Benjamin Franklin has been attributed with suggesting the Bald Eagle be replaced with a rattlesnake as the proper symbol of American resolve. Politicians, ministers, and other orators are not averse to referencing rattlesnakes for effect in their speeches. Usually they are referenced in a negative connotation, such as "mean as a rattler," "sneaky as an old rattlesnake," or "dangerous as a rattlesnake."

During World War II several American forces included rattlesnakes in the design of their group insignia. It was not uncommon during that era for impressionist paintings of them to personalize fighter planes and boats. A potent air-to-air missile called "Sidewinder" was a lethal weapon during the Vietnam War because of its position on the helicopter and its accuracy.

A massive roller coaster in San Antonio is called The Rattler. Several high schools and colleges have chosen rattlesnakes as their mascots or namesakes. Perhaps the most visible of these is Florida A&M University. A vivid, highly stylized likeness of an aroused eastern diamondback is used as the symbol of their sports teams. Their slogan is "Who do you fear?" A football team in Phoenix is known as Arizona Rattlers. Not to be outdone, Phoenix's recently organized major league baseball team was named Arizona Diamondbacks.

Literature and Film

Aside from their obvious legitimate place among factual natural history writings, rattlesnakes are forced into a dubious role in many fictional works. Their place in paperback Western novels is nearly always the same—a hackneyed cliché. They are little more than extras to spice up a scene. Usually, it is an accidental meeting, a precarious brush with death.

Cast as feisty, aggressive, incessantly rattling bad guys, they ferociously strike at the hapless cowboy. Occasionally they may be entwined in the plot. Spooking a horse and throwing the rider (likely the heroine) or biting a subordinate character are two overused story lines. Their fate is invariably the same: They are killed with one bullet or beheaded with a trusty Bowie knife. Frequently a cover illustration depicts the confrontation with a dramatically stylized, aroused rattlesnake in a menacing position—its mouth agape, fangs erect and dripping venom.

The culprit in these Westerns is the western diamondback, *Crotalus atrox*. In truth, depiction of this snake as a villain is not far from the mark: This species' temperament, abundance, and wide distribution make it responsible for more bites than any other rattlesnake. Even though its venom is only moderately potent, the amount injected is plentiful enough to cause death in some cases.

Rattlesnakes are used as heavies in many movie Westerns, too, but they have reached their greatest (or worst) heights in horror films. Three "B" films, *Stanley* in 1972, *Rattlers* in 1976, and *Fangs* in 1991, elevated rattlesnakes into starring roles. *Rattlers* was rewritten and remade as a television movie in 1996.

Stanley attained some cult status and is occasionally shown as a late-night rerun on television. In it, the lead (Tom) saves an eastern diamondback (Stanley) from being attacked by a hawk. Thereafter, they become inseparable friends. Soon his cabin is literally crawling with snakes. While confronting a group of commercial snake collectors, he discovers a clothing manufacturer is using the snake skins to produce belts, shoes, purses, and other apparel. He and Stanley make a pact to become the protectors of all snakes. Following Tom's orders Stanley and an assorted cast of other snakes kill several people.

The plot of *Rattlers* is slightly more original and elaborate. Unknown to the developer and builder, a luxury California resort is built atop a massive den containing thousands of hibernating rattlesnakes. When the lodge opens to the public in the spring, the conflict and carnage begins. This quotation from the rear cover of the book from which the screenplay was adapted sets the scene: "There was no way that anyone could know that they were holidaying above the dens of a seething mass of rattlesnakes. And there was no way anyone could escape the fiendish hissing horror, or the nightmare struggle that would erupt" (J. L. Gilmore, *Rattlers: A Novel of Relentless Flesh-Creeping Horror!*, New York: Signet, 1976).

Of the three movies, *Fangs* gives rattlesnakes the smallest roles. Snakey Bender is an old eccentric who collects snakes for a university. All is going well until the pressure from a series of events causes him to lose control. His best friend marries a young exotic dancer and casts Snakey aside. The local schoolmarm, who has had an unusual, albeit perverse, relationship with Snakey and his snakes, suddenly refuses his nocturnal visits. When the country store owner kills Snakey's favorite "python" (actually a large indigo snake), Snakey lures them, and other characters that have wronged him, to the ranch and, as the promo goes, "Even if you're partial to skin-crawling scares of the serpent kind, nothing will prepare you for the flesh-piercing pain of *Fangs*!"

Accounts of rattlesnakes in adventure and outdoor magazines are usually accompanied by sensationalized illustrations demonstrating viciousness. The tired portrayal of them as savage beasts is always fallaciously overdone. They are viewed from ground level, with their mouths agape, fangs raised and dripping venom. As mentioned earlier, the depiction is preposterous, because rattlesnakes do not normally gape or leak precious venom. An equally stale variation has fangs being deeply embedded in the hero's muscular arm, blood dripping from the punctures. The victim's face is contorted with intense pain and fear as he prepares to kill the snake with an ever-handy knife or handgun. The narratives are heavily embellished, and they are little more than fantasy.

The majority of these representations do little to educate the public. They promote additional fear, misunderstanding, and further exploitation of rattlesnakes. A study of the nearly three dozen North American animals that people find most offensive placed rattlesnakes high on the list. Only the cockroach, rat, mosquito, and wasp rated as more loathsome, and surely such fictional portrayals are at least in part to blame.

Members of the world-famous, outrageously entertaining Florida A&M Rattler marching band performing at a football game at half-time.

ENSURING RATTLESNAKE SURVIVAL

If there is a just god, how humanity would writhe in its attempt to justify its treatment of animals.

—Isaac Asimov

Rattlesnakes are part of the complex interrelationship of our natural inheritance. They are important predators in the convoluted food web that includes all living things. A few U.S. states understand and accept that there is a serious problem in declining populations of rattlesnakes. They have taken the lead by protecting certain rattlesnakes along with a cross section of other vertebrates and plants. There is no time or grounds for debate: Endangered species are truly in danger of extinction.

Protected Rattlesnakes

Recent studies of the intricate natural history of the timber rattlesnakes, *Crotalus horridus horridus,* have exposed that the future of these snakes is in jeopardy. They have been protected as threatened or endangered in Connecticut, New Hampshire, Massachusetts, Vermont, New Jersey, New York, Ohio, and Indiana, as well as Ontario in Canada. Unfortunately, the impact of years—since the 1920s—of carrying bounties (all of which have been eliminated recently) and wanton persecution in many of these states leave such meager populations that survival throughout much of its northern and midwestern range is tenuous. Several researchers are conducting a survey to

Crawling near a building site that has all but eradicated its habitat, a southern Pacific rattlesnake, *Crotalus viridis helleri,* wanders aimlessly, looking for clues to its former turf. At best, its future is tenuous. If it survives the construction and landscaping, inhabitants almost certainly will kill it.

ascertain whether federal listing by the U.S. Fish and Wildlife Service is warranted under the U.S. Endangered Species Act. Although the very existence of the law has come under the assault of politicians who appear to have little interest in the survival of our wildlife heritage, and listing any reptile or amphibian may prove difficult, a state by state timber rattlesnake conservation action plan is being drafted by a group of biologists.

In addition, the eastern massasauga, *Sistrurus catenatus catenatus,* another form perhaps more quickly approaching extinction, is afforded some legal protection in every state throughout its range (the Great Lakes states). Federal protection is also being considered for this small rattlesnake.

Federal law fully protects all wildlife and plants in U.S. national parks, national monuments, and national wildlife refuges. Nearly all states require scientific permits, hunting licenses, or nongame licenses to legally collect snakes, as well as other reptiles and amphibians, and they set possession limits. Enforcement, however, is difficult to monitor and rarely accomplished. In some states fines for taking are as much as $5,000 per snake (for multiple offenses), plus a prison sentence. Federally listed endangered species carry fines of as much as $250,000 per taken animal and several years in jail. Such penalties may be a deterrent to many, but commercial collecting continues nevertheless.

One infamous collector brags about having taken an estimated 9,000 timber rattlesnakes in the U.S. Northeast over the past 45 years, first as a commercial collector and later as an outright poacher. What is even worse, he is driven by maliciousness. He "delights in purposely removing these snakes from study populations of researchers, and . . . has a penchant for using the telephone or the mail to harass individuals involved in conservation work or scientific study of the timber rattlesnake" (W. S. Brown, L. Jones, and R. Stechert, "A Case in Herpetological Conservation: Notorious Poacher Convicted of Illegal Trafficking in Timber Rattlesnakes," *Bulletin of the Chicago Herpetological Society* 29:74–76 [1994]). Although he had been arrested and fined several times in New York, it was not until a federal indictment in November 1992 that he was to be imprisoned. This time he was incriminated by a compatriot who cooperated in a sting operation as a plea bargain in an effort to secure his own release. Shortly after the poacher's release from four months in federal prison, he telephoned a longtime timber rattlesnake researcher and boasted about his plan to move west and south to continue his exploitation.

North Carolina has listed the eastern diamondback, *Crotalus adamanteus,* the canebrake rattlesnake, *Crotalus horridus atricaudatus,* and the pigmy rattlesnake, *Sistrurus miliarius,* as protected species. The canebrake rattlesnake is listed as endangered in Virginia. Arizona protects three montane forms—the twin-spotted rattlesnake, *Crotalus pricei,* the banded rock rattlesnake, *Crotalus lepidus klauberi,* and the ridgenose rattlesnake, *Crotalus willardi*—as well as the desert-grassland massasauga, *Sistrurus catenatus edwardsii.* The

New Mexican ridgenose rattlesnake, *Crotalus willardi obscurus,* is the only U.S. rattlesnake afforded federal protection as a threatened species. Fortunately, the Nature Conservancy, a private land conservation organization, controls the stewardship of nearly all of its U.S. range (in the Animas Mountains of southwestern New Mexico). The Aruba Island rattlesnake, *Crotalus unicolor,* is protected by that island's government and also is listed as an internationally endangered species with the Convention of International Trade in Endangered Species (CITES).

Legislative Action

A recent excursion to Coronado Island off the Baja California coast disclosed that the endemic rattlesnake *Crotalus viridis caliginis* is in serious trouble. In the past few years, goats and mules have been released, and the threat of habitat destruction through grazing is readily apparent. The island flora is almost exclusively grasses and low shrubs, with some cacti. Without this ground cover, basking rattlesnakes will be exposed to additional predation by birds. Western gulls maintain an expanding rookery on the highest point of the island, within the rattlesnakes' densest population. If funding is made available, studies could be made to assess the status, importance, and future of these interesting endemic rattlesnakes, as well as studies of many other endangered snakes before they are imperiled.

A federally funded, scientifically based study would likely conclude that the skin trade ought to be abolished. Florida originated a series of studies on the number of rattlesnakes that are taken locally and imported for their skins. K. M. Enge (*Herptile Use and Trade in Florida: Final Performance Report,* Tallahassee: Florida Game and Freshwater Fish Commission, 1993) presented data clearly demonstrating that action needs to be taken. In the two-year study, 21,776 eastern diamondback rattlesnakes and 4,782 timber rattlesnakes were reported as being purchased by two Florida skin dealers. He suggested that "the Eastern Diamondback Rattlesnake is the most likely candidate for some sort of protection from human harvest" (p. 79). A major step would be to stop rattlesnake roundups. Protection of the dwindling populations of the eastern diamondback has been proposed in Georgia but has met with strong opposition from unreceptive, poorly informed, and deeply entrenched legislators (mostly from the southern part of the state where roundups are held).

Serious legal consequences for gassing must be written into law and strictly enforced. Gassing was tolerated in Georgia until 1994 because of an eleven-word addendum affixed to the associated protection amendment of the state's Fish and Wildlife Code (italicized in the cited regulation) that follows:

27-3-30 Disturbing, etc., of wildlife habitats; use of explosives, chemicals electric or mechanical devices for taking wildlife.

Except as otherwise provided by law or regulation, it shall be unlawful to disturb, mutilate, or destroy the dens, holes, or homes of any wildlife; to blind wildlife with lights; or to use explosives, chemicals, electric or mechanical devices, or smokers of any kind in order to drive such wildlife out of such habitats; *provided that this code section shall not apply to poisonous snakes.*

Finally, the Metro Toronto Zoo in Canada is engaged in an elaborate public awareness campaign to protect the Canadian population of eastern massasaugas, *Sistrurus catenatus catenateus,* that remains in southeastern Canada. The serious concern shown by attendees of a 1992 international symposium and workshop on the conservation of the subspecies all but ensures some protective legislation is imminent.

Captive Breeding

To date the Aruba Island rattlesnake, *Crotalus unicolor,* is the only rattlesnake taxon included in the International Endangered Species Captive Breeding Program. With the island's increasing development as a resort and with the ongoing use of the island for oil drilling, refining, and exploration, the rattlesnake population is being confined to a constantly decreasing thorn scrub habitat at the

Left: Ecologist Hugh McCrystal injecting a pit tag into a banded rock rattlesnake, *Crotalus lepidus klauberi,* in the field where it was captured. McCrystal has been studying the Huachuca Mountain, Arizona, population of this snake for several years. Note that the rattlesnake has been tubed.

Above, top: A pit tag (approximately the size of a grain of rice) being injected subcutaneously into the venter of an immature canebrake rattlesnake, *Crotalus horridus atricaudatus.* Each pit tag has a unique number that will be recorded in a logbook along with relevant data, such as weight, length, and the capture site.

Above, bottom: A pit-tag reader electronically excites the internal tag and displays its unique number on the LED screen. Each time this canebrake rattlesnake, *Crotalus horridus atricaudatus,* is recaptured, it will be examined and scanned, the number read, and new data entered into the logbook. Because the tag will remain readable for the life of the snake, it is an excellent method of studying many facets of the snake's natural history. Scott Pfaff holds the tubed snake while Wade Kalanowsky reads the tag's number.

Field biologist Andy Holycross checking traps along a drift fence he has set out to study the movements and population density of a relictual population of the desert-grassland massasauga, *Sistrurus catenatus edwardsii,* in western New Mexico.

center of the small island. The snake's entire range is believed to be less than 7 square miles (18 square kilometers).

Funding was made available, leading to a preliminary field study and evaluation in 1987 under the Species Survival Plan developed by the American Association of Zoological Parks and Aquariums. Another field study began in 1994. Before the latter study began, the wild population was believed to be fewer than 500; now it is estimated that fewer than 225 adults survive. The population remains in decline.

In addition to the field studies, captive reproduction is carefully monitored. A studbook, listing all the specimens of Aruba Island rattlesnakes in captivity and their genetic lineage, is kept, and selective breeding is vigilantly maintained and controlled among specified institutions. When the project started, 107 animals in twelve zoos were registered. Five pairs were added to the founder

stock in 1989, and five additional pairs in 1991. The intention is to maintain a genetically viable colony (with 95 percent genetic diversity) that could be used to reintroduce captive propagated offspring into the wild when the habitat is stabilized. From its inception until January 1994, more than 330 specimens were registered in the studbook. The captive population currently is considered viable and stable in forty participating locations.

Two high-tech innovations have simplified natural history studies of mobile vertebrates: radio tagging and PIT tagging. In radio tagging, a thumb-sized radio transmitter is either forced into the stomach or surgically implanted into the body cavity of a rattlesnake. The snake is released and its movements are tracked telemetrically. There is no need to actually touch or disturb the animal. Some transmitters are equipped to transmit thermal data as well. The transmitters operate on a variety of frequencies, so several ani-

Left: Naturalist Greg Greer demonstrates how a homeowner can safely trap a rattlesnake that has wandered onto the premises. A large plastic trashcan is quickly and deliberately placed over the snake with a sweeping motion. The head is contained first. Note how one lip of the can is held close to the ground, effectively shielding the captor from any contact with the snake, and care is taken to keep hands and feet safely out of striking range. The snake, in this case a large canebrake rattlesnake, *Crotalus horridus atricaudatus,* is contained until an experienced person can remove it to a safe area.

Right: In this variation, the rattlesnake is simply swept into the trashcan with a broom. When the can is quickly righted and covered, the snake is safely contained. This method should be used with extreme caution with a rattlesnake of this size, but it is a very effective method of capturing smaller ones.

mals can be identified and tracked simultaneously. The battery lasts as long as six months.

In PIT tagging, a glass-enclosed chip the size of a grain of rice is inserted into the snake's body cavity with a special syringe, and the snake is released. Each tag has a unique number encoded on it and will last indefinitely. When a tagged snake is found, a hand-held reader is held several inches from the snake. It transmits a harmless micro charge, and the chip becomes electronically excited, producing the number on the reader.

Several zoos, under the progressive eyes of a handful of curators and keepers, have committed to similar captive propagation of some other taxa that are potentially threatened, notably the ridgenose rattlesnake, *Crotalus willardi.* However, many zoos, as well as the private sector, have placed their emphasis and energies on maintaining and breeding exotic reptile species. Many make no attempt at captive reproduction whatsoever.

Snakes and Humans in Conflict

Whether it is within our new suburbia or in the distant reaches of civilization, snakes that survived the onslaught are usually destroyed on sight. Rattlesnakes become "lost," wandering aimlessly through what was their territory. Desperately, they search out food, mates, or ancient scent trails. Those not dispatched directly by the hand of humans are threatened by automobiles. Wide interstate highways slice through uninhabited regions, contributing an impassable barrier laden with a seemingly endless chain of eighteen-wheelers.

Thousands of rattlesnakes are killed annually crossing roads, commonly by drivers purposely bent on hitting them. This is evidenced by skid marks passing over flattened carcasses. An immoderate number are found lacking rattles, doubtless the reward and proof of a "brave" act. A study done in Louisiana, using rubber turtles and snakes on a specific stretch of road, showed most drivers swerved to miss the turtles yet drove directly at the snakes in order to kill them.

Unlike many snake species, rattlesnakes rarely choose to live near human habitations. They are relatively nervous, preferring natural, undisturbed areas. As we have seen, however, humanity has invaded the rattlesnake's domain at such a rapid pace that the two have been forced into conflict. If rattlesnakes, or any large rodent-eating snakes, are known to be in the vicinity of a house, certain precautions will make the homesite less suitable for the snakes.

Rattlesnakes are attracted by food. Simply put, if a person upsets the food chain by limiting or eradicating the rodent population, snakes will move away. Some mice, rats, ground squirrels, and rabbits are attracted to humans, mostly by an abundance of food, thus greater care must be taken to reduce its availability. Properly discarded trash and covered containers discourage vermin and other small mammals.

Bird feeders and spreading seeds and baked goods not only attract birds but ground feeding small mammals as well. These in turn attract mammal predators such as rattlesnakes. Naturalists in fact discourage these practices during warmer weather, preferring that birds seek wild forage. Bird feeding is acceptable in colder weather when (coincidentally) snakes and many small mammals (snake food) are hibernating.

Care should be taken in the placement of woodpiles, rock piles, and thickets. They provide near-perfect shelters for a variety of small mammals. High grass affords cover, enabling greater mobility and access to their food supply. Poorly attended and harvested vegetable gardens contribute a variety of foodstuffs for small mammals. Again, their predators, including rattlesnakes, may follow.

In some areas, under certain conditions (such as having constructed a building within a rattlesnake's paths to and from a den), fencing may be of value to keep the snakes out. When an impenetrable fence obstructs the path of many snakes, as well as of many other reptiles and small vertebrates, they usually follow its course rather than attempt to crawl over it. Field biologists frequently use these, known as drift fences, to direct migrating or foraging animals to traps or collecting containers buried in the ground. It is important that drift fences are made of materials that completely block the snake's passage and that they are judiciously maintained. In general, to deter rattlesnakes, the barrier need not be more than 3 feet (1 meter) in height, but it must fit closely to the ground or be buried 1 or 2 inches (4 centimeters) so snakes cannot crawl under it. Careful placement will steer the animals away.

Avoiding Confrontation with a Rattlesnake

No doubt, there are occasions when rattlesnakes may impose a threat to humans, usually when humans are in the wrong place at the wrong time. It is always the best and safest alternative to maintain one's calm and to confront the situation logically.

When confronting a snake of any kind, the first question should be, "Are you certain it is a venomous snake?" Then, "Does it pose an immediate, realistic danger?" Finally, "What needs to be done to properly dispose of it?" One important consideration is whether *you* are merely temporarily invading *its* territory, as would be the case on a hike into the back country. Here the logical course is to leave the snake undisturbed and continue on your way. Simply walk around a rattlesnake coiled along a hiking trail, giving it berth. Remember: Most snakebites occur when handling, capturing, or attempting to kill a snake!

Assuming the situation presents a realistic danger (for example, a rattlesnake has been found in your backyard), be sure to keep children and pets away, and do not provoke the snake with any undo movements or disturbance, such as prodding. It is best not to approach the snake too closely. A sensible primary action is to safely

observe the snake, not preventing its escape. An undisturbed rattlesnake most likely will be sitting loosely coiled and immobile. If this is the situation, there is probably time to call a trained animal control officer to capture the snake. However, if the snake is aroused or moving, great care should be taken to not get too close to the snake.

A coiled undisturbed rattlesnake should be a relatively simple matter to cover with a suitable trash can or sizable cardboard box. While maintaining a safe distance beyond striking range, and using the container as a shield (between you and the snake), the can should be placed over the snake in a rapid sweeping motion. Be sure to keep hands and feet safely away, shielded by the container. If done carefully and quickly, without disturbing the snake, this procedure is simple and effective. In addition, place an adequate weight (such as a rock or brick) on top of the container. Professional help can then be sought. The respondent should be knowledgeable in removing venomous snakes. Rather than kill the trespasser, it should be transported to a safer, more appropriate habitat away from inhabited areas and released. In most circumstances, released "nuisance" rattlesnakes do not return.

"Snake Busters"

In an attempt to provide a better understanding of the human–snake relationship, while preventing the death of many luckless snakes, several avocational herpetological societies have a network of so-called snake busters. They go to the home of a person with a wayward snake and capture it, sometimes for a fee.

With some experience, it is a simple matter to capture a venomous snake, either by using specially designed snake tongs or by coaxing it into a suitable container with a snake hook. Venomous snakes are pinned and picked up only as a last resort, because this type of handling is extremely stressful for the snake and could cause vertebral or internal injury.

There are dozens of avocational herpetological groups throughout the United States. Most are associated with zoos, natural history museums, nature centers, or universities. A listing of amateur or regional societies, many of which provide snake removal services, is provided in Appendix 3.

Not all societies provide this service, which may require licensing, special permits, or insurance, and it is a very time-consuming, expensive operation. Fortunately, snake busters are most active in areas with the biggest problems. The Tucson Herpetological Society, and its counterpart in Phoenix, the Arizona Herpetological Society, respond and save hundreds of rattlesnakes annually. There is a well-publicized group in Gainesville, Florida, and there are a half dozen groups in various other Florida cities. At least two groups provide the service in southern California. Some zoos and nature centers may be willing to catch an occasional rattlesnake, but time constraints usually make it impossible. However, they, local fire and police departments, and some Game and Fish departments will

Above: Herpetologists using a safe method of transporting a large, heavy eastern diamondback rattlesnake, *Crotalus adamanteus,* from a South Carolina field.

Far left: Herpetologist Craig Avanyi of the Arizona-Sonora Desert Museum in Tucson demonstrates the clamp-and-hook method as he captures a northern blacktail rattlesnake, *Crotalus molossus molossus,* on the museum grounds. It is the safest capture method for both the snake and captor. The box is specially made with a screened, hinged inner lid as an extra precaution against bites.

Left: Researcher Wade Kalanowsky demonstrates the proper technique for "tubing" a rattlesnake. Plastic tubes of varying diameters and lengths are used, depending on the size of the snake. Once the snake's head and neck are inside the tube, the snake is restrained at the opening and along its body. Because the snake is unable to turn and bite its captor, it can be examined safely.

have a snake busters number. Most humane societies will not deal with snake problems, but frequently they can recommend someone who can. Wildlife trappers can usually be found in a local telephone directory.

Needed Research

Additional research on the ecology and behavior of rattlesnakes is essential to better understand their importance in nature. The fact that most of the current rattlesnake-oriented scientific literature deals with biochemistry and behavior, largely performed under

Herpetological Consultants' owner Bob Zappalorti *(left)*, using a portable radio receiver, tracks the movements of a timber rattlesnake, *Crotalus horridus horridus (below)*. He has been studying the natural history of the New Jersey Pine Barrens populations for several years. The installed radio enabled Zappalorti to pinpoint his quarry. Because the rattlesnake is opaque (about to shed), it has limited eyesight, making it vulnerable to predation.

controlled laboratory conditions, demonstrates that few researchers are doing fieldwork. Aside from a few long-term, ongoing studies of eastern massasauga, *Sistrurus catenatus catenatus,* prairie rattlesnake, *Crotalus viridis viridis,* timber rattlesnake, *Crotalus horridus horridus,* eastern diamondback, *Crotalus adamanteus,* and dusky pigmy rattlesnake, *Sistrurus miliarius barbouri,* little is being investigated or being published about the natural history of other species. A great deal needs to be done with all aspects of the neotropical rattlesnake, *Crotalus durissus.* Several montane Mexican rattlesnake species are considered rare, but most likely their habits and habitats are simply unknown or misunderstood. Further scrutiny, using molecular biology of DNA and venom, is needed to clarify the relationships and taxonomy of all rattlesnakes.

Klauber has noted some physical differences that, with additional research, may lead to a better understanding of the affinities and evolution of the various species. Some of these research suggestions include the function and systematic implications of (1) the elongated, thin head in the Mexican lance-headed rattlesnake, *Crotalus polystictus,* and the exceptionally long tail in the long-tailed rattlesnake, *Crotalus stejnegeri;* (2) the lack of palatine teeth in both of these forms; (3) the differing head proportions in the otherwise similar speckled rattlesnake, *Crotalus mitchellii,* and tiger rattlesnake, *Crotalus tigris;* and (4) the rudimentary left lung in neotropical rattlesnake, *Crotalus durissus,* Mexican west-coast rattlesnake, *Crotalus basiliscus,* timber rattlesnake, *Crotalus horridus,* and blacktail rattlesnake, *Crotalus molossus.*

It is my deeply held belief that rattlesnake roundups should be stopped immediately. These barbaric events, I believe, should be illegal. However, if roundups continue, researchers could collect a sizable amount of natural history data. For the decades of their existence, little information has been accurately recorded about the ecological impact of the over-collecting or the physical characteristics (size, weight, age, maturity, and gender and pattern differences) of the snakes that are brought to the roundups. Weir has suggested that by carefully controlling collecting procedures, some scientific credibility may be derived. By selecting a specific territory and time limits of sampling, collecting biological data would provide a basis to "help gauge the broader, ecosystematic impact of the hunts" (J. Weir, "The Sweetwater Rattlesnake Round-Up: A Case Study in Environmental Ethics," *Conservation Biology* 6:116–27 [1992]). Such studies have been recently undertaken at Oklahoma roundups.

Course of Action

The public must be educated! People must be made aware of the importance of maintaining our entire natural world. A foremost authority on snake conservation, Kenneth Dodd, suggests, "Education is likely to be more effective when aimed at children, because children are less prejudicial than adults who may have ingrained negative feelings toward snakes" ("Strategies for Snake Conservation,"

in *Snakes: Ecology and Behavior,* ed. R. A. Seigel and J. T. Collins, New York: McGraw-Hill, 1993).

Rattlesnake den sites and nearby birthing rookeries must be protected. Entire populations of the timber rattlesnake, *Crotalus horridus horridus,* have been extirpated by continued commercial collecting at these sites, when the snakes have aggregated and are most susceptible. Taking pregnant females quickly destroys the reproductive ability and maintenance of a population. Although statutes against collecting any rattlesnakes exist in several states, few local and state wildlife officers arrest and prosecute offenders.

Habitat destruction must be stopped or seriously curtailed. Although extremely controversial and in need of serious investigation and planning, restrictions should be considered on draining, mining, grazing, housing, and industrial development—and these restrictions must be enforced. Careless road building is a major destructive factor. Through education and action, people can be made to understand the far-reaching and permanent effects made by changes to the habitat.

Lobbyists, often funded by big money interests, wield tremendous power among elected and appointed politicians and officials. National and local watchdog conservation groups need more support from the populace. Elected officials, particularly at the higher levels of government, must be monitored for their views and stands on environmental issues, and the public should vote in future elections accordingly.

The Nature Conservancy (TNC) appears to be one of the most successful private conservation groups at stopping destruction and saving natural areas. TNC actively seeks out and trades for or buys large or small endangered tracts of land. This affords protection to whole landscapes or vulnerable habitats that are certainly in peril. Several other conservation organizations, such as the National Audubon Society, the Sierra Club, the Natural Resources Defense Council, the Environmental Defense Fund, the National Wildlife Federation, the Defenders of Wildlife, and various state natural heritage programs, show special concern for snakes and all wildlife.

The Ecosystem and Its Future

It is appallingly obvious that plants and animals are in jeopardy all over the earth. Daily, the media disclose new difficulties with the environment. The public is constantly deluged with accounts of destruction and loss, so much so that the scope and immediacy have become diluted, lost in a myriad of other human problems that preoccupy humanity. The causes of worldwide decline of animal populations are complex and universal, and the responsibility is shared by all nations. Sheer human numbers are overwhelming. The human animal is so narcissistically enmeshed in its own space that priorities for long-term survival have been misappropriated. Regardless of how insignificant the loss of rattlesnakes may appear as a global environmental problem, any interference with the pre-

carious web of life jeopardizes the whole. Certainly, some deterioration may be part of a natural cycle, but there is no doubt most is caused by humans.

As with global warming, the cost of the loss of rattlesnakes in the world's ecosystem cannot be fully anticipated. Global warming brings about changes in regional precipitation and temperature, altering the seasons. Ozone depletion places ecosystems in serious jeopardy as a result of increased ultraviolet penetration. In Chile, so far the only populous nation sitting underneath an ozone hole, there has been a 1,000-fold increase in ultraviolet-B radiation. Ozone depletion is thought to be a major culprit in the alarmingly rapid, worldwide decline in amphibian populations as well. Elevated levels of UV radiation cause increased rates of skin cancers in humans. Uncontrolled burning and logging in rain forests modifies the carbon dioxide–oxygen cycles, while eliminating millions of acres of habitat. Acid rain, mining, and logging runoff, non-biodegradable debris, unchecked vehicle emissions, and pesticides are other ecological time bombs. These, combined with leveling and irrigating deserts, clear-cut logging, strip mining, draining wetlands for agriculture, cattle grazing, and building housing developments, produce damage of catastrophic proportions.

Charles Lowe, a leading American authority on desert ecology in the Americas, recently said, "It's all over! It's a matter of time! And there's nothing you and I can do about it! Population growth, which is sex, and greed, are the keys" (quoted in M. Rubio, "The Conference on the Herpetology of North American Deserts," *Sonoran Herpetologist* 3:56–57 [1991]). Although he was referring directly to the plight of the Mojave Desert environment, he was in fact describing all environments. Humanity's desire to procreate (at an alarming rate), combined with our personal need to own and abuse our natural surroundings, is causing irreparable damage. These changes are evident everywhere.

Final Word

"It's only a snake!"

The stigma attached to snakes retains its centuries-old acceptance. If something is not done, Lowe's prophecy will become historical fact. Rattlesnakes will exist as museum specimens, bygone curiosities in the minds of those who were fortunate to have studied them.

Opposite: The richly mottled Nuevo Leon rock rattlesnake, *Crotalus lepidus castenaeus,* was described from that Mexican state in 1978 but has not been accepted as a valid subspecies.

Right: Although this snake has several characteristics that differ from those of other subspecies of the neotropical rattlesnake group, the Nuevo Leon neotropical rattlesnake, *Crotalus durissus neoleonensis,* has not been officially recognized. If the description is submitted to and published in a peer-reviewed journal, the subspecies likely would be accepted.

The eastern twin-spotted rattlesnake, *Crotalus pricei miquihuanus*, brownish in color, inhabits open rocky areas in Nuevo Leon and Tamaulipas, Mexico. It frequently is encountered among the bases of agaves. When threatened, it quickly escapes into recesses of the needle-sharp spines of this plant.

APPENDIX 1

COMPLETE SCIENTIFIC AND COMMON ENGLISH AND SPANISH NAMES OF RECENT RATTLESNAKES

Spanish names are given whenever they exist; snakes not indigenous to Spanish-speaking countries do not, of course, have Spanish names.

Scientific Name	Common Name (English)	Common Name (Spanish)
Crotalus adamanteus	eastern diamondback rattlesnake	—
Crotalus aquilus[a]	Queretaran blotched rattlesnake	cascabel oscuro de Queretaro[a]
Crotalus atrox	western diamondback rattlesnake	vibora serrana
Crotalus basiliscus	Mexican west-coast rattlesnake	saye
Crotalus catalinensis	Santa Catalina Island rattlesnake	cascabel de la Isla Santa Catalina
Crotalus cerastes cerastes	Mojave Desert sidewinder	—
Crotalus cerastes cercobombus	Sonoran Desert sidewinder	vibora cornuda de Sonora
Crotalus cerastes laterorepens	Colorado Desert sidewinder	vibora cornuda del Desierto de Colorado
Crotalus durissus cascavella	northeastern Brazilian rattlesnake	cascabel de cuatro ventas
Crotalus durissus collilineatus	central Brazilian rattlesnake	maraca
Crotalus durissus culminatus	northwestern neotropical rattlesnake	shunu
Crotalus durissus cumanensis	Venezuelan rattlesnake	culebra de cascabel
Crotalus durissus dryinus	Guianian rattlesnake	crotale
Crotalus durissus durissus	neotropical rattlesnake	vibora real
Crotalus durissus marajoensis	Marajoan rattlesnake	boicininga
Crotalus durissus neoleonensis[b]	Nuevo Leon neotropical rattlesnake	—
Crotalus durissus ruruima	Mt. Roraima rattlesnake	—
Crotalus durissus terrificus	South American rattlesnake	vibora de cascabel
Crotalus durissus totonacus	Totonacan rattlesnake	tepocolcoatl
Crotalus durissus trigonicus[c]	Rupunini rattlesnake	—
Crotalus durissus tzabcan	Yucatan neotropical rattlesnake	tzab-can
Crotalus enyo cerralvensis	Cerralvo Island rattlesnake	cascabel de la Isla Cerralvo
Crotalus enyo enyo	Baja California rattlesnake	cascabel de Baja California
Crotalus enyo furvus	Rosario rattlesnake	cascabel de Rosario
Crotalus exsul exsul	Cedros Island diamond rattlesnake	cascabel de la Isla Cedros
Crotalus horridus atricaudatus	canebrake rattlesnake	—
Crotalus horridus horridus	timber rattlesnake	—

[a]Previously *Crotalus triseriatus aquilus*.
[b]Synonymized as *Crotalus durissus totonacus*.
[c]Synonymized as *Crotalus durissus ruruima*.

APPENDIX 2

COMMON ENGLISH AND SCIENTIFIC NAMES OF RECENT RATTLESNAKES

Common Name (English)	Scientific Name	Common Name (English)	Scientific Name
Angel de la Guarda Island speckled rattlesnake	*Crotalus mitchellii angelensis*	Mexican dusky rattlesnake	*Crotalus triseriatus armstrongi*
		Mexican lance-headed rattlesnake	*Crotalus polystictus*
Arizona black rattlesnake	*Crotalus viridis cerberus*	Mexican west-coast rattlesnake	*Crotalus basiliscus*
Arizona ridgenose rattlesnake	*Crotalus willardi willardi*	Midget faded rattlesnake	*Crotalus viridis concolor*
Aruba Island rattlesnake	*Crotalus unicolor*	Mojave Desert sidewinder	*Crotalus cerastes cerastes*
Autlan rattlesnake	*Crotalus lannomi*	Mojave rattlesnake	*Crotalus scutulatus scutulatus*
		Mottled rock rattlesnake	*Crotalus lepidus lepidus*
Baja California rattlesnake	*Crotalus enyo enyo*	Mt. Roraima rattlesnake	*Crotalus durissus ruruima*
Banded rock rattlesnake	*Crotalus lepidus klauberi*		
		Neotropical rattlesnake	*Crotalus durissus durissus*
Canebrake rattlesnake	*Crotalus horridus atricaudatus*	New Mexican ridgenose rattlesnake	*Crotalus willardi obscurus*
Carolina pigmy rattlesnake	*Sistrurus miliarius miliarius*	Northeastern Brazilian rattlesnake	*Crotalus durissus cascavella*
Cedros Island diamond rattlesnake	*Crotalus exsul exsul*	Northern blacktail rattlesnake	*Crotalus molossus molossus*
Central Brazilian rattlesnake	*Crotalus durissus collilineatus*	Northern Pacific rattlesnake	*Crotalus viridis oreganus*
Central Plateau dusky rattlesnake	*Crotalus triseriatus triseriatus*	Northwestern neotropical rattlesnake	*Crotalus durissus culminatus*
Central Plateau pigmy rattlesnake	*Sistrurus ravus ravus*	Nuevo Leon neotropical rattlesnake	*Crotalus durissus neoleonensis*
Cerralvo Island rattlesnake	*Crotalus enyo cerralvensis*	Nuevo Leon rock rattlesnake	*Crotalus lepidus castenaeus*
Colorado Desert sidewinder	*Crotalus cerastes laterorepens*		
Coronado Island rattlesnake	*Crotalus viridis caliginis*	Oaxacan blacktail rattlesnake	*Crotalus molossus oaxacus*
Cross-banded mountain rattlesnake	*Crotalus transversus*	Oaxacan pigmy rattlesnake	*Sistrurus ravus brunneus*
		Oaxacan small-headed rattlesnake	*Crotalus intermedius gloydi*
Del Nido ridgenose rattlesnake	*Crotalus willardi amabilis*	Omilteman small-headed rattlesnake	*Crotalus intermedius omiltemanus*
Desert-grassland massasauga	*Sistrurus catenatus edwardsii*		
Durango rock rattlesnake	*Crotalus lepidus maculosus*	Panamint rattlesnake	*Crotalus mitchellii stephensi*
Dusky pigmy rattlesnake	*Sistrurus miliarius barbouri*	Prairie rattlesnake	*Crotalus viridis viridis*
Eastern diamondback rattlesnake	*Crotalus adamanteus*	Queretaran blotched rattlesnake	*Crotalus aquilus*
Eastern massasauga	*Sistrurus catenatus catenatus*		
Eastern twin-spotted rattlesnake	*Crotalus pricei miquihuanus*	Red diamond rattlesnake	*Crotalus ruber ruber*
El Muerto Island rattlesnake	*Crotalus mitchellii muertensis*	Rosario rattlesnake	*Crotalus enyo furvus*
		Rupunini rattlesnake	*Crotalus durissus trigonicus*
Grand Canyon rattlesnake	*Crotalus viridis abyssus*		
Great Basin rattlesnake	*Crotalus viridis lutosus*	San Esteban Island blacktail rattlesnake	*Crotalus molossus estebanensis*
Guerreran pigmy rattlesnake	*Sistrurus ravus exiguus*	San Lorenzo Island diamond rattlesnake	*Crotalus ruber lorenzoensis*
Guianian rattlesnake	*Crotalus durissus dryinus*	San Lucan Island diamond rattlesnake	*Crotalus ruber lucasensis*
		San Lucan speckled rattlesnake	*Crotalus mitchellii mitchellii*
Hopi rattlesnake	*Crotalus viridis nuntius*	Santa Catalina Island rattlesnake	*Crotalus catalinensis*
Humantlan rattlesnake	*Crotalus scutulatus salvini*	Sonoran Desert sidewinder	*Crotalus cerastes cercobombus*
		South American rattlesnake	*Crotalus durissus terrificus*
Long-tailed rattlesnake	*Crotalus stejnegeri*	Southern Pacific rattlesnake	*Crotalus viridis helleri*
		Southern ridgenose rattlesnake	*Crotalus willardi meridionalis*
Marajoan rattlesnake	*Crotalus durissus marajoensis*	Southwestern speckled rattlesnake	*Crotalus mitchellii pyrrhus*
Mexican blacktail rattlesnake	*Crotalus molossus nigrescens*		

APPENDIX 1

COMPLETE SCIENTIFIC AND COMMON ENGLISH
AND SPANISH NAMES OF RECENT RATTLESNAKES

Spanish names are given whenever they exist; snakes not indigenous
to Spanish-speaking countries do not, of course, have Spanish names.

Scientific Name	Common Name (English)	Common Name (Spanish)
Crotalus adamanteus	eastern diamondback rattlesnake	—
Crotalus aquilus[a]	Queretaran blotched rattlesnake	cascabel oscuro de Queretaro
Crotalus atrox	western diamondback rattlesnake	vibora serrana
Crotalus basiliscus	Mexican west-coast rattlesnake	saye
Crotalus catalinensis	Santa Catalina Island rattlesnake	cascabel de la Isla Santa Catalina
Crotalus cerastes cerastes	Mojave Desert sidewinder	—
Crotalus cerastes cercobombus	Sonoran Desert sidewinder	vibora cornuda de Sonora
Crotalus cerastes laterorepens	Colorado Desert sidewinder	vibora cornuda del Desierto de Colorado
Crotalus durissus cascavella	northeastern Brazilian rattlesnake	cascabel de cuatro ventas
Crotalus durissus collilineatus	central Brazilian rattlesnake	maraca
Crotalus durissus culminatus	northwestern neotropical rattlesnake	shunu
Crotalus durissus cumanensis	Venezuelan rattlesnake	culebra de cascabel
Crotalus durissus dryinus	Guianian rattlesnake	crotale
Crotalus durissus durissus	neotropical rattlesnake	vibora real
Crotalus durissus marajoensis	Marajoan rattlesnake	boicininga
Crotalus durissus neoleonensis[b]	Nuevo Leon neotropical rattlesnake	—
Crotalus durissus ruruima	Mt. Roraima rattlesnake	—
Crotalus durissus terrificus	South American rattlesnake	vibora de cascabel
Crotalus durissus totonacus	Totonacan rattlesnake	tepocolcoatl
Crotalus durissus trigonicus[c]	Rupunini rattlesnake	—
Crotalus durissus tzabcan	Yucatan neotropical rattlesnake	tzab-can
Crotalus enyo cerralvensis	Cerralvo Island rattlesnake	cascabel de la Isla Cerralvo
Crotalus enyo enyo	Baja California rattlesnake	cascabel de Baja California
Crotalus enyo furvus	Rosario rattlesnake	cascabel de Rosario
Crotalus exsul exsul	Cedros Island diamond rattlesnake	cascabel de la Isla Cedros
Crotalus horridus atricaudatus	canebrake rattlesnake	—
Crotalus horridus horridus	timber rattlesnake	—

[a]Previously *Crotalus triseriatus aquilus*.
[b]Synonymized as *Crotalus durissus totonacus*.
[c]Synonymized as *Crotalus durissus ruruima*.

Scientific Name	Common Name (English)	Common Name (Spanish)
Crotalus intermedius gloydi	Oaxacan small-headed rattlesnake	viborilla de Oaxaca
Crotalus intermedius intermedius	Totalcan small-headed rattlesnake	viborilla sorda
Crotalus intermedius omiltemanus	Omilteman small-headed rattlesnake	viborilla de Omilteme
Crotalus lannomi	Autlan rattlesnake	cascabel de Autlan
Crotalus lepidus castenaeus[d]	Nuevo Leon rock rattlesnake	cascabel de piedras de Nuevo Leon
Crotalus lepidus klauberi	banded rock rattlesnake	cascabel rayada de piedra
Crotalus lepidus lepidus	mottled rock rattlesnake	cascabel de rocas
Crotalus lepidus maculosus	Durango rock rattlesnake	cascabel de piedras de Durango
Crotalus lepidus morulus	Tamaulipan rock rattlesnake	cascabel cafe de las rocas
Crotalus mitchellii angelensis	Angel de la Guarda Island speckled rattlesnake	vibora blanca de Isla Angel
Crotalus mitchellii mitchellii	San Lucan speckled rattlesnake	vibora blanca
Crotalus mitchellii muertensis	El Muerto Island rattlesnake	vibora blanca de Isla El Muerto
Crotalus mitchellii pyrrhus	southwestern speckled rattlesnake	vibora blanca del suroeste
Crotalus mitchellii stephensi	panamint rattlesnake	—
Crotalus molossus estebanensis	San Esteban Island blacktail rattlesnake	cascabel de la Isla Esteban
Crotalus molossus molossus	northern blacktail rattlesnake	cascabel de colinegra nortena
Crotalus molossus nigrescens	Mexican blacktail rattlesnake	palanca
Crotalus molossus oaxacus[e]	Oaxacan blacktail rattlesnake	tleua
Crotalus pifanorum[f]	—	—
Crotalus polystictus	Mexican lance-headed rattlesnake	hocico de puerco
Crotalus pricei miquihuanus	eastern twin-spotted rattlesnake	cascabel de miquihuana
Crotalus pricei pricei	western twin-spotted rattlesnake	cascabel manchas-gamelas de Price
Crotalus pusillus	Tancitaran dusky rattlesnake	cascabel oscura del Tancitaro
Crotalus ruber lorenzoensis	San Lorenzo Island diamond rattlesnake	cascabel de Isla San Lorenzo
Crotalus ruber lucasensis[g]	San Lucan Island diamond rattlesnake	cascabel de San Lucan
Crotalus ruber ruber[h]	red diamond rattlesnake	cascabel diamante rojo
Crotalus scutulatus salvini	Humantlan rattlesnake	chiauhcoatl de Salvin
Crotalus scutulatus scutulatus	Mojave rattlesnake	cascabel llanera
Crotalus stejnegeri	long-tailed rattlesnake	cascabel cola-larga
Crotalus tigris	tiger rattlesnake	cascabel tigre
Crotalus tortugensis	Tortuga Island diamond rattlesnake	cascabel de Isla Tortuga
Crotalus transversus	cross-banded mountain rattlesnake	cascabel cruz-rayada de montana

[d]Suggested as synonym of *Crotalus lepidus morulus*.

[e]Suggested reassignment from *Crotalus basiliscus oaxacus* to *Crotalus molossus oaxacus*.

[f]The only known specimen was placed into the synonymy of *Crotalus durissus cumanensis* by J. R. McCranie ("*Crotalus durissus*." Catalogue of American Amphibians and Reptiles 577:1–11 [1993]).

[g]It has been suggested that *Crotalus ruber lucasensis* is a junior synonym of *Crotalus exsul exsul* (L. L. Grismer, J. A. McGuire, and B. D. Hollingsworth. "A Report on the Herpetofauna of the Vizcaino Peninsula, Baja California, Mexico, with a Discussion of Its Biogeographic and Taxonomic Implications." *Bulletin, Southern California Academy of Sciences* 93:45–80 [1994]).

[h]Grismer et al. (in the 1994 article cited in footnote *g*) have suggested that *Crotalus ruber* be reassigned as a subspecies of *Crotalus exsul (Crotalus exsul ruber)* and the subspecies reassigned to follow suit. I feel there will be considerable discussion about the proposal and chose to retain *Crotalus ruber* until the matter is settled by systematic herpetologists.

Scientific Name	Common Name (English)	Common Name (Spanish)
Crotalus triseriatus armstrongi	Mexican dusky rattlesnake	chiauhcoatl chiauitl de Armstrong
Crotalus triseriatus triseriatus	Central Plateau dusky rattlesnake	cascabel oscura Mexicana
Crotalus unicolor	Aruba Island rattlesnake	colebra
Crotalus vegrandis	Uracoan rattlesnake	cascabel Uracoa
Crotalus viridis abyssus	Grand Canyon rattlesnake	—
Crotalus viridis caliginis	Coronado Island rattlesnake	cascabel de Isla Coronado
Crotalus viridis cerberus	Arizona black rattlesnake	—
Crotalus viridis concolor	midget faded rattlesnake	—
Crotalus viridis helleri	southern Pacific rattlesnake	cascabel del Pacifico meridional
Crotalus viridis lutosus	Great Basin rattlesnake	—
Crotalus viridis nuntius	Hopi rattlesnake	—
Crotalus viridis oreganus	northern Pacific rattlesnake	—
Crotalus viridis viridis	prairie rattlesnake	cascabel de pradera
Crotalus willardi amabilis	Del Nido ridgenose rattlesnake	cascabel de nariz-surcada Del Nido
Crotalus willardi meridionalis	southern ridgenose rattlesnake	cascabel meridional de nariz-surcada
Crotalus willardi obscurus	New Mexican ridgenose rattlesnake	cascabel de nariz-surcada Nuevo Mexico
Crotalus willardi silus	western Chihuahuan ridgenose rattlesnake	cascabel de nariz-surcada Chihuahua
Crotalus willardi willardi	Arizona ridgenose rattlesnake	cascabel de nariz-surcada Arizona
Sistrurus catenatus catenatus	eastern massasauga	—
Sistrurus catenatus edwardsii	desert-grassland massasauga	cascabel del desierto
Sistrurus catenatus tergeminus	western massasauga	—
Sistrurus miliarius barbouri	dusky pigmy rattlesnake	—
Sistrurus miliarius miliarius	Carolina pigmy rattlesnake	—
Sistrurus miliarius streckeri	western pigmy rattlesnake	—
Sistrurus ravus brunneus	Oaxacan pigmy rattlesnake	vibora de cascabel de Oaxaca
Sistrurus ravus exiguus	Guerreran pigmy rattlesnake	cascabel enana de Guerrero
Sistrurus ravus ravus	Central Plateau pigmy rattlesnake	viborita hocico de puerco

APPENDIX 2

COMMON ENGLISH AND SCIENTIFIC NAMES OF RECENT RATTLESNAKES

Common Name (English)	Scientific Name	Common Name (English)	Scientific Name
Angel de la Guarda Island speckled rattlesnake	*Crotalus mitchellii angelensis*	Mexican dusky rattlesnake	*Crotalus triseriatus armstrongi*
Arizona black rattlesnake	*Crotalus viridis cerberus*	Mexican lance-headed rattlesnake	*Crotalus polystictus*
Arizona ridgenose rattlesnake	*Crotalus willardi willardi*	Mexican west-coast rattlesnake	*Crotalus basiliscus*
Aruba Island rattlesnake	*Crotalus unicolor*	Midget faded rattlesnake	*Crotalus viridis concolor*
Autlan rattlesnake	*Crotalus lannomi*	Mojave Desert sidewinder	*Crotalus cerastes cerastes*
		Mojave rattlesnake	*Crotalus scutulatus scutulatus*
Baja California rattlesnake	*Crotalus enyo enyo*	Mottled rock rattlesnake	*Crotalus lepidus lepidus*
Banded rock rattlesnake	*Crotalus lepidus klauberi*	Mt. Roraima rattlesnake	*Crotalus durissus ruruima*
Canebrake rattlesnake	*Crotalus horridus atricaudatus*	Neotropical rattlesnake	*Crotalus durissus durissus*
Carolina pigmy rattlesnake	*Sistrurus miliarius miliarius*	New Mexican ridgenose rattlesnake	*Crotalus willardi obscurus*
Cedros Island diamond rattlesnake	*Crotalus exsul exsul*	Northeastern Brazilian rattlesnake	*Crotalus durissus cascavella*
Central Brazilian rattlesnake	*Crotalus durissus collilineatus*	Northern blacktail rattlesnake	*Crotalus molossus molossus*
Central Plateau dusky rattlesnake	*Crotalus triseriatus triseriatus*	Northern Pacific rattlesnake	*Crotalus viridis oreganus*
Central Plateau pigmy rattlesnake	*Sistrurus ravus ravus*	Northwestern neotropical rattlesnake	*Crotalus durissus culminatus*
Cerralvo Island rattlesnake	*Crotalus enyo cerralvensis*	Nuevo Leon neotropical rattlesnake	*Crotalus durissus neoleonensis*
Colorado Desert sidewinder	*Crotalus cerastes laterorepens*	Nuevo Leon rock rattlesnake	*Crotalus lepidus castenaeus*
Coronado Island rattlesnake	*Crotalus viridis caliginis*		
Cross-banded mountain rattlesnake	*Crotalus transversus*	Oaxacan blacktail rattlesnake	*Crotalus molossus oaxacus*
		Oaxacan pigmy rattlesnake	*Sistrurus ravus brunneus*
Del Nido ridgenose rattlesnake	*Crotalus willardi amabilis*	Oaxacan small-headed rattlesnake	*Crotalus intermedius gloydi*
Desert-grassland massasauga	*Sistrurus catenatus edwardsii*	Omilteman small-headed rattlesnake	*Crotalus intermedius omiltemanus*
Durango rock rattlesnake	*Crotalus lepidus maculosus*		
Dusky pigmy rattlesnake	*Sistrurus miliarius barbouri*	Panamint rattlesnake	*Crotalus mitchellii stephensi*
		Prairie rattlesnake	*Crotalus viridis viridis*
Eastern diamondback rattlesnake	*Crotalus adamanteus*		
Eastern massasauga	*Sistrurus catenatus catenatus*	Queretaran blotched rattlesnake	*Crotalus aquilus*
Eastern twin-spotted rattlesnake	*Crotalus pricei miquihuanus*		
El Muerto Island rattlesnake	*Crotalus mitchellii muertensis*	Red diamond rattlesnake	*Crotalus ruber ruber*
		Rosario rattlesnake	*Crotalus enyo furvus*
Grand Canyon rattlesnake	*Crotalus viridis abyssus*	Rupunini rattlesnake	*Crotalus durissus trigonicus*
Great Basin rattlesnake	*Crotalus viridis lutosus*		
Guerreran pigmy rattlesnake	*Sistrurus ravus exiguus*	San Esteban Island blacktail rattlesnake	*Crotalus molossus estebanensis*
Guianian rattlesnake	*Crotalus durissus dryinus*	San Lorenzo Island diamond rattlesnake	*Crotalus ruber lorenzoensis*
		San Lucan Island diamond rattlesnake	*Crotalus ruber lucasensis*
Hopi rattlesnake	*Crotalus viridis nuntius*	San Lucan speckled rattlesnake	*Crotalus mitchellii mitchellii*
Humantlan rattlesnake	*Crotalus scutulatus salvini*	Santa Catalina Island rattlesnake	*Crotalus catalinensis*
		Sonoran Desert sidewinder	*Crotalus cerastes cercobombus*
Long-tailed rattlesnake	*Crotalus stejnegeri*	South American rattlesnake	*Crotalus durissus terrificus*
		Southern Pacific rattlesnake	*Crotalus viridis helleri*
Marajoan rattlesnake	*Crotalus durissus marajoensis*	Southern ridgenose rattlesnake	*Crotalus willardi meridionalis*
Mexican blacktail rattlesnake	*Crotalus molossus nigrescens*	Southwestern speckled rattlesnake	*Crotalus mitchellii pyrrhus*

MARYLAND

Maryland Herpetological Society
Natural History Society
2643 N. Charles Street
Baltimore, MD 21218

MASSACHUSETTS

New England Herpetological Society
P.O. Box 1082
Boston, MA 02103

MICHIGAN

Michigan Herpetological Society
P.O. Box 13037
Lansing, MI 48906

MINNESOTA

Minnesota Herpetological Society
Bell Museum of Natural History
10 Church Street S.E.
Minneapolis, MN 55455-0104

NEVADA

Northern Nevada Herpetological Society
P.O. Box 21282
Reno, NV 89502-1282

NEW MEXICO

New Mexico Herpetological Society
University of New Mexico
Department of Biology
Albuquerque, NM 87131

NEW YORK

New York Herpetological Society
P.O. Box 1245
Grand Central Station
New York, NY 10163-1245

NORTH CAROLINA

North Carolina Herpetological Society
North Carolina State Museum
P.O. Box 29555
Raleigh, NC 27626

OHIO

Greater Cincinnati Herpetological Society
Cincinnati Museum of Natural History
1720 Gilbert Avenue
Cincinnati, OH 45202

Northern Ohio Association of Herpetologists
Department of Biology
Case Western University
Cleveland, OH 44106
Toledo Herpetological Society
1587 Jermain Drive
Toledo, OH 43606

OKLAHOMA

Oklahoma Herpetological Society
Tulsa Chapter
5701 E. 36th Street N.
Tulsa, OK 74115

Oklahoma Herpetological Society
Oklahoma City Chapter
Oklahoma Zoo
2101 N.E. 50th
Oklahoma City, OK 73111

PENNSYLVANIA

Philadelphia Herpetological Society
P.O. Box 52261
Philadelphia, PA 19115

Pittsburgh Herpetological Society
Pittsburgh Zoo
1 Hill Road
Pittsburgh, PA 15206

SOUTH CAROLINA

South Carolina Herpetological Society
P.O. Box 100107
Columbia, SC 29230

TENNESSEE

Tennessee Valley Herpetological Society
P.O. Box 360
Ooltewah, TN 37363

TEXAS

East Texas Herpetological Society
P.O. Box 34028
Trinity, TX 75862-9470

El Paso Herpetological Society
7505 Demsey
El Paso, TX 79925

North Texas Herpetological Society
P.O. Box 1043
Euless, TX 76039

Texas Herpetological Society
Hutchison Hall of Science
31st at Canton
Lubbock, TX 79410

WASHINGTON

Pacific Northwest Herp Society
P.O. Box 70231
Bellevue, WA 98008

WISCONSIN

Wisconsin Herpetological Society
P.O. Box 366
Germantown, WI 53022

Canada

ONTARIO

Canadian Amphibian and Reptile Conservation
Society
9 Mississauga Road
North Mississauga, Ontario L5H 2H5

Ontario Herpetological Society
P.O. Box 244
Port Credit, Ontario L5G 4L8

QUEBEC

Canadian Association of Herpetologists
Redpath Museum
McGill University
859 Sherbrooke Street West
Montreal, Quebec H3A 2K6

GLOSSARY

The definitions in this glossary relate most specifically to rattlesnakes and to the contents of this book. They may have additional meanings and implications in a different biological context, however. For more information, I recommend *The Concise Oxford Dictionary of Zoology* (M. Allaby [ed.], New York: Oxford University Press, 1992).

activity period   The time an animal is moving about, fulfilling its biological needs.

aestivation   A period of dormancy to avoid dry and hot, potentially lethal periods in a refuge providing adequate moisture and sublethal temperatures.

aglyphous   Pertaining to or possessing solid teeth, without a venom-carrying canal (i.e., not fangs).

alarm scent   A distinctive odor produced when an animal is under stress. In theory it excites (alarms) conspecifics.

albinism   A deficiency of pigment leaving the skin almost colorless (yellowish) and the eyes pink. This is caused by a recessive gene.

alluvium   Soil that has been transported and deposited by a stream or by runoff.

ambush feeder   An animal that hunts by remaining secluded or immobile, waiting for prey to pass into range.

amelanism   A condition in which black pigment is lacking.

amino acid   The chemical component (building block) of proteins.

anal scute   The last enlarged ventral scale covering the anus, or cloacal opening, in snakes (also called anal plate). The urinary and reproductive tracts also end in the cloaca.

anaphylactic shock   An immediate, intense, hypersensitive reaction to the introduction of an antigen (such as snake venom). The resulting drop in blood pressure may be so severe that it may be fatal.

anerythrism   A condition in which red pigment is lacking.

anterior   Toward the head (front). The part of an animal that moves forward first during locomotion.

antitoxin   An antibody (e.g., antivenom) that combats and neutralizes a toxin (e.g., venom).

antivenom   Serum containing antibodies against venom proteins. It is usually extracted from the blood of horses that have been injected with specific venoms.

anuran   A tailless amphibian (frog or toad).

arachnid   An invertebrate belonging to the class Arachnida (e.g., spiders, scorpions, ticks, and mites).

arboreal   Living above the ground, in trees or vegetation.

assimilation   The act of changing digested and absorbed nutrients into protoplasm or living tissues.

axanthism   A condition in which yellow pigmentation is lacking.

biennial   Occurring every two years (in reference to female reproductive frequency).

binomial   A two-name classification consisting of the genus classification and the species designation, names for each species of animal or plant (see **scientific name**).

biochemistry   Scientific study of the chemical makeup of biological systems in plants and animals.

biome   A major geographic community type with all the plants and animals necessary to be self-sustaining in a large region.

bolus   A food mass that has entered the digestive tract.

canaliculate   Pertaining to or possessing a tooth or fang with a longitudinal channel or groove for injecting venom.

A vividly patterned and large banded rock rattlesnake, *Crotalus lepidus klauberi,* from Rancho Santa Barbara in Durango, Mexico.

canopy   High tree and shrub foliage in a woodland or forest that prevents direct sunlight from passing through to the ground below.

canthus rostralus   A group of (usually) enlarged scales lying between the internasal and the supraocular and forming a distinct ridge on the head (e.g., as found in *Crotalus willardi*).

capillary action   Retention and movement of a liquid between very closely positioned objects.

carnivorous   Pertaining to an animal that eats other animal matter.

carrion   Dead animal matter that is decomposing and putrefying.

catalyst   A chemical or enzyme that enables two other chemicals or compounds to interact or undergo chemical change.

caudal luring   Waving of a brightly colored tail tip in an elevated position to attract prey. Most commonly seen in immature sidewinder, massasauga, banded rock, and pigmy rattlesnakes.

chromatophore   A pigment cell that, in a group or series, produces pattern and coloration in an animal.

circadian rhythm   A pattern of metabolic activities within a twenty-four-hour cycle controlled by an internal biological clock.

cloaca   An internal chamber or expansion of the gut tube into which urinary, reproductive, and digestive discharge is received. Located at the distal end of the large intestine, immediately anterior to the anus, the cloaca is covered and protected by the anal scute.

common name   The vernacular name given to a species. The same animal may be called something totally different in another state or country. Attempts are being made to standardize common names. The only universally accepted name is the scientific (Latin) name given by taxonomists.

conspecific   Another individual of the same species.

convergent evolution   A process of two distinct and unrelated animals evolving similar characteristics or structures because of similar ecological pressures.

crotalid   A snake belonging to the family Crotalidae.

cryptic coloration   A blend of color and pattern that enables the animal to be inconspicuous in its surroundings.

deme   A local interbreeding population of a taxon.

desertified   Altered in a way that results in a drier habitat with sparser vegetation. Of the many relevant causal factors, depleting the underground water supply or destroying the vegetation are most common.

digestion   Changing of complex, usually insoluble organic matter into simpler soluble compounds by the gut for assimilation or storage by the body. The major chemicals involved are digestive enzymes in the stomach and small intestine.

distal   Away from the point of attachment.

diurnal   Of or pertaining to an animal that is active during daylight hours.

DNA   Deoxyribonucleic acid, the major component of chromosomes and substance of genes; the building matter of all living things.

dormancy   A period in which metabolic activity is reduced (e.g., hibernation and aestivation).

dorsal   Of or pertaining to the top or back of the body, the portion away from the ground or the opposite of ventral.

Duvernoy's gland   A modified salivary gland in colubrid snakes that produces a toxic substance (venom).

ecchymosis   Discoloration of the skin caused by destruction of smaller blood vessels, a common result of envenomation.

ecdysis   Shedding of the outer layer of keratinized skin.

ecology   Biological study of the interrelationships of plants and animals and their environment.

ecosystem   A self-sustaining natural community in which all plants and animals survive in an interacting system with the nonliving environment.

ectotherm   An animal that regulates its body heating and cooling from external sources, mostly by behavior (e.g., thermoregulation). Often such animals are improperly termed "cold-blooded."

edema   An abnormal accumulation of fluid beneath the skin or within the body, causing swelling.

egg tooth   A pointed, somewhat sharp, perhaps vestigial structure at the end of the snout in newborn reptiles. Its function was to break egg membranes or slit the outer shell to enable birth or hatching.

elapid   One of a group of mostly venomous tropical snakes with nonmovable fangs at the front of their mouths (e.g., coralsnakes, mambas, cobras).

elliptical pupil   The pupil of a rattlesnake's eye, which is elongated along the dorsal–ventral axis. In bright light it may appear little more than a slit. The majority of snakes have round pupils.

endemic   Of or living within a defined region (in reference to a plant or animal).

endotherm   An animal that regulates its body heating and cooling from internal sources, mostly physiological (e.g., metabolism), and thus has a relatively stable body temperature. Often such animals are improperly termed "warm-blooded."

envenomation   The introduction of a toxic foreign substance (a venom) into the tissues of an animal.

enzyme   A protein that is produced by the body to aid in a specific chemical reaction, most commonly associated with digestion and with metabolism.

epidermis   The outer layer of the skin.

erythrism   A condition in which there is a predominance of red pigmentation.

erythrophore   A chromatophore containing red pigment.

ethnology   Scientific study of the social groups and customs of humankind.

ethology   Biological study of animal behavior.

evolutionary biology   Scientific study of the structure, relationships, and characteristics of animals based on evolutionary changes.

family   A taxonomic group of related genera.

fang   An elongated, scimitar-shaped, enameled, modified tooth at the front of the upper jaw, articulating with the maxillary bone. When retracted, the fang lies in a protective membranous sheath. As with all snake teeth, additional fangs are in various stages of development directly posterior to their attachment within the sheath.

food chain   A prey–predator continuum of the plants and animals consuming one another in nature; a process of energy transfer.

forage   To actively seek and pursue food.

fossorial   Of or pertaining to an animal that burrows in the soil or in another medium.

gamete   A reproductive sex cell, either sperm or ova.

gangrene   A destructive condition within tissue that is a combination of infection with bacteria and obstructed blood supply. The result is necrosis and, if left untreated, further complications and possibly death.

genus   (plural, **genera**) A taxonomic group of related species with similar characteristics. The name of a genus (generic name) is always capitalized and italicized (see **scientific name**).

glaciation   The covering of an area by the ice of a glacier.

gonad   A major sex organ (testis or ovary) producing gametes (sperm or ova) as well as certain sex hormones.

habitat   The vegetative environment and physical conditions of a specific area occupied by an organism or by a plant and animal community.

harmless snake   A snake that does not have the ability to inject venom or cause serious harm to a human.

head scales   Skin scales on the head.

hemipenis   (plural, **hemipenes**) One of the paired male copulatory organs.

hemolysis   Destruction of red blood cells, which causes release of hemoglobin.

herpetology   Biological study of amphibians and reptiles.

hibernaculum   (plural, **hibernacula**) The site chosen by a reptile to avoid extremes of cold; a den.

hibernation   A dormant period to avoid extreme cold (e.g., winter) within a refuge (hibernaculum) with adequate moisture and above-freezing temperatures.

home range   The area in which an animal conducts most of its normal daily activities.

hormone   A chemical substance produced by an endocrine gland. The hormone is transported by the bloodstream and used in a chemical reaction somewhere else in the animal.

hybrid   The progeny of genetic cross-breeding between a male and female of different species (which may be of the same genus or, more rarely, of different genera).

hypomelanism   A condition in which there is a distinct but incomplete reduction of melanin (black pigment).

igneous   A form of rock produced by volcanic activity.

imprint   To induce learning in an immature or newborn animal by exposing it to a significant stimulus, such as adult trailing pheromones.

insular   Pertaining to or living in a geographically isolated environment (usually an island).

intergradation   Interbreeding of two subspecies, producing animals with a blend of characteristics and coloration of both. The area in which these intermediates occur is called a zone of intergradation.

iridophore   A chromatophore that refracts light, producing a rainbow effect.

isolation   Separation from other populations by geological, climatical, geographical, or ecological factors.

Jacobson's organ   The collection of nerve-rich receptors located in paired indentations in the palate of a lizard or snake. They receive particles delivered into the mouth cavity by the flicking tongue. The brain interprets the nerve signals, thereby identifying the chemical that has been sensed.

keeled scale   A dorsal scale with a longitudinally raised portion (ridge). Together, keeled scales impart a highly texturized, file-like appearance to the skin.

keratin   A fibrous protein that is a major component of skin and rattles.

kinetics   The study of physical movement.

kinin   A polypeptide produced by the body to regulate the permeability of capillaries by affecting the contraction of isolated smooth muscles.

labial pits   A series of thermosensitive indentations along the upper labials (lips) and, in some snake species, along the lower labials. They are similar to loreal pits but are less defined in function. Some snakes (e.g., the ball python, *Python regius*) have additional labial pits below the rostrum, on the front of the face.

labial   One of a continuous row of scales forming either the upper or the lower lips.

lateral   To the side.

leucism   A condition in which the skin is colorless, almost snow white, and devoid of pattern, but in which the eyes retain normal pigmentation.

lipid   An oil or fat produced and stored in the body.

loreal pits   A pair of complex thermoreceptors set within deep indentations (pits). Outwardly, the pits resemble nostrils. Situated between the eye and the nostril on either side of the head, the pits are found only in pitvipers and are the structures for which this group of snakes is named.

lymphatics   Vessels on the lymphatic circulatory system that carry a clear fluid (lymph) containing lymphocytes, cells that kill and remove other body cells and carry out certain immune functions.

maxillary bone   One of a pair of elongated upper jaw bones. In rattlesnakes the fang is attached to a shortened, modified maxillary bone.

melanism   A condition in which there is a high level of black pigment and thus decidedly dark skin. Some snakes retain only vestiges of pattern and are almost totally black.

melanophore   A chromatophore consisting of an amorphous, heavily branching system of granules of melanin, producing black or very dark brown coloration.

mesic   Of or pertaining to a wet environment or a habitat with a moderate amount of moisture.

metabolic fluid   Water produced within the cells of certain specialized, mostly desert-inhabiting animals, either by the chemical breakdown of larger molecules or by the combination of hydrogen and oxygen.

metamorphic   Pertaining to a rock that has been crystallized and hardened by extreme heat or pressure.

microhabitat   A small environment that supports life (e.g., a tree stump).

molecular biology   The study of cell functions and chemical processes of plants and animals through biochemical methods.

monotypic   Having one type, in reference to a species for which there are no described subspecies or geographic races.

montane   Of or living in a mountainous environment.

morph   A form within a species that differs from closely related forms by subtle characteristics of structure, pattern, or color.

morphology   The biological study of the structure and form of the body and its development.

musk gland   One of a pair of glands that are situated near the cloacal opening and that produce a very strong, pungent secretion used to deter predators.

natural selection   A major mechanism of evolutionary change that postulates that poorly adapted plants or animals are eliminated from a population before they are mature so that their traits are not passed on. Better adapted individuals will survive and reproduce, passing on their genes to their offspring.

necrosis   Death and destruction of animal tissue.

neonate   A newborn animal.

neurotoxin   Venom that primarily affects the nervous system.

niche   The unique part of a habitat in which a species lives; all attributes of ecology and behavior that define a species' role in nature.

nocturnal   Of or pertaining to an animal that is active at night.

nominate species   The first described member of a genus.

olfaction   The process of sensing particles when they contact epithelial cells lining nasal passages (e.g., smelling).

ophiophagy   Consumption of snakes as food.

opisthoglyphous   Pertaining to an animal that has normally enlarged grooved teeth at the back of the mouth on the upper jaw for injecting venom (rear fangs).

opportunistic feeder   An animal that happens on prey while wandering, usually while foraging.

optimum condition   The most favorable climatic situation for maintaining life.

osteology   The biological study of the development and characteristics of bones.

oviparous   Pertaining to a species in which the embryo develops outside the mother in a shelled egg; egg-laying.

oxidation   Chemical change of a substance, usually when it combines with oxygen.

paleontology   The biological study of extinct forms of life through fossils.

parthenogenesis   The development of an egg without fertilization.

phaneric coloration   Bright pigmentation and pattern meant to startle a predator (also called aposmatic coloration).

pheromone   An odorous chemical substance produced by glands to attract or to stimulate other animals (e.g., female sex pheromones stimulate males to pursue receptive females).

phylogeny   The evolutionary history and relationships of a group of animals.

physiology   The biological study of the functions that occur within an animal and that make it carry out its various life processes.

piebaldism   A condition in which normally pigmented skin contains distinct random blotches of abnormal white.

placenta   A vascularized membranous structure that attaches the chorionic sac (containing a fetus) to the uterine wall of the mother and provides for the transfer of nutrients, wastes, and respiratory gasses.

plant association   A group of plants growing in a defined community with certain specific interrelationships that permit long-term survival.

polyvalent   Of or pertaining to an antivenom with antibodies for more than one species.

population   A group of interacting animals of the same species inhabiting a common environment.

posterior   Toward the rear; away from the head.

predator   An animal that attacks other animals, usually as prey.

primitive   Of or pertaining to an animal that is in the early stages of evolution and has many simple, nonspecialized characteristics when compared with related animals (also termed "less derived").

protein   A complex, nitrogenous organic molecule composed of chains of amino acids.

proteroglyphous   Pertaining to or possessing fairly short, mostly nonmovable teeth with canals for injecting venom; fangs of certain venomous snakes such as elapids.

proximal   Close to the body or point of attachment.

relict population   A remnant of a previously larger, formerly widespread group of animals or plants.

resting coil   Platter-like coil in which a snake lies flat out with its body in concentric coils and its head and neck resting on top toward the center of the coils.

riparian   Pertaining to an animal that lives along a stream, river, lake, or other aquatic habitat.

RNA   Ribonucleic acid, a major component in the cytoplasm of cells.

rostrum   The most anterior and dorsal protruding portion of the head; "nose."

salmonella   A complex group of gram-negative, enteric bacteria of the genus *Salmonella*. They cause serious food poisoning in humans.

saurian   Of or related to lizards.

saxicolous   Living among rocks.

scale   The small, individual subdivisions of the outermost skin of reptiles. Unlike the scales of fish, which are individual, the scales of snakes form a continuous sheet. These horny epidermal outgrowths develop into a variety of shapes and sizes with specific functions.

scientific name   A Latin name given to an organism by a taxonomist, who describes it to distinguish the species from all others. The scientific name, which is the only universally accepted name for that taxon, consists of a generic name (e.g., *Crotalus*), a specific name (e.g., *viridis*), and, in many wide-ranging, diverse populations, a subspecific name (e.g., *helleri*). Thus, *Crotalus viridis helleri* is the scientific name for the southern Pacific rattlesnake, a subspecies of the species *Crotalus viridis*.

scree   A form of talus or fallen rock, mostly in a loose, smaller state (e.g., broken rock and rubble), that is not associated with a cliff.

sexual dichromatism   A condition in which colors specific to one gender differentiate it from the opposite gender of the same species.

sexual dimorphism   A condition in which physical characteristics specific to one gender differentiate it from the opposite gender of the same species (e.g., size, coloration, tail length, and shape).

solenoglyphous   Of or pertaining to movable teeth, or fangs, on the upper maxilla bone that have canals for injecting venom. Occasionally these fangs are very long.

speciation   The evolutionary process in which new species are formed.

species   A group of individual plants or animals of common ancestry sharing similar physiological and morphological traits. Interbreeding in nature produces fertile offspring. This evolutionary or phylogenetic concept of a species is the most widely accepted species concept. However, because it is thought to be somewhat ambiguous, it is subject to considerable heated debate. Specific names are always in lowercase type, are either italicized or underlined, and are always preceded by the capitalized generic name (see **scientific name**).

spectacle   A nearly transparent, hardened, immovable continuation of the epidermis covering the eye.

strike   A forceful, directional, rapid movement of the head toward an annoyance or prey. The length of a strike is determined by the neck position. Nearly all rattlesnake strikes include an opened mouth with erected fangs in an attempt at penetration. Venom is not always injected.

striking coil   An aroused, threatening position with the anterior third of the body (head and neck) raised in an S-shape above the anchoring body coils. The head faces the annoyance, the tongue is flicked, and the rattle is shaken.

stun gun   A high-voltage electric device producing a quick jolt of energy, strong enough to render a person unconscious. Used by law enforcement officers for subduing unruly persons or by ranchers for prodding cattle, the stun gun is also used as an unorthodox treatment for snakebite.

subcaudal   Pertaining to ventral tail scales posterior to the anal scute. Unlike ventrals, they may be divided into two rows (in some rattlesnakes).

subspecies   A morphologically distinct, geographically separated race of a species that is formally named by a taxonomist. Subspecies usually interbreed where their ranges come into contact (see intergrade). They produce fertile offspring that usually have characteristics of both races. Subspecific names are always in lowercase type and are underlined (see **scientific name**).

supraocular   Pertaining to prominent scales positioned directly above the eye. For sidewinders those scales are modified, more elongated, and somewhat pointed.

sympatric   Pertaining to two or more species inhabiting the same geographic region or occurring together.

synonymy   The full list of scientific names, including former names applied to a taxon, often accompanied by the author, date, and publication of each name.

systematics   The biological study of the evolutionary relationships and diversity of organisms that leads to their classification and naming (also called taxonomy).

tail   The portion of the body posterior to the anal scute. The male's hemipenes are the only major organ (other than the rattle) in or on the tail. It contains vertebrae but no prominent ribs. A snake usually survives even when the majority of its tail has been severed.

talus   An open area of fallen rocks, usually in an assortment of sizes from boulders or slabs to pebbles, below a steep slope or a cliff.

taxon   (plural, **taxa**) A member of any taxonomic rank (family, genus, species, subspecies) or an actual animal that has been described and named.

taxonomy   The biological field of naming and classifying organisms into a highly organized, systematic group following all the modern scientific methods of systematics.

temperate zone   The portion of the earth lying between the tropics and polar regions in which the climate demonstrates mild changes without prolonged periods of life-threatening extremes.

terrestrial   Living on land.

thermoregulation   The alteration of body temperature by behavioral patterns (e.g., basking in the sun or seeking refuge underground).

toxin   A chemical compound produced by an animal that causes a deleterious, toxic reaction when injected into another animal. If it produces a similar reaction when ingested, it is called a poison.

trinomial   Relating to a three-part name that uses genus, species, and subspecies names for a subspecific taxon (see **scientific name**).

venom   A viscous, usually amber-colored liquid produced in a specialized salivary gland of a venomous snake that produces toxic reactions when injected into animal tissues. Its primary function is subduing and digesting prey, but it has defensive value as well.

venom gland   A modified salivary gland that lies posterior to the eye and is connected to the fang by an elongated duct that runs internally below the eye, pit, and nostril (also called a parotid gland).

ventral   Pertaining to the underside, opposite of dorsal; also a term for one in a series of transversely elongated scales on the "belly" (ventral surface) of a snake. Starting at the neck, immediately posterior to the head, ventral scales extend to the anal scute. Beyond the anal scute they are called subcaudals.

vestigial   Pertaining to an organ or part of an animal that has lost its function during evolution and of which only a small portion remains.

vitellogenesis   The biochemical process of producing yolk in an egg. It may occur in either spring or fall and is not necessarily an annual occurrence. Many physical and chemical factors control yolk production.

viviparous   Bearing live offspring; of or pertaining to an animal in which the embryo develops in an amniotic sac within the mother's uterus and is born alive.

vomeronasal organ   See **Jacobson's organ.**

watershed   An area of elevated land where water runs off and is collected.

xanthism   A condition in which yellow or red pigmentation predominates.

xanthophore   A chromatophore producing yellow or red pigmentation.

xeric   Pertaining to a dry habitat.

zoogeography   The biological study of the geographic distribution of animals.

BIBLIOGRAPHY

This bibliography represents a cross section of the literature that I consulted for this book and consider pertinent to understanding rattlesnakes. It is by no means complete. Because Laurence Klauber's book *Rattlesnakes: Their Habits, Life Histories, and Influence on Mankind* (Berkeley: University of California Press, 1956) has a nearly complete bibliography of earlier works on rattlesnakes, I limited this list mostly to sources that have been published since then. Another excellent bibliography, which includes many recent publications from outside the United States and Canada, is in J. A. Campbell and W. W. Lamar's 1989 book, *The Venomous Reptiles of Latin America* (Ithaca, N.Y.: Cornell University Press).

This bibliography is divided into two parts: general and subject. The general portion cites broad-based works and popular writings about herpetology, rattlesnakes in particular, and related sciences. The subject portion lists, by subject, works that are narrower in scope and are the most recent or interesting herpetological findings about rattlesnakes. No doubt, students of rattlesnakes will take exception to some of my selections.

Aside from monographs, books, and technical journals, I have included in this bibliography many citations from regional herpetological society publications. Such publications contain a wealth of natural history data and observations but commonly follow an erratic publishing schedule or are limited in availability, and so researchers tend to overlook them.

An asterisk denotes sources that I have consulted frequently or that I consider to be of key importance.

General

DANGEROUS ANIMALS

Burcherl, W., and E. E. Buckley, eds. 1968. *Venomous animals and their venoms.* Vol. 1. New York: Academic Press.

Burton, R. 1977. *Venomous animals.* The Colour Nature Library. London: Colour Library International.

Caras, R. 1964. *Dangerous to man.* New York: Chilton Books.

———. 1974. *Venomous animals of the world.* Englewood Cliffs, N.J.: Prentice-Hall.

Edstrom, A. 1992. *Venomous and poisonous animals.* Melbourne, Fla.: Kreiger.

Freiberg, M., and J. G. Walls. 1984. *The world of venomous animals.* Neptune, N.J.: T.F.H. Publications.

Gadd, L. 1980. *Deadly beautiful: The world's most poisonous animals and plants.* New York: Macmillan.

Golay, P., H. M. Smith, D. G. Broadley, J. R. Dixon, V. C. McCarthy, J. C. Rage, B. Schatti, and M. Toriba. 1993. *Endoglyphs and other major venomous snakes of the world: A checklist.* Geneva, Switzerland: *Azemiops* Herpetological Data Center.

Habermehl, G. 1981. *Venomous animals and their toxins.* New York: Springer-Verlag.

Mara, W. P. 1993. *Venomous snakes of the world.* Neptune, N.J.: T.F.H. Publications.

Minton, S. A., Jr., and M. R. Minton. 1969. *Venomous reptiles.* New York: Scribner.

HERPETOLOGY: GENERAL WORKS AND POPULAR ACCOUNTS

Bartlett, R. D. 1988. *In search of reptiles and amphibians.* New York: E. J. Brill.

Bauchot, R. ed. 1994. *Snakes: A natural history.* New York: Sterling.

Bellairs, A. 1970. *The life of reptiles.* 2 vols. New York: Universe Books.

Bellairs, A., and G. Underwood. 1951. The origin of snakes. *Biological Review of the Cambridge Philosophy Society* 26:193–237.

Brattstrom, B. H. 1964. Evolution of the pit vipers. *Transactions of the San Diego Society of Natural History* 13:185–268.

*Campbell, J. A., and E. D. Brodie, Jr., eds. 1992. *Biology of the pitvipers.* Tyler, Tex.: Selva.

*Collins, J. T. 1990. Standard common and current scientific names for North American amphibians and reptiles. 3d ed. *Society for the Study of Amphibians and Reptiles Herpetological Circular* 12:1–41.

Engleman, W., and F. J. Obst. 1981. *Snakes: Biology, behavior, and relationships to man.* New York: Exeter Books.

Fenton, M. B., and L. E. Licht. 1990. Why rattle snake? *Journal of Herpetology* 24:274–79.

Gans, C., and A. M. Taub. 1969. Precautions for keeping poisonous snakes in captivity. *Curator* 7:196–205.

Gibbons, J. W. 1983. *Their blood runs cold: Adventures with reptiles and amphibians.* Tuscaloosa: University of Alabama Press.

Gloyd, H. K., and R. Conant. 1990. *Snakes of the Agkistrodon complex.* Contributions to Herpetology, no. 6. Oxford, Ohio: Society for the Study of Amphibians and Reptiles.

Goin, C. J., O. B. Goin, and G. R. Zug. 1978. *Introduction to herpetology.* 3d ed. San Francisco: Freeman.

Golay, P., H. M. Smith, D. G. Broadley, J. R. Dixon, V. C. McCarthy, J. C. Rage, B. Schatti, and M. Toriba. 1993. *Endoglyphs and other major venomous snakes of the world: A checklist.* Geneva, Switzerland: *Azemiops* Herpetological Data Center.

Gotch, A. F. 1986. *Reptiles: Their Latin names explained.* Poole, U.K.: Blanford Press.

*Greene, H. W. 1992. The ecological and behavioral context for pitviper evolution. In *Biology of the pitvipers,* ed. J. A. Campbell and E. D. Brodie, Jr. Tyler, Tex.: Selva.

———. 1992. Vipers: The evolution of mystery in nature. *Sonoran Herpetologist* 5:96–102.

*———. 1997. *Snakes: The evolution of mystery in nature.* Los Angeles: University of California Press.

Grenard, S. 1994. *Medical herpetology.* Pottsville, Pa.: NG Publishing.

Hardy, D. L., ed. 1992. *Collected papers of the Tucson Herpetological Society.* Tucson, Ariz.: Tucson Herpetological Society.

Hylander, C. J. 1951. *Adventures with reptiles: The story of Ross Allen.* New York: Julian Messner.

Ipsen, D. C. 1970. *Rattlesnakes and scientists.* Reading, Mass.: Addison-Wesley.

Kauffeld, C. F. 1957. *Snakes and snake hunting.* Garden City, N.Y.: Hanover House.

———. 1969. *Snakes: The keeper and the kept.* New York: Doubleday.

Liner, E. A. 1994. Scientific and common names for the amphibians and reptiles of Mexico in English and Spanish. *Society for the Study of Amphibians and Reptiles Herpetological Circular* 23:1–113.

Mara, W. P. 1993. *Venomous snakes of the world.* Neptune, N.J.: T.F.H. Publications.

Minton, S. A., Jr., and M. R. Minton. 1969. *Venomous reptiles.* New York: Scribner.

Neill, W. T. 1958. The occurrence of amphibians and reptiles in saltwater areas, and a bibliography. *Bulletin of Marine Science of the Gulf and Caribbean* 8:1–97.

Oliver, J. A. 1955. *The natural history of North American amphibians and reptiles.* Princeton, N.J.: Van Nostrand.

———. 1958. *Snakes in fact and fiction.* New York: Macmillan.

Parker, H. W. 1963. *Snakes.* New York: Norton.

———. 1965. *Natural history of snakes.* London: Trustees of the British Museum of Natural History.

Peters, J. A. 1964. *Dictionary of herpetology.* Hafner.

Pinney, R. 1981. *The snake book.* Garden City, N.Y.: Doubleday.

Pope, C. H. 1937. *Snakes alive and how they live.* New York: Viking Press.

Porter, K. R. 1972. *Herpetology.* Philadelphia: Saunders.

Pough, F. H., R. M. Andrews, J. E. Cadle, M. L. Crump, A. H. Savitzky, and K. D. Wells. 1998. *Herpetology.* Upper Saddle River, N.J.: Prentice Hall.

Rossi, J. V. 1992. *Snakes of the United States and Canada: Keeping them healthy in captivity.* Vol. 1: *Eastern area.* Malabar, Fla.: Krieger.

Rossi, J. V., and R. Rossi. 1995. *Snakes of the United States and Canada: Keeping them healthy in captivity.* Vol. 2: *Western area.* Malabar, Fla.: Krieger.

Scott, N. J., Jr., ed. 1982. Herpetological communities. *U.S. Department of the Interior, Fish and Wildlife Service, Wildlife Resources Report* 13:1–239.

Seigel, R. A., and J. T. Collins, eds. 1993. *Snakes: Ecology and behavior.* New York: McGraw-Hill.

Seigel, R. A., J. T. Collins, and S. S. Novak, eds. 1987. *Snakes: Ecology and evolutionary biology.* New York: Macmillan.

Shine, R. 1991. *Australian snakes: A natural history.* Ithaca, N.Y.: Cornell University Press.

Snider, A. T., and J. K. Bowler. 1992. Longevity of reptiles and amphibians in North American collections. 2d ed. *Society for the Study of Amphibians and Reptiles Circular* 21:1–44.

Stimson, A. C., and D. E. Justman. 1982. *The snake's advocate.* Austin, Tex.: Eakin Press.

Wareham, D. C. 1993. *The reptile and amphibian keeper's dictionary.* London: Blanford Books.

Zug, G. R. 1993. *Herpetology: An introductory biology of amphibians and reptiles.* San Diego, Calif.: Academic Press.

HERPETOLOGY: REGIONAL ACCOUNTS

Anderson, P. 1965. *The reptiles of Missouri.* Columbia: University of Missouri Press.

Ashton, R. E., Jr. 1981. *Handbook of the amphibians and reptiles of Florida. Part 1. The snakes.* Miami, Fla.: Windward.

Barbour, R. W. 1971. *Amphibians and reptiles of Kentucky.* Lexington: University of Kentucky Press.

Bogert, C. M., and J. A. Oliver. 1945. A preliminary analysis of the herpetofauna of Sonora. *Bulletin of the American Museum of Natural History* 83:297–426.

Breckenridge, W. J. 1944. *Reptiles and amphibians of Minnesota.* Minneapolis: University of Minnesota Press.

*Campbell, J. A., and W. W. Lamar. 1989. *The venomous reptiles of Latin America.* Ithaca, N.Y.: Cornell University Press.

Carr, A. F., Jr. 1940. A contribution to the herpetology of Florida. *University of Florida Publication, Biological Science Series* 3:1–118.

Carr, A. F., Jr., and C. J. Goin. 1955. *Guide to the reptiles, amphibians, and fresh-water fishes of Florida.* Gainesville: University of Florida Press.

Collins, J. T., and S. L. Collins. 1993. Amphibians and reptiles in Kansas. 3d ed. *University of Kansas Museum of Natural History Public Education Series* 13:1–397.

Conant, R. 1951. The reptiles of Ohio. 2d ed. *American Midland Naturalist* 20:1–284.

———. 1975. *A field guide to reptiles and amphibians of eastern and central North America.* 2d ed. Boston: Houghton Mifflin.

Conant, R., and J. T. Collins. 1991. *A field guide to reptiles and amphibians (eastern/central North America).* 3d ed. Boston: Houghton Mifflin.

Degenhardt, W. G., C. W. Painter, and A. H. Price. 1996. *Amphibians and reptiles of New Mexico.* Albuquerque: University of New Mexico Press.

Dixon, J. R. 1987. *Amphibians and reptiles of Texas.* College Station: Texas A&M University Press.

Duellman, W. E. 1961. The amphibians and reptiles of Michoacan, Mexico. *University of Kansas, Publications of the Museum of Natural History* 15:1–148.

———. 1965. Amphibians and reptiles from the Yucatan Peninsula, Mexico. *University of Kansas, Publications of the Museum of Natural History* 15:577–614.

———. 1965. Biogeographic account of the herpetofauna of Michoacan, Mexico. *University of Kansas, Publications of the Museum of Natural History* 15:627–709.

Dundee, H. A., and D. A. Rossman. 1989. *The amphibians and reptiles of Louisiana.* Baton Rouge: Louisiana State University Press.

Ernst, C. H. 1992. *Venomous reptiles of North America.* Washington, D.C.: Smithsonian Institution Press.

Ernst, C. H., and R. W. Barbour. 1989. *The snakes of eastern North America.* Fairfax, Va.: George Mason University Press.

Florez-Villela, O. A. 1993. Herpetofauna Mexicana. *Carnegie Museum of Natural History Special Publication* 17:1–17.

Fowlie, J. A. 1965. *The snakes of Arizona.* Falbrook, Calif.: Author.

Green, N. B., and T. K. Pauley. 1987. *Amphibians and reptiles in West Virginia.* Pittsburgh, Pa.: University of Pittsburgh Press.

Grismer, L. L. 1993. The insular herpetofauna of the Pacific coast of Baja California, Mexico. *Herpetological Natural History* 1:1–10.

Hardy, L. M., and R. W. McDiarmid. 1969. The amphibians and reptiles of Sinaloa, Mexico. *University of Kansas, Publications of the Museum of Natural History* 18:39–252.

Hunter, M. L., Jr., J. Albright, and J. Arbuckle. 1992. Amphibians and reptiles of Maine. *Bulletin of the Maine Amphibian and Reptile Atlas Project* 838:1–88.

Johnson, T. R. 1987. *The amphibians and reptiles of Missouri.* Jefferson City: Missouri Department of Conservation.

Lowe, C. H. 1964. *Vertebrates of Arizona.* Tucson: University of Arizona Press.

Lowe, C. H., C. R. Schwalbe, and T. B. Johnson. 1986. *The venomous reptiles of Arizona.* Phoenix: Arizona Game and Fish Commission.

Martin, P. S. 1958. A biogeography of reptiles and

amphibians in the Gomez Farias region, Tamaulipas, Mexico. *Miscellaneous Publications, Museum of Zoology, University of Michigan* 101:1–102.

Martof, B. S., W. M. Palmer, J. R. Bailey, J. R. Harrison III, and J. Dermid. 1980. *Amphibians and reptiles of the Carolinas and Virginia*. Chapel Hill: University of North Carolina Press.

McDiarmid, R. W., ed. 1978. *Rare and endangered biota of Florida*. Vol. 3: *Amphibians and reptiles*. Gainesville: University of Florida Press.

Means, D. B. 1994. Venomous snakes of South America. *Newsletter of the League of Florida Herpetological Societies* (December).

Miller, D. M., R. A. Young, T. W. Gatlin, and J. A. Richardson. 1982. *Amphibians and reptiles of the Grand Canyon National Park* (Monograph no. 4). Arizona: Grand Canyon Natural History Association.

Minton, S. A., Jr. 1972. *Amphibians and reptiles of Indiana*. Indianapolis: Indiana Academy of Science.

Moler, P. E., ed. 1992. *Rare and endangered biota of Florida*. Vol. 3: *Amphibians and reptiles*. Gainesville: University of Florida Press.

Mount, R. H. 1975. *Reptiles and amphibians of Alabama*. Auburn, Ala.: Auburn University, Agricultural Experiment Station.

Palmer, W. M., and A. L. Braswell. 1995. *Reptiles of North Carolina*. Chapel Hill: University of North Carolina Press.

Shaw, C. E., and S. Campbell 1974. *Snakes of the American West*. New York: Albert A. Knopf.

Smith, H. M., and R. B. Smith. *Synopsis of the herpetofauna of Mexico*. 7 vols. North Bennington, Vt.: Johnson.

Smith, P. W. 1961. The amphibians and reptiles of Illinois. *Illinois Natural History Survey Bulletin* 28:1–298.

Stebbins, R. C. 1985. *A field guide to western amphibians and reptiles*. 2d ed. Boston: Houghton Mifflin.

Tennant, A. 1984. *The snakes of Texas*. Austin: Texas Monthly Press.

———. 1985. *A field guide to the snakes of Texas*. Austin: Texas Monthly Press.

Vermersch, T. G., and R. E. Kunz. 1986. *Snakes of south-central Texas*. Austin, Tex.: Eakin Press.

Webb, R. G. 1969. *Reptiles of Oklahoma*. Norman: University of Oklahoma Press.

Werler, J. E. 1978. Poisonous snakes of Texas. *Texas Parks and Wildlife Department Bulletin* 31:1–53.

Wittner, D. 1978. A discussion of venomous snakes of North America. *Herp: Bulletin of the New York Herpetological Society* 14(1): 12–17.

Wright, A. H., and A. A. Wright. 1957. *Handbook of snakes of the United States and Canada*. Ithaca, N.Y.: Comstock.

OTHER NATURAL SCIENCES

Gibbons, J. W. 1993. *Keeping all the pieces*. Washington, D.C.: Smithsonian Institution Press.

Krutch, J. W. 1961. *The world of animals*. New York: Simon and Schuster.

Lean, G., D. Hinrichsen, and A. Markham. 1990. *Atlas of the environment*. New York: Prentice Hall.

Lydekker, R. 1896. *The new natural history*. Vol. 5. New York: Merrill and Baker.

Mayr, E. 1970. *Populations, species, and evolution*. Cambridge, Mass.: Harvard University Press.

Shelford, V. E. 1963. *The ecology of North America*. Urbana: University of Illinois Press.

Sinclair, S. 1985. *How animals see: Other visions of our world*. New York: Facts on File.

Van Dyke, J. C. 1901. *The desert*. New York: Scribner.

Watkins, T. H. 1995. Desert extraordinaire. *Audubon* 97:42–57.

Wood, J. G. 1855. *Animate creation, "Our living world."* New York: Selmar Hess.

RATTLESNAKES: GENERAL WORKS AND POPULAR ACCOUNTS

*Armstrong, B. L., and J. B. Murphy. 1979. The natural history of Mexican rattlesnakes. *University of Kansas, Museum of Natural History Special Publication* 5:1–88.

Beltz, E. 1988. Selections from the writings of early travelers in North America concerning rattlesnakes. *Tucson Herpetological Society Newsletter* 1:84–88.

Brennan, C. E. 1995. *Rattler tales from north-central Pennsylvania*. Pittsburgh, Pa.: University of Pittsburgh Press.

Brown, W. S. 1987. Hidden life of the timber rattler. *National Geographic Magazine* 172:128–38.

Dobie, J. F. 1965. *Rattlesnakes*. Boston: Little, Brown.

*Gloyd, H. K. 1940. The rattlesnakes, genera *Sistrurus* and *Crotalus*. *Chicago Academy of Sciences Special Publication* 4:1–266.

King, W. A., Jr. 1964. *Rattling yours . . . snake king*. Brownsville, Tex.: Springman-King Lithograph.

Klauber, L. M. 1956. *Rattlesnakes: Their habits, life histories, and influence on mankind*. 2 vols. Berkeley: University of California Press.

Lawler, H. E. 1981. So elegante a beaste, the bell-tailed serpent: The rattlesnake. *Sonorensis* 3:4–11.

Lowe, C. 1996. The tale of the rattler. *Florida Living* (August): 12–15.

Mattison, C. 1996. *Rattler! A natural history of rattlesnakes*. London: Blandford Press.

Medden, R. V. 1930. Tales of the rattlesnake: From the works of early travelers in America. *Bulletin of the Antivenin Institute of America* 4:17–23.

Meek, G. 1946. *Creatures of mystery*. Macon, Ga.: J. W. Burke.

Scheidt, V., and J. H. Tashjian. 1990. Small rattlesnakes. *The Vivarium* 2:15–18.

Walls, J. G. 1996. *Rattlesnakes: Their natural history and care in captivity*. Neptune, N.J.: T.F.H. Publications.

RATTLESNAKES: SPECIES ACCOUNTS

Beaman, K. R., and L. L. Grismer. 1994. *Crotalus enyo. Catalogue of American Amphibians and Reptiles* 589:1–6.

Campbell, J. A. 1988. *Crotalus transversus. Catalogue of American Amphibians and Reptiles* 450:1–3.

Collins, J. T. 1982. *Crotalus stejnegeri. Catalogue of American Amphibians and Reptiles* 303:1–2.

Collins, J. T., and J. L. Knight. 1980. *Crotalus horridus. Catalogue of American Amphibians and Reptiles* 253:1–2.

Fabian, H., and A. Simmons. 1988. The massasauga rattlesnake. *The Vivarium* 1:25–26.

Glenn, J. L., and H. E. Lawler. 1987. *Crotalus scutulatus salvani* (Huamantian rattlesnake). *Behavioral Herpetology Review* 18:15–16.

Haller, R. 1971. The diamondback rattlesnakes. *Herpetology* 3:1–34.

Kauffeld, C. F., and H. K. Gloyd. 1939. Notes on the Aruba Island rattlesnake, *Crotalus unicolor*. *Herpetologica* 1:156–60.

McCranie, J. R. 1976. *Crotalus polystictus. Catalogue of American Amphibians and Reptiles* 180:1–2.

———. 1980. *Crotalus pricei. Catalogue of American Amphibians and Reptiles* 266:1–2.

———. 1980. *Crotalus adamanteus. Catalogue of American Amphibians and Reptiles* 267:1–2.

———. 1981. *Crotalus basiliscus. Catalogue of American Amphibians and Reptiles* 283:1–2.

———. 1983. *Crotalus pusillus. Catalogue of American Amphibians and Reptiles* 313:1–2.

———. 1984. *Crotalus vegrandis. Catalogue of American Amphibians and Reptiles* 350:1–2.

———. 1986. *Crotalus unicolor. Catalogue of American Amphibians and Reptiles* 389:1–2.

———. 1991. *Crotalus intermedius. Catalogue of American Amphibians and Reptiles* 519:1–4.

———. 1993. *Crotalus durissus. Catalogue of American Amphibians and Reptiles* 577:1–11.

McCrystal, H. K., and M. J. McCoid. 1986. *Crotalus mitchellii. Catalogue of American Amphibians and Reptiles* 388:1–4.

Minton, S. A., Jr. 1983. *Sistrurus catenatus. Catalogue of American Amphibians and Reptiles* 332:1–2.

Palmer, W. M. 1978. *Sistrurus miliarius. Catalogue of American Amphibians and Reptiles* 220:1–2.

Price, A. 1980. *Crotalus molossus. Catalogue of American Amphibians and Reptiles* 242:1–2.

———. 1982. *Crotalus scutulatus. Catalogue of American Amphibians and Reptiles* 291:1–2.

Strimple, P. 1983. *Crotalus mitchellii,* the speckled rattlesnake. *The Forked Tongue* 8(9): 8–13.

———. 1984. *Crotalus cerastes,* the sidewinder. *The Forked Tongue* 9(8): 6–9.

———. 1984. *Crotalus molossus,* the black-tailed rattlesnake. *The Forked Tongue* 9(1): 10–13.

———. 1984. *Crotalus pricei,* the twin-spotted rattlesnake. *The Forked Tongue* 9(12): 11–14.

———. 1984. *Crotalus pusillus* Klauber, the Tancitaran rattlesnake. *The Forked Tongue* 9(5): 7–8.

———. 1985. *Crotalus polystictus* (Cope), the Mexican lance-headed rattlesnake. *The Forked Tongue* 10(7): 7–9.

———. 1985. *Crotalus scutulatus* (Kennicott), the Mojave rattlesnake. *The Forked Tongue* 10(2): 7–9.

———. 1985. *Crotalus stejnegeri* Dunn, the long-tailed rattlesnake. *The Forked Tongue* 10(12): 5–7.

———. 1985. *Crotalus tigris* Kennicott, the tiger rattlesnake. *The Forked Tongue* 10(2): 11–12.

———. 1986. *Crotalus atrox* Baird and Girard, the western diamondback rattlesnake. *The Forked Tongue* 11(6): 7–9.

———. 1987. *Crotalus unicolor* van Lidth de Jeude (Aruba Island rattlesnake). *The Forked Tongue* 12(12): 3–15.

———. 1987. *Crotalus vegrandis* Klauber (Uracoan rattlesnake). *The Forked Tongue* 12(8): 7–12.

———. 1989. *Crotalus transversus* Taylor 1944 (the cross-banded mountain rattlesnake). *The Forked Tongue* 14(11): 7–15.

Tanner, W. W. 1986. *Crotalus lannomi. Catalogue of American Amphibians and Reptiles* 387:1–2.

Subject

CONFLICT WITH HUMANS

Bury, R. B., R. A. Luckenbach, and S. D. Busack. 1977. Effects of off-road vehicles on vertebrates in the California desert. *Wildlife Resources Report* 8:1–20.

Busack, S. D., and R. B. Bury. 1974. Some effects of off-road vehicles and sheep grazing on lizard populations in the Mojave Desert. *Biological Conservation* 6:179–83.

Bushey, C. L. 1985. Man's effect upon a colony of *Sistrurus c. catenateus* (Raf.) in northwestern Illinois (1834–1975). *Bulletin of the Chicago Herpetological Society* 20:1–12.

Minton, S. A., Jr. 1968. The fate of amphibians and reptiles in a suburban area. *Journal of Herpetology* 2:113–16.

Prior, K. A., and P. J. Weatherhead. 1994. Response of free-ranging eastern massasauga rattlesnakes to human disturbance. *Journal of Herpetology* 28:255–57.

Stebbins, R. C. 1974. Off-road vehicles and the fragile desert. *American Biology Teacher* 36:203–8, 294–304.

Volmer, A. T., B. G. Maza, P. A. Medica, F. B. Turner, and S. A. Bamberg. 1976. The impact of off-road vehicles on a desert ecosystem. *Environmental Management* 1:115–29.

Wilson, L. D., and L. Porras. 1983. The ecological impact of man on the south Florida herpetofauna. *University of Kansas, Museum of Natural History Special Publication* 9:1–89.

CONSERVATION

Adams, C. E., S. L. Jester, and J. K. Thomas. 1995. National overview of regulations to conserve amphibians and reptiles. *Wildlife Society Bulletin* 23:391–96.

Applegarth, J. S. 1980. *The ridge-nosed rattlesnake in New Mexico: A review of existing information and a search for suitable habitat on public lands.* Las Cruces, N.M.: U.S. Bureau of Land Management.

Bogert, C. M. 1948. The problem of snake control. *Natural History Magazine* 57:185–88.

Breisch, A. R. 1992. Summary of state and provincial regulations concerning the timber rattlesnake. In *Conservation of the timber rattlesnake in the Northeast,* ed. T. F. Tyning. Lincoln: Massachusetts Audubon Society.

Brown, W. S. 1992. Biology and conservation of the timber rattlesnake. In *Conservation of the timber rattlesnake in the Northeast,* ed. T. F. Tyning. Lincoln: Massachusetts Audubon Society.

*———. 1993. Biology, status, and management of the timber rattlesnake *(Crotalus horridus):* A guide for conservation. *Society for the Study of Amphibians and Reptiles Herpetological Circular* 22:1–78.

Brown, W. S., L. Jones, and R. Stechert. 1994. A case in herpetological conservation: Notorious poacher convicted of illegal trafficking in timber rattlesnakes. *Bulletin of the Chicago Herpetological Society* 29:74–76.

Dodd, C. K., Jr. 1993. Strategies for snake conservation. In *Snakes: Ecology and behavior,* ed. R. A. Seigel and J. T. Collins. New York: McGraw-Hill.

Freda, J. 1977. Fighting a losing battle: The story of a timber rattlesnake. *Herp: Bulletin of the New York Herpetological Society* 13(2): 35–38.

Greene, H. W. 1990. The sound defense of the rattlesnake. *Pacific Discovery* 43:10–19.

———. 1994. Systematics and natural history: Foundations for understanding and conserving biodiversity. *American Zoologist* 34:48–56.

Greene, H. W., and J. A. Campbell. 1992. The future of pitvipers. In *Biology of the pitvipers,* ed. J. A. Campbell and E. D. Brodie, Jr. Tyler, Tex.: Selva.

Grossmann, J. 1993. How green are these fairways? *Audubon* 95:90–99.

Hare, T. A., and J. T. McNally. 1997. Evaluation of

a rattlesnake relocation program in the Tucson, Arizona, area. *Sonoran Herpetologist* 10:26–31.

*Johnson, B., and V. Menzies, eds. 1993. *International symposium and workshop on the conservation of the eastern massasauga rattlesnake, Sistrurus catenatus catenatus.* Ontario: Metro Toronto Zoo.

Johnson, T. B. 1983. Status report: *Crotalus willardi willardi* (Meek, 1905). Publication No. 14-16-0002-81-224. U.S. Fish and Wildlife Service, Washington, D.C.

Johnson, T. B., and G. S. Mills. 1982. A preliminary report on the status of *Crotalus lepidus, C. pricei,* and *C. willardi* in southeastern Arizona. Publication No. 14-16-0002-81-24. U.S. Fish and Wildlife Service, Washington, D.C.

Kellert, S. R., and M. Westervelt. 1983. *Children's attitudes, knowledge, and behaviors toward animals.* Washington, D.C.: U.S. Fish and Wildlife Service.

Odum, R. A. 1995. *Aruba Island rattlesnake conservation action plan.* 2d ed. Toledo, Ohio: American Zoo and Aquarium Association.

Sealy, J. B. 1997. Short-distance translocations of timber rattlesnakes in a North Carolina state park: A successful conservation and management program. *Sonoran Herpetologist* 10:94–99.

Seigel, R. A. 1986. Ecology and conservation of an endangered rattlesnake, *Sistrurus catenatus,* in Missouri. *Biological Conservation* 35:333–46.

Speake, D. W., J. Diemer, and J. McGlincy. 1982. *Eastern indigo snake recovery plan.* Atlanta, Ga.: U.S. Fish and Wildlife Service.

Stechert, R. 1981. Historical depletion of timber rattlesnake colonies in New York State. *Herp: Bulletin of the New York Herpetological Society* 17(2): 23–24.

Tyning, T. F., ed. 1992. *Conservation of the timber rattlesnake in the Northeast.* Lincoln: Massachusetts Audubon Society.

DISTRIBUTION

Atkinson, D. A., and M. G. Netting. 1927. The distribution and habits of the massasauga. *Bulletin of Antivenin Institution of America* 1:40–44.

Martin, B. E. 1974. Distribution and habitat adaptations in rattlesnakes of Arizona. *Herp: Bulletin of the New York Herpetological Society* 10(2): 3–12.

Martin, W. H. 1981. The timber rattlesnake in the Northeast: Its range, past and present. *Herp: Bulletin of the New York Herpetological Society* 17(2): 15–20.

———. 1992. Phenology of the timber rattlesnake *(Crotalus horridus)* in an unglaciated section of the Appalachian Mountains. In *Biology of the pitvipers,* ed. J. A. Campbell and E. D. Brodie, Jr. Tyler, Tex.: Selva.

———. 1992. The timber rattlesnake: Its distribution and natural history. In *Conservation of the timber rattlesnake in the Northeast,* ed. T. F. Tyning. Lincoln: Massachusetts Audubon Society.

Murphy, R. W., and J. R. Ottley. 1984. Distribution of amphibians and reptiles on islands in the Gulf of California. *Annals for the Carnegie Museum* 53:207–30.

Odum, R. A. 1979. The distribution and status of the New Jersey timber rattlesnake, including an analysis of Pine Barrens populations. *Herp: Bulletin of the New York Herpetological Society* 15(1): 27–35.

Palmer, W. M. 1971. Distribution and variation of the Carolina pigmy rattlesnake, *Sistrurus miliarius miliarius* Linnaeus, in North Carolina. *Journal of Herpetology* 5:39–44.

Wilkinson, J. A., J. L. Glenn, R. C. Straight, and J. W. Sites, Jr. 1991. Distribution and genetic variation in venom A and B populations of the Mojave rattlesnake (*Crotalus scutulatus scutulatus*). *Herpetologica* 47:54–68.

FANGS AND VENOM

Allen, W. B., Jr. 1956. The effects of a massasauga bite. *Herpetologica* 12:151.

Barton, A. J. 1950. Replacement fangs in newborn timber rattlesnakes. *Copeia* 1950:235–36.

Bush, C. R. 1994. The effects of whole and fractionated venom on preference for prey in rattlesnakes (*Crotalus atrox*). Master's thesis, University of Colorado, Boulder.

Dart, R., J. T. McNally, D. W. Spaite, and R. Gustafson. 1992. The sequelae of pitviper envenomation in the United States. In *Biology of the pitvipers,* ed. J. A. Campbell and E. D. Brodie, Jr. Tyler, Tex.: Selva.

Eppie, D. R., J. D. Johnson, O. Molina, and H. K. McCrystal. 1992. Distribution of a Mojave toxin-like protein in rock rattlesnake (*Crotalus lepidus*) venom. In *Biology of the pitvipers,* ed. J. A. Campbell and E. D. Brodie, Jr. Tyler, Tex.: Selva.

Gennaro, J. F., R. S. Leopold, and T. W. Merriam. 1961. Observations on the actual quantity of venom introduced by several species of crotalid snakes in their bites. *Anatomical Record* 139:303.

Githens, T. S., and J. D. George. 1931. Comparative studies of the venoms of certain rattlesnakes. *Bulletin of the Antivenin Institute of America* 5:31–34.

Glenn, J. L. 1994. New snakebite antivenom in human clinical trials. *Intermontanus* 3:26.

Glenn, J. L., and R. C. Straight. 1993. Human fatalities caused by venomous animals in Utah, 1900–90. *Great Basin Naturalist* 53:390–94.

Hardy, D. L. 1988. Epidemiology of rattlesnake envenomation in Tucson, Arizona, 1973–1980: A preliminary report. *Tucson Herpetological Society Newsletter* 1:33–36.

———. 1991. Epidemiology and medical management of rattlesnake bite in southern Arizona. *Sonoran Herpetologist* 4:153–58.

———. 1992. A review of first aid measures for pitviper bite in North America, with an appraisal of Extractor suction and stun gun electroshock. In *Biology of the pitvipers,* ed. J. A. Campbell and E. D. Brodie, Jr. Tyler, Tex.: Selva.

———. 1997. Fatal bite by a captive rattlesnake in Tucson, Arizona. *Sonoran Herpetologist* 10:38–39.

Hardy, L. M. 1995. The Aruba Island rattlesnake (*Crotalus durissus unicolor*): Epidemiology and treatment aspects of envenomation. In *Aruba Island rattlesnake conservation action plan,* ed. R. A. Odum. American Zoo and Aquarium Association Report 5.

Harris, H. H., Jr. 1965. Case reports of two dusky pigmy rattlesnake bites (*Sistrurus miliarius barbouri*). *Bulletin of the Maryland Herpetological Society* 2:8–10.

Hutchison, R. H. 1929. On the incidence of snake bite poisoning in the United States and the results of the newer methods of treatment. *Bulletin of the Antivenin Institute of America* 3:43–57.

Johnson, B. D., J. Hoppe, R. Rogers, and H. L. Stahnke. 1968. Characteristics of venom from the rattlesnake *Crotalus horridus atricaudatus. Journal of Herpetology* 2:107–12.

*Kardong, K. V. 1982. The evolution of the venom apparatus in snakes from colubrids to viperids and elapids. *Memorias do Instituto Butantan* 46:105–18.

Kardong, K. V. 1995. Snake toxins and venoms: An evolutionary perspective. *Herpetologica* 52:36–46.

———. 1996. Mechanical damage inflicted by fangs on prey during predatory strikes by rattlesnakes, *Crotalus viridis oreganus. Bulletin of the Maryland Herpetological Society* 32:113–18.

Kardong, K. V., and P. A. Lavin-Murcio. 1993. Venom delivery of snakes as high-pressure and low-pressure systems. *Copeia* 1993:644–50.

Klauber, L. M. 1928. The collection of snake venom. *Bulletin of the Antivenin Institute of America* 2:11–18.

Kochva, E., and C. Gans. 1966. Histology and histochemistry of venom glands of some crotaline snakes. *Copeia* 1966:506–15.

Mackessy, S. P. 1988. Venom ontogeny in the Pacific rattlesnakes, *Crotalus viridis helleri* and *C. v. oreganus. Copeia* 1988:92–101.

McKinistry, D. M. 1983. Morphologic evidence of toxic saliva in colubrid snakes: A checklist of world genera. *Herpetological Review* 14:12–14.

Mebs, D., and F. Kornalik. 1984. Intraspecific variation in content of a basic toxin in eastern diamondback rattlesnake (*Crotalus adamanteus*) venom. *Toxicon* 22:831–33.

Minton, S. A., Jr. 1967. Observations on toxicity and antigenic makeup of venoms from juvenile snakes. *Toxicon* 4:294.

Mitchell, S. W., and E. T. Reichert. 1886. Researches upon the venoms of poisonous serpents. *Smithsonian Contributions to Knowledge* 647:1–186.

Parrish, H. M. 1980. *Poisonous snakebites in the United States.* New York: Vantage Press.

Russell, F. E. 1983. *Snake venom poisoning.* Great Neck, N.Y.: Scholium.

Schaeffer, N. 1976. The mechanism of venom transfer from the venom duct to the fang in snakes. *Herpetologica* 32:71–76.

Tu, A. T., ed. 1977. *Venoms: Chemistry and molecular biology.* New York: John Wiley and Sons.

———. 1982. *Rattlesnake venoms: Their action and treatment.* New York: Marcel Dekker.

Weinstein, S. A., and L. A. Smith 1990. Preliminary fractionation of tiger rattlesnake (*Crotalus tigris*) venom. *Toxicon* 28:1447–55.

Wilkinson, J. A., J. L. Glenn, R. C. Straight, and J. W. Sites, Jr. 1991. Distribution and genetic variation in venom A and B populations of the Mojave rattlesnake (*Crotalus scutulatus scutulatus*). *Herpetologica* 47:54–68.

FOOD AND FEEDING

Brown, W. S., and D. B. Greenberg. 1992. Vertical-tree ambush posture in *Crotalus horridus. Herpetological Review* 23:67.

Chiszar, D., D. Duvall, K. Scudder, and C. W. Radcliffe. 1980. Simultaneous and successive discriminations between envenomated and nonenvenomated mice by rattlesnakes (*Crotalus durissus* and *C. viridis*). *Behavioral Neural Biology* 29:518–21.

Chiszar, D., R. K. Lee, H. M. Smith, and C. W. Radcliffe. 1992. Searching behaviors by rattlesnakes following predatory strikes. In *Biology of the pitvipers,* ed. J. A. Campbell and E. D. Brodie, Jr. Tyler, Tex.: Selva.

Chiszar, D., C. Radcliffe, B. O'Connell, and H. M. Smith. 1983. Analysis of the behavioral sequence emitted by rattlesnakes during feeding episodes. II. Duration of strike-induced chemosensory searching in rattlesnakes (*Crotalus viridis, C. enyo*). *Behavioral Neural Biology* 34:261–70.

Chiszar, D., and K. Scudder. 1977. Analysis of the behavioral sequence emitted by rattlesnakes during feeding episodes. I. Striking and chemosensory searching. *Behavioral Biology* 21:418–25.

Chiszar, D., H. M. Smith, and A. R. Hoge. 1982. Post-strike trailing behavior in rattlesnakes. *Memorias do Instituto Butantan* 46:195–206.

Chiszar, D., S. V. Taylor, C. W. Radcliffe, H. M. Smith, and B. O'Connell. 1981. Effects of chemical and visual stimuli upon chemosensory searching by garter snakes and rattlesnakes. *Journal of Herpetology* 15:415–23.

Diller, L. V., and D. R. Johnson. 1988. Food habits, consumption rates, and predation rates of western rattlesnakes and gopher snakes in southwestern Idaho. *Herpetologica* 44:228–33.

Duvall, D., K. Scudder, and D. Chiszar. 1980. Rattlesnake predatory behavior: Mediation of prey discrimination and release of swallowing by cues arising from envenomated mice. *Animal Behaviour* 28:674–83.

Funderburg, J. B. 1968. Eastern diamondback rattlesnake feeding on carrion. *Journal of Herpetology* 2:161–62.

Golan, L., C. Radcliffe, T. Miller, B. O'Connell, and D. Chiszar. 1982. Trailing behavior in the western diamondback rattlesnake, *Crotalus atrox*. *Behavioral Neural Biology* 32:235–40.

———. 1982. Trailing behavior in prairie rattlesnakes *(Crotalus viridis)*. *Journal of Herpetology* 16:287–93.

Hayes, W. K., P. Lavin-Murcio, and K. V. Kardong. 1995. Northern Pacific rattlesnakes *(Crotalus viridis oreganus)* meter venom when feeding on prey of different sizes. *Copeia* 1995:337–49.

Hamilton, W. J., Jr., and J. A. Pollack. 1955. The food of some crotalid snakes from Fort Benning, Georgia. *Natural History Miscellanea, Chicago Academy of Sciences* 140:1–4.

Jackson, J. F., and D. L. Martin. 1980. Caudal luring in the dusky pygmy rattlesnake, *Sistrurus miliarius barbouri*. *Copeia* 1980:926–27.

Kardong, K. V. 1986. The predatory strike of the rattlesnake: When things go amiss. *Copeia* 1986:816–20.

———. 1996. Mechanical damage inflicted by fangs on prey during predatory strikes by rattlesnakes, *Crotalus viridis oreganus*. *Bulletin of the Maryland Herpetological Society* 32:113–18.

Kardong, K. V., and S. P. Mackessy. 1991. The strike behavior of a congenitally blind rattlesnake. *Journal of Herpetology* 25:208–11.

Kauffeld, C. F. 1943. Growth and feeding of newborn Price's and green rock rattlesnakes. *American Midland Naturalist* 29:607–14.

Keenlyne, K. D. 1972. Sexual differences in feeding habits of *Crotalus horridus horridus*. *Journal of Herpetology* 6:234–37.

Keenlyne, K. D., and J. R. Beer. 1973. Food habits of *Sistrurus catenatus catenatus*. *Journal of Herpetology* 7:382–84.

Lardie, R. L. 1976. Large centipede eaten by a western massasauga. *Bulletin of the Oklahoma Herpetological Society* 1:40.

Lavin-Murcio, P., B. G. Robinson, and K. V. Kardong. 1993. Cues involved in relocation of struck prey by rattlesnakes, *Crotalus viridis oreganus*. *Herpetologica* 49:463–69.

Melcer, T., and D. Chiszar. 1989. Striking prey creates a specific chemical search image in rattlesnakes. *Animal Behaviour* 37:477–86.

Minton, S. A., Jr. 1969. The feeding strike of the timber rattlesnake. *Journal of Herpetology* 3:121–24.

Neill, W. T. 1960. The caudal lure of various juvenile snakes. *Quarterly Journal of the Florida Academy of Science* 23:173–200.

Parker, S. A., and D. Stotz. 1977. An observation on the foraging behavior of the Arizona ridgenosed rattlesnake, *Crotalus willardi willardi* (Serpentes: Crotalidae). *Bulletin of the Maryland Herpetological Society* 13:123.

Rabatsky, A. M., and T. M. Farrell. 1997. The effects of age and light level on foraging posture and frequency of caudal luring in the rattlesnake, *Sistrurus milarius barbouri*. *Journal of Herpetology* 30:558–61.

Reinert, H. K., D. Cundall, and L. M. Bushar. 1984. Foraging behavior of the timber rattlesnake, *Crotalus horridus*. *Copeia* 1984:976–81.

Robinson, B. G., and K. V. Kardong. 1991. Relocation of struck prey by venomoid (venom-less) rattlesnakes, *Crotalus viridis oreganus*. *Bulletin of the Maryland Herpetological Society* 32:23–30.

Schuett, G. W., D. L. Clark, and F. Kraus. 1984. Feeding mimicry in the rattlesnake *Sistrurus catenatus*, with comments on the evolution of the rattle. *Animal Behaviour* 32:625–26.

HEALTH

Jacobson, E. R., and J. M. Gaskin. 1992. Paramyxovirus infection of viperid snakes. In *Biology of the pitvipers*, ed. J. A. Campbell and E. D. Brodie, Jr. Tyler, Tex.: Selva.

Mader, D. R., and K. DeRemer. 1993. Salmonellosis in reptiles. *The Vivarium* 4:12–13, 22.

Minton, S. A., Jr. 1992. Reptiles as a source of human infections. In *Contributions in Herpetology*, ed. P. D. Strimple and J. L. Strimple. Cincinnati, Ohio: Greater Cincinatti Herpetological Society.

Murphy, J. B., and B. L. Armstrong. 1978. Maintenance of rattlesnakes in captivity. *University of Kansas, Museum of Natural History Special Publication* 3:1–40.

Snellings, E., and J. T. Collins. 1996. *Sistrurus miliarius barbouri* (dusky pigmy rattlesnake): Maximum size. *Herpetology Review* 27:84.

HIBERNATION

Brown, W. S. 1982. Overwintering body temperatures of timber rattlesnakes *(Crotalus horridus)* in northeastern New York. *Journal of Herpetology* 16:145–50.

———. 1992. Emergence, ingress, and seasonal captures at dens of northern timber rattlesnakes, *Crotalus horridus*. In *Biology of the pitvipers*, ed. J. A. Campbell and E. D. Brodie, Jr. Tyler, Tex.: Selva.

Charland, M. B. 1989. Size and winter survivorship in neonatal western rattlesnakes *(Crotalus viridis)*. *Canadian Journal of Zoology* 67:1620–25.

Duvall, D., M. J. Goode, W. K. Hayes, J. K. Leonhart, and D. G. Brown. 1990. Prairie rattlesnake vernal migration: Field experimental analyses and survival value. *National Geographic Research* 6:457–69.

Graves, M., D. Duvall, M. B. King, S. L. Lindstedt, and W. A. Gern. 1986. Initial den location by neonatal prairie rattlesnakes: Functions, causes, and natural history in chemical ecology. In *Chemical signals in vertebrates,* vol. 4, ed. D. Duvall, D. Muller-Schwarze, and R. M. Silverstein. New York: Plenum Press.

Jacob, J. S., and C. W. Painter. 1980. Overwintering thermal ecology of *Crotalus viridis* in the north-central plains of New Mexico. *Copeia* 1980:799–805.

Macartney, J. M., K. W. Larsen, and P. T. Gregory. 1989. Body temperatures and movements of hibernating snakes *(Crotalus and Thamnophis)* and thermal gradients of natural hibernacula. *Canadian Journal of Zoology* 67:108–14.

Maple, W. T., and L. P. Orr. 1968. Overwintering adaptations of *Sistrurus catenatus* in northeastern Ohio. *Journal of Herpetology* 2:179–80.

Parker, W. S., and W. S. Brown. 1974. Mortality and weight changes of Great Basin rattlesnakes *(Crotalus viridis)* at a hibernaculum in northern Utah. *Herpetologica* 30:234–39.

Pough, F. H., and M. B. Pough. 1971. How cold are cold snakes? Comments on the reliability of low temperature records. *Herpetological Review* 3:102.

Sexton, O. J., P. Jacobson, and J. E. Bramble. 1992. Geographic variation in some activities associated with hibernation in Nearctic pitvipers. In *Biology of the pitviper,* ed. J. A. Campbell and E. D. Brodie, Jr. Tyler, Tex.: Selva.

Stechert, R. 1980. Observations on northern snake dens. *Herp: Bulletin of the New York Herpetological Society* 15(2): 7–14.

———. 1981. Historical depletion of timber rattlesnake colonies in New York State. *Herp: Bulletin of the New York Herpetological Society* 17(2): 23–24.

HYBRIDS

Bailey, R. M. 1942. An intergeneric hybrid rattlesnake. *American Naturalist* 76:376–85.

Murphy, R. W., and C. B. Crabtree. 1985. Genetic identification of a natural hybrid rattlesnake: *Crotalus scutulatus scutulatus* × *C. viridis viridis*. *Herpetologica* 44:451–70.

Perkins, C. B. 1951. Hybrid rattlesnakes. *Herpetologica* 7:146.

LOCOMOTION

Bogert, C. M. 1947. Rectilinear locomotion in snakes. *Copeia* 1947:253–54.

Bonati, R. L. 1978. Adaptive locomotion in snakes. *Bulletin of the Chicago Herpetological Society* 13:19–28.

Cowles, R. B. 1956. Sidewinding locomotion in snakes. *Copeia* 1965:211–14.

Gans, C. 1962. Terrestrial locomotion without limbs. *American Zoologist* 2:167–82.

Jayne, B. C. 1986. Kinematics of terrestrial snake locomotion. *Copeia* 1986:915–27.

Mosauer, W. 1932. On the locomotion of snakes. *Science* 76:583–85.

Muir, J. H. 1982. Notes on the climbing ability of a captive timber rattlesnake, *Crotalus horridus*. *Bulletin of the Chicago Herpetological Society* 17:22–23.

MISCELLANEOUS BEHAVIORS

Aird, S. D., and M. E. Aird. 1990. Rain-collecting behavior in a Great Basin rattlesnake, *Crotalus viridis lutosus*. *Bulletin of the Chicago Herpetological Society* 25:217.

Brown, W. S., and F. M. MacLean. 1983. Conspecific scent-trailing by newborn timber rattlesnakes, *Crotalus horridus*. *Herpetologica* 39:430–36.

Carpenter, C. C., and J. C. Gillingham. 1975. Postural response of kingsnakes to crotaline snakes. *Herpetologica* 31:293–302.

Chiszar, D., J. Perelman, H. M. Smith, and D. Duvall. 1992. "Shouldering" in prairie rattlesnakes: A new hypothesis. *Bulletin of the Maryland Herpetological Society* 28:69–76.

Cowles, R. B. 1938. Unusual defense postures assumed by rattlesnakes. *Copeia* 1938:13–16.

Graves, B. M., and D. Duvall. 1983. Occurrence and function of prairie rattlesnake mouth gaping in a non-feeding context. *Journal of Experimental Zoology* 227:471–74.

———. 1985. Mouth gaping and head shaking by prairie rattlesnakes associated with vomeronasal organ olfaction. *Copeia* 1985:496–97.

Landreth, H. F. 1973. Orientation and behavior of the rattlesnake *Crotalus atrox*. *Copeia* 1973:26–31.

Lowe, C. H., and K. S. Norris. 1950. Aggressive behavior in male sidewinders, *Crotalus cerastes*, with a discussion of aggressive behavior and territoriality in snakes. *Natural History Miscellanea, Chicago Academy of Sciences* 66:1–13.

Marchisin, A. 1978. Observations on an audiovisual "warning" signal in the pigmy rattlesnake, *Sistrurus miliarius* (Reptilia, Serpentes, Crotalidae). *Herpetological Review* 9:92–93.

Wharton, C. H. 1960. Birth and behavior of a brood of cottonmouths, *Agkistrodon piscivorus*

piscivorus, with notes on tail luring. *Herpetologica* 16:125–29.

MYTHOLOGY AND RELIGION

Bogert, C. M. 1933. Notes on the dance of the Hopi Indians. *Copeia* 1933:219–21.

———. 1941. The Hopi snake dance. *Natural History Magazine* 47:276–83.

Burton, T. 1993. *Serpent-handling believers.* Knoxville: University of Tennessee Press.

Covington, D. 1995. *Salvation on sand mountain.* Reading, Mass.: Addison-Wesley.

Fewkes, J. W. 1891. A suggestion as to the meaning of the Moki snake dance. *Journal of American Folklore* 4:129–38.

Ricks, J. B., and A. E. Anthony, Jr., eds. 1986. *Hopi snake ceremonies.* (Reprint of selected writings of J. W. Fewkes from the Bureau of American Ethnology Annual Reports, no. 16 [1894–95] and no. 19 [1897–98]). Albuquerque, N.M.: Avanyu.

Sterling, M. W. 1942. Snake bites and the Hopi snake dance. *Smithsonian Report* 1941:551–55.

NATURAL HISTORY

Applegarth, J. S. 1980. *The ridge-nosed rattlesnake in New Mexico: A review of existing information and a search for suitable habitat on public lands.* Las Cruces, N.M.: U.S. Bureau of Land Management.

*Armstrong, B. L., and J. B. Murphy. 1979. The natural history of Mexican rattlesnakes. *University of Kansas, Museum of Natural History Special Publication* 5:1–88.

Barker, D. G. 1990. Variation, intraspecific relationships, and biogeography of the ridgenose rattlesnake, *Crotalus willardi:* A report to the Endangered Species Program. New Mexico Department of Game and Fish, Las Cruces.

———. 1992. Variation, intraspecific relationships, and biogeography of the ridgenose rattlesnake, *Crotalus willardi*. In *Biology of the pitvipers,* ed. J. A. Cambell and E. D. Brodie Jr. Tyler, Tex.: Selva.

Bartlett, R. D. 1992. Pygmies afield: Reflections on herping for the red pygmy rattlesnake (*Sistrurus m. miliarius*). *The Vivarium* 3:16–18.

Beaupre, S. J. 1995. Comparative ecology of the mottled rock rattlesnake, *Crotalus lepidus,* in Big Bend National Park. *Herpetologica* 51:45–56.

———. 1995. Sexual size dimorphism in the western diamondback rattlesnake (*Crotalus atrox):* Integrating natural history, behavior, and physiology. *Sonoran Herpetologist* 8:112–18.

Beck, D. D. 1995. Ecology and energetics of three sympatric rattlesnake species in the Sonoran Desert. *Journal of Herpetology* 29:211–23.

Brown, C. W., and C. H. Ernst. 1986. A study of the variation in eastern timber rattlesnakes, *Crotalus horridus* Linnaeus (Serpentes: Viperidae). *Brimleyana* 12:57–74.

Brown, D. G., and D. Duvall. 1993. Habitat associations of prairie rattlesnakes (*Crotalus viridis*) in Wyoming. *Herpetological Natural History* 1:5–12.

Brown, T. W., and H. B. Lillywhite. 1992. Autecology of the Mojave Desert sidewinder (*Crotalus cerastes cerastes*) at Kelso Dunes, Mojave Desert, California. In *Biology of the pitvipers,* ed. J. A. Campbell and E. D. Brodie, Jr. Tyler, Tex.: Selva.

Brown, W. S. 1992. Biology and conservation of the timber rattlesnake. In *Conservation of the timber rattlesnake in the Northeast,* ed. T. F. Tyning. Lincoln: Massachusetts Audubon Society.

*———. 1993. Biology, status, and management of the timber rattlesnake (*Crotalus horridus):* A guide for conservation. *Society for the Study of Amphibians and Reptiles Herpetological Circular* 22:1–78.

Brown, W. S., D. W. Pyle, K. R. Greene, and J. B. Friedlaender. 1982. Movements and temperature relationships of timber rattlesnakes (*Crotalus horridus*) in northeastern New York. *Journal of Herpetology* 16:151–61.

Cavanaugh, C. J. 1994. *Crotalus horridus* (timber rattlesnake): Longevity. *Herpetological Review* 25:71.

Clarke, J. A., J. T. Chopko, and S. P. Mackessy. 1995. The effect of moonlight on activity patterns of adult and juvenile prairie rattlesnakes (*Crotalus viridis viridis*). *Journal of Herpetology* 30:192–97.

Diller, L. V., and R. L. Wallace. 1996. Comparative ecology of two snake species (*Crotalus viridis* and *Pituophis melanoleucus*) in southwestern Idaho. *Herpetologica* 52:343–60.

Dorcas, M. E. 1992. Relationships among montane populations of *Crotalus lepidus* and *Crotalus triseriatus*. In *Biology of the pitvipers,* ed. J. A. Campbell and E. D. Brodie, Jr. Tyler, Tex.: Selva.

Duvall, D., M. B. King, and K. J. Gutzwiller. 1985. Behavioral ecology and ethology of the prairie rattlesnake. *National Geographic Research* 1:80–111.

Fitch, H. S., and G. R. Pisani. 1993. Life history traits of the western diamondback rattlesnake (*Crotalus atrox*) studied from roundup samples in Oklahoma. *Occasional Papers of the Museum of Natural History, University of Kansas* 156:1–24.

Galligan, J. H., and W. A. Dunson. 1979. Biology and status of the timber rattlesnake (*Crotalus horridus*) populations in Pennsylvania. *Biological Conservation* 15:13–58.

Gannon, V. P. J., and D. M. Secoy. 1985. Seasonal and daily activity patterns in a Canadian population of the prairie rattlesnake, *Crotalus viridis viridis*. *Canadian Journal of Zoology* 63:86–91.

Goode, M., and D. Duvall. 1997. Living on the edge: Prairie rattlesnakes in Wyoming. *Sonoran Herpetologist* 10:82–87.

Greene, H. W., and G. V. Oliver, Jr. 1965. Notes on the natural history of the western massasauga. *Herpetologica* 21:225–28.

Grismer, L. L. 1994. The origin and evolution of the peninsular herpetofauna of Baja California, Mexico. *Herpetological Natural History* 2:51–106.

Grismer, L. L., J. A. McGuire, and B. D. Hollingsworth. 1994. A report on the herpetofauna of the Vizcaino Peninsula, Baja California, Mexico, with a discussion of its biogeographic and taxonomic implications. *Bulletin, Southern California Academy of Sciences* 93:45–80.

Jacob, J. S. 1981. *Population density and ecological requirements of the western pigmy rattlesnake in Tennessee.* Denver, Colo.: U.S. Fish and Wildlife Service.

Jemison, J. F., L. A. Bishop, P. G. May, and T. M. Farrell. 1995. The impact of PIT-tags on growth and movement of the rattlesnake, *Sistrurus miliarius barbouri. Journal of Herpetology* 28:129–32.

Kauffeld, C. F. 1943. Field notes on some Arizona reptiles and amphibians. *American Midland Naturalist* 29:342–59.

———. 1961. Massasauga land. *Bulletin of the Philadelphia Herpetological Society* 9:7–13.

Kimball, D. W., ed. 1992. *The timber rattlesnake in New England: A symposium.* Lincoln: Massachusetts Audubon Society. (Originally published 1978, revised 1992.)

Klauber, L. M. 1940. Notes from a herpetological diary. II. *Copeia* 1940:15–18.

Martin, B. E. 1974. Distribution and habitat adaptations in rattlesnakes of Arizona. *Herp: Bulletin of the New York Herpetological Society* 10(2): 3–12.

Martin, P. S. 1958. A biogeography of reptiles and amphibians in the Gomez Farias region, Tamaulipas, Mexico. *Miscellaneous Publications, Museum of Zoology, University of Michigan* 101:1–102.

Martin, W. H. 1981. The timber rattlesnake in the Northeast: Its range, past and present. *Herp: Bulletin of the New York Herpetological Society* 17(2): 15–20.

———. 1992. Phenology of the timber rattlesnake *(Crotalus horridus)* in an unglaciated section of the Appalachian Mountains. In *Biology of the pitvipers,* ed. J. A. Campbell and E. D. Brodie, Jr. Tyler, Tex.: Selva.

———. 1992. The timber rattlesnake: Its distribution and natural history. In *Conservation of the timber rattlesnake in the Northeast,* ed. T. F. Tyning. Lincoln: Massachusetts Audubon Society.

May, P. G., T. M. Farrell, S. T. Heulett, M. A. Pilgrim, L. A. Bishop, D. J. Spence, A. M. Rabatsky, M. G. Campbell, A. D. Aycrigg, and W. E. Richardson II. 1996. Seasonal abundance and activity of a rattlesnake *(Sistrurus miliarius barbouri)* in central Florida. *Copeia* 1996:389–401.

May, P. G., T. M. Farrell, and A. M. Rabatsky. 1994.

Researching the real serpent: Studies of pigmy rattlesnakes. *Newsletter of the League of Florida Herpetological Societies,* May issue.

May, P. G., S. T. Heulett, T. M. Farrell, and M. A. Pilgrim. 1997. Live fast, love hard, and die young: Ecology of pigmy rattlesnakes. *Reptiles and Amphibians* 45:36–49.

Means, D. B. 1985. Radio-tracking the eastern diamondback rattlesnake. *National Geographic Research* 1:529–36.

Moore, R. G. 1978. Seasonal and daily activity patterns and thermoregulation in the southwestern speckled rattlesnake *(Crotalus mitchellii pyrrus)* and the Colorado Desert sidewinder *(Crotalus cerastes laterorepens). Copeia* 1978:439–42.

Neill, W. T. 1958. The occurrence of amphibians and reptiles in saltwater areas, and a bibliography. *Bulletin of Marine Science of the Gulf and Caribbean* 8:1–97.

Palmer, W. M., and G. M. Williamson. 1971. Observations on the natural history of the Carolina pigmy rattlesnake, *Sistrurus miliarius miliarius* Linnaeus. *Elisha Mitchell Science Society Journal* 87:20–25.

Pough, F. H. 1966. Ecological relationships of rattlesnakes in southeastern Arizona, with notes on other species. *Copeia* 1966:676–83.

Reinert, H. K. 1984. Habitat separation between sympatric snake populations. *Ecology* 65:478–86.

———. 1984. Habitat variation among sympatric snake populations. *Ecology* 65:1673–82.

———. 1993. Habitat selection in snakes. In *Snakes: Ecology and behavior,* ed. R. A. Seigel and J. T. Collins. New York: McGraw-Hill.

Reinert, H. K., and W. R. Kodrich. 1982. Movements and habitat utilization by the massasauga, *Sistrurus catenatus catenatus. Journal of Herpetology* 6:162–71.

Reinert, H. K., and R. T. Zappalorti. 1988. Timber rattlesnakes *(Crotalus horridus)* in the Pine Barrens: Their movement patterns and habitat preference. *Copeia* 1988:964–78.

Rubio, M. 1972. In search of the rare cascabel. *Herp: Bulletin of the New York Herpetological Society* 8(3–4): 6–15.

———. 1991. The conference on the herpetology of North American deserts. *Sonoran Herpetologist* 3:56–57.

Secor, S. M. 1992. A preliminary analysis of the movement and home range size of the sidewinder, *Crotalus cerastes.* In *Biology of the pitvipers,* ed. J. A. Campbell and E. D. Brodie, Jr. Tyler, Tex.: Selva.

———. 1994. Ecological significance of movements and activity range for the sidewinder, *Crotalus cerastes. Copeia* 1994:631–45.

———. 1994. Sidewinder natural history. In *Her-*

petology of the North American deserts: Proceedings of a symposium, ed. P. R. Brown and J. W. Wright. Van Nuys, Calif.: Southwestern Herpetologists Society.

Seigel, R. A. 1986. Ecology and conservation of an endangered rattlesnake, *Sistrurus catenatus,* in Missouri. *Biological Conservation* 35:333–46.

Starrett, B. 1995. In search of the Grand Canyon rattlesnake. *Sonoran Herpetologist* 8:22–27.

Stewart, G. R. 1994. An overview of the Mojave Desert and its herpetofauna. In *Herpetology of the North American deserts: Proceedings of a symposium,* ed. P. R. Brown and J. W. Wright. Van Nuys, Calif.: Southwestern Herpetologists Society.

Sweet, S. S. 1985. Geographic variation, convergent crypsis, and mimicry in gopher snakes *(Pituophis melanoleucus)* and western rattlesnakes *(Crotalus viridis). Journal of Herpetology* 19:55–67.

Swinford, G. 1991. Collecting the banded rock rattlesnake. *The Vivarium* 3:8–11.

Timmerman, W. W. 1989. Home range, habitat use, and behavior of the eastern diamondback rattlesnake. Doctoral dissertation, University of Florida, Gainesville.

———. 1995. Home range, habitat use, and behavior of the eastern diamondback rattlesnake *(Crotalus adamanteus)* on the Ordway Preserve. *Bulletin of the Florida Museum of Natural History* 38:127–58.

Vogt, R. C. 1981. *Natural history of amphibians and reptiles of Wisconsin.* Milwaukee: Milwaukee Public Museum.

Weatherhead, P. J., and K. A. Prior. 1992. Preliminary observations on the habitat use and movements of the eastern massasauga rattlesnake *(Sistrurus c. catenatus). Journal of Herpetology* 26:447–52.

Weldon, P. J., R. Ortiz, and T. R Sharp. 1992. The chemical ecology of crotaline snakes. In *Biology of the pitvipers,* ed. J. A. Campbell and E. D. Brodie, Jr. Tyler, Tex.: Selva.

PHYSICAL CHARACTERISTICS

Antonio, F. B., and J. B. Barker. 1983. An inventory of phenotypic aberrancies in the eastern diamondback rattlesnake *(Crotalus adamanteus). Herpetological Review* 14:108–110.

Bagnara, J. 1983. Developmental aspects of vertebrate chromatophores. *American Zoology* 23:465–78.

Barton, A. J. 1950. Replacement fangs in newborn timber rattlesnakes. *Copeia* 1950:235–36.

Beaupre, S. J. 1995. Sexual size dimorphism in the western diamondback rattlesnake *(Crotalus atrox):* Integrating natural history, behavior, and physiology. *Sonoran Herpetologist* 8:112–18.

Bechtel, H. B. 1978. Color and pattern in snakes (Reptila; Serpentes). *Journal of Herpetology* 12:521–32.

———. 1991. Inherited color defects: Comparison between humans and snakes. *International Journal of Dermatology* 30:243–46.

———. 1995. *Naturally occurring variants of reptiles and amphibians.* Melbourne, Fla.: Kreiger.

Bechtel, H. B., and E. Bechtel. 1985. Genetics of color mutations in the snake *Elaphe obsoleta. Journal of Heredity* 76:7–11.

———. 1989. Color mutations in the corn snake *(Elaphe guttata guttata):* Review and additional breeding data. *Journal of Heredity* 80:272–76.

Bishop, L. A., T. M. Farrell, and P. G. May. 1996. Sexual dimorphism in a Florida population of the rattlesnake *Sistrurus miliarius. Herpetologica* 52:360–64.

Bogert, C. M. 1941. Sensory cues used by rattlesnakes in their recognition of ophidian enemies. *Annals of the New York Academy of Science* 41:329–44.

Brown, W. S. 1988. Shedding rate and rattle growth in timber rattlesnakes. *American Zoology* 28:198A.

Bullock, T. H., and R. B. Cowles. 1952. Physiology of an infrared receptor: The facial pit of pit vipers. *Science* 115:541–3.

Bullock, T. H., and F. P. J. Diecke. 1956. Properties of an infra-red sense organ in the facial pit of pit vipers. *Journal of Physiology* 134:47–87.

Bullock, T. H., and W. Fox. 1957. The anatomy of the infra-red sense organ in the facial pit vipers. *Quarterly Journal of Microscopic Science* 98:219–34.

Burghardt, G. M. 1970. Chemical perception in reptiles. In *Communications by chemical signals,* ed. J. W. Johnson, D. G. Moulton, and A. Turk. New York: Appleton-Century-Crofts.

Chiszar, D., D. Dickman, and J. Colton. 1986. Sensitivity to thermal stimulation in prairie rattlesnakes *(Crotalus viridis)* after bilateral anesthetization of the facial pits. *Behavioral and Neural Biology* 45:143–49.

Cohen, A. C., and B. C. Myres. 1970. A function of the horns (supraocular scales) in the sidewinder rattlesnake, *Crotalus cerastes,* with comments on other horned snakes. *Copeia* 1970:574–75.

Conley, K. E., and S. I. Lindstedt. 1996. Minimal cost per twitch in rattlesnake tail muscle. *Nature* 383:71–72.

Cook, P. M., M. P. Rowe, and R. W. Van Devender. 1994. Allometric scaling and interspecific differences in the rattling sounds of rattlesnakes. *Herpetologica* 50:358–68.

Cowles, R. B., and R. L. Phelan. 1958. Olfaction in rattlesnakes. *Copeia* 1958:77–83.

Fitch, H. S. 1985. Observations on the rattle size and demography of prairie rattlesnakes *(Crotalus viridis)* and timber rattlesnakes *(Crotalus horridus)* in Kansas. *Occasional Papers of the Museum of Natural History, University of Kansas* 118:1–11.

Ford, N. B., and G. M. Burghardt. 1993. Perceptual mechanisms and the behavioral ecology of snakes. In *Snakes: Ecology and behavior,* ed. R. A. Seigel and J. T. Collins. New York: McGraw-Hill.

Gamow, R. I., and J. F. Harris. 1963. The infrared receptors of snakes. *Scientific American* 228:94–100.

Gillingham, J. C., and D. L. Clark. 1981. Snake tongue-flicking: Transfer mechanics to Jacobson's organ. *Canadian Journal of Zoology* 59:1651–57.

Gloyd, H. K. 1958. Aberrations in the color patterns of some crotalid snakes. *Bulletin of the Chicago Academy of Sciences* 10:185–95.

Hartline, P. H., L. Kass, and M. S. Loop. 1978. Merging of modalities in the optic tectum: Infrared and visual integration in rattlesnakes. *Science* 199:1225–29.

Jackson, J. F., W. Ingram III, and H. W. Campbell. 1976. The dorsal pigmentation pattern of snakes as an antipredator strategy: A multivariate approach. *American Naturalist* 110:1029–53.

Klauber, L. M. 1936–40. A statistical study of the rattlesnakes. Parts I–VII. *Occasional Papers of the San Diego Society of Natural History.*

———. 1943. Tail-length differences in snakes with notes on sexual dimorphism and the coefficient of divergence. *Bulletin of the Zoological Society of San Diego* 18:1–60.

Lillywhite, H. B., and A. W. Smits. 1992. The cardiovascular adaptations of viperid snakes. In *Biology of the pitvipers,* ed. J. A. Campbell and E. D. Brodie, Jr. Tyler, Tex.: Selva.

Lynn, W. G. 1931. The structure and function of the facial pit of the pit vipers. *American Journal of Anatomy* 49:97–139.

Messler, R. M., and D. B. Webster. 1968. Histochemistry of the rattlesnake facial pit. *Copeia* 1968:722–28.

Molenar, G. J. 1974. An additional trigeminal system in certain snakes possessing infrared receptors. *Brain Research* 78:340–44.

Newman, E. A., and P. H. Hartline. 1981. Integration of visual and infrared information in bimodal neurons of the rattlesnake optic tedum. *Science* 213:789–91.

Powers, A. 1973. A review of the purpose of the rattle in crotalids as a diversionary mechanism. *Bulletin of the Maryland Herpetological Society* 9:30–32.

Romer, A. S. 1956. *Osteology of the reptiles.* Chicago: University of Chicago Press.

Schaeffer, G. C. 1969. Sex independent ground color in the rattlesnake, *Crotalus horridus horridus. Herpetologica* 25:65–66.

Schaeffer, N. 1976. The mechanism of venom transfer from the venom duct to the fang in snakes. *Herpetologica* 32:71–76.

Schuett, G. W., D. L. Clark, and F. Kraus. 1984. Feeding mimicry in the rattlesnake *Sistrurus catenatus,* with comments on the evolution of the rattle. *Animal Behaviour* 32:625–26.

Schwenk, K. 1994. Why snakes have forked tongues. *Science* 263:1573–77.

———. 1995. The serpent's tongue. *Natural History Magazine* 104:48–54.

Schwenk, K., and H. W. Greene. 1995. No electrostatic sense in snakes. *Nature* 373:26.

Shine, R. 1993. Sexual dimorphism in snakes. In *Snakes: Ecology and behavior,* ed. R. A. Seigel and J. T. Collins. New York: McGraw-Hill.

Sisk, N. R., and J. F. Jackson. 1997. Two hypotheses for the origin of the crotaline rattle. *Copeia* 1997:485–95.

Stille, B. 1987. Dorsal scale microdermatoglyphics and rattlesnake *(Crotalus* and *Sistrurus)* phylogeny (Reptilia: Viperidae: Crotalinae). *Herpetologica* 43:98–104.

Taub, A. M. 1967. Comparative histological studies of Duvernoy's gland of colubrid snakes. *Bulletin of the American Museum of Natural History* 138:1–50.

Vonstille, W. T., and W. T. Stille III. 1994. Electrostatic sense in rattlesnakes. *Nature* 370:184–85.

Wever, E. G., and J. A. Vernon. 1960. The problem of hearing in snakes. *Journal of Auditory Research* 1:77–83.

Whitt, A. L., Jr. 1970. Some mechanisms with which *Crotalus horridus horridus* responds to stimuli. *Transactions of the Kentucky Academy of Science* 31:45–48.

Young, B. 1990. Is there a direct link between the ophidian tongue and Jacobson's organ? *Amphibia-Reptilia* 11:263–76.

Zimmerman, A. A., and C. H. Pope. 1948. Development and growth of the rattle of rattlesnakes. *Fieldiana Zoology* 32:355–413.

RATTLESNAKES AS PREY

Graves, B. M. 1989. *Crotalus viridis* predation. *Herpetological Review* 20:71–72.

Keegan, H. L. 1944. Indigo snakes feeding upon poisonous snakes. *Copeia* 1969:59.

Neill, W. T. 1961. River frog swallows eastern diamondback rattlesnake. *Bulletin of the Philadelphia Herpetological Society* 9:19.

Ross, D. A. 1991. Amphibians and reptiles in the diets of North American raptors. *Wisconsin Endangered Resources Report* 59:1–33.

ROUNDUPS

Adams, C. E., K. J. Strnadel, and S. L. Lester. 1991. Texas rattlesnake roundups: Evaluation report. Texas Parks and Wildlife Department, Austin.

Adams, C. E., J. K. Thomas, K. J. Strnadel, and S. L. Jester. 1994 Texas rattlesnake roundups: Implications of unregulated commercial use of wildlife. *Wildlife Society Bulletin* 22:324–30.

Black, J. H. 1981. Oklahoma rattlesnake hunts—1981. *Bulletin of the Oklahoma Herpetological Society* 6:39–43.

Campbell, J. A., D. R. Formanowicz, and E. D. Brodie, Jr. 1989. The effects of gasoline fumes on selected reptiles and amphibians. Report of the Texas Parks and Wildlife Department, Austin.

———. 1989. Potential impact of rattlesnake roundups on natural populations. *Texas Journal of Science* 41:301–317.

Enge, K. M. 1991. Herptile exploitation: Annual performance report. Florida Game and Freshwater Fish Commission, Tallahassee.

———. 1993. Herptile use and trade in Florida: Final performance report. Florida Game and Freshwater Fish Commission, Tallahassee.

Fitzgerald, L. A., and C. W. Painter. 1994. A critical evaluation of rattlesnake commercialization: Roundups and the rattlesnake trade. Final report. World Wildlife Fund/Traffic (U.S.A.).

Garrett, C. M. 1994. Rattlesnake roundups: Messin' with Texas. *The Vivarium* 6:6.

Jester, S. L., C. E. Adams, and J. K. Thomas. 1990. *Commercial trade in Texas nongame wildlife.* Austin: Texas Parks and Wildlife Department.

Kilmon, J., and H. Shelton. 1981. *Rattlesnakes in America, and the history of the Sweetwater Jaycees' rattlesnake roundup.* Sweetwater, Tex.: Shelton Press.

Lawler, H. E. 1976. A zoo perspective on rattlesnake roundups in the southeastern U.S. *Proceedings of the American Association of Zoological Parks and Aquariums Regional Conference* 3:27–32.

———. 1977. Rattlesnake roundups revisited. *Proceedings of the American Association of Zoological Parks and Aquariums Regional Workshop* 4:376–81.

———. 1992. Rattlesnake roundups in Georgia: An environmental travesty. *Tucson Herpetological Society Newsletter* 1:25–27.

Lawler, H. E., and R. Lee-Fulgham. 1977. Rattlesnake roundups. *Defenders Magazine, Defenders of Wildlife* 52:360–66.

Pisani, G. R., and H. S. Fitch. 1994. A survey of Oklahoma's rattlesnake roundups. *Kansas Herpetological Society Newsletter* 92:7–15.

Reinert, H. K. 1990. A profile and impact assessment of organized rattlesnake hunts in Pennsylvania. *Journal of the Pennsylvania Academy of Science* 64:136–44.

Speake, D., and R. H. Mount. 1973. Some possible ecological effects of "rattlesnake roundups" in the southeastern coastal plain. *Proceedings of the Annual Conference, Southeastern Association of Game and Fish Commissioners* 1973:267–77.

Warwick, C. 1990. Disturbance of natural habitats arising from rattlesnake roundups. *Environmental Conservation* 17:173–74.

———. 1991. Observations on collection, handling, storage, and slaughter of western diamondback rattlesnakes *(Crotalus atrox). Herpetopathologia* 2:31–37.

Warwick, C., C. Steedman, and T. Holford. 1991. Rattlesnake collection drives: Their implications for species and environmental conservation. *Oryx* 25:399–440.

Weir, J. 1992. The Sweetwater rattlesnake roundup: A case study in environmental ethics. *Conservation Biology* 6:116–27.

SEX AND REPRODUCTION

Aldridge, R. D. 1993. Male reproductive anatomy and seasonal occurrence of mating and combat behavior of the rattlesnake *Crotalus v. viridis. Journal of Herpetology* 27:481–84.

Aldridge, R. D., and W. S. Brown. 1995. Male reproductive cycle, age at maturity, and cost of reproduction in the timber rattlesnake *(Crotalus horridus). Journal of Herpetology* 29:399–407.

Blem, C. R. 1982. Biennial reproduction in snakes: An alternative hypothesis. *Copeia* 1982:961–63.

Brown, W. S. 1991. Female reproductive ecology in a northern population of the timber rattlesnake, *Crotalus horridus. Herpetologica* 47:101–115.

———. 1995. Heterosexual groups and the mating season in the northern population of timber rattlesnakes, *Crotalus horridus. Herpetological Natural History* 3:127–33.

Butler, J. A., and T. W. Hull. 1995. Neonate aggregations and maternal attendance of young in the eastern diamondback rattlesnake, *Crotalus adamanteus. Copeia* 1995:196–98.

Carpenter, C. C., J. C. Gillingham, and J. B. Murphy. 1976. The combat ritual of the rock rattlesnake *(Crotalus lepidus). Copeia* 1976:319–31.

Chiszar, D., K. Scudder, H. M. Smith, and C. W. Radcliffe. 1976. Observations of the courtship behavior in the western massasauga *(Sistrurus catenatus tergeminus). Herpetologica* 32:337–38.

Darevsky, I. S. 1994. Evolution and ecology of parthenogenesis in reptiles. *Society for the Study of Amphibians and Reptiles Contributions to Herpetology* 9:21–39.

Dubach, J., A. Sajewicz, and R. Pawley. 1997. Parthenogenesis in the Arafuran filesnake. *Herpetological Natural History* 5:11–18.

Diller, L. V., and R. L. Wallace. 1984. Reproductive biology of the northern Pacific rattlesnake *(Crotalus viridis oreganus)* in northern Idaho. *Herpetologica* 40:182–93.

Duvall, D., S. J. Arnold, and G. W. Schuett. 1992. Pitviper mating systems: Ecological potential, sexual selection, and microevolution. In *Biology of the pitvipers,* ed. J. A. Campbell and E. D. Brodie, Jr. Tyler, Tex.: Selva.

Duvall, D., G. W. Schuett, and S. J. Arnold. 1993. Ecology and evolution of snake mating systems. In *Snakes: Ecology and behavior,* ed. R. A. Seigel and J. T. Collins. New York: McGraw-Hill.

Farrell, T. M., P. G. May, and M. A. Pilgrim. 1996. Reproduction in the rattlesnake, *Sistrurus miliarius barbouri,* in central Florida. *Journal of Herpetology* 29:21–27.

Fitch, H. S. 1985. Variation in the clutch and litter size in New World reptiles. *University of Kansas, Museum of Natural History Publication* 76:1–76.

Fleet, R. R., and J. C. Kroll. 1978. Litter size and parturition behavior in *Sistrurus miliarius streckeri. Herpetological Review* 9:11.

Ford, N. B., and J. R. Low, Jr. 1984. Sex pheromone source location by garter snakes: A mechanism for detection of direction in non-volatile trails. *Journal of Chemical Ecology* 10:1193–99.

Gibbons, J. W. 1972. Reproduction, growth, and sexual dimorphism in the canebrake rattlesnake *(Crotalus horridus atricaudatus). Copeia* 1972:222–26.

Gillingham, J. C., C. C. Carpenter, and J. B. Murphy. 1983. Courtship, male combat, and dominance in the western diamondback rattlesnake, *Crotalus atrox. Journal of Herpetology* 17:265–70.

Gloyd, H. K. 1947. Notes on the courtship and mating behavior of certain snakes. *Natural History Miscellanea, Chicago Academy of Sciences* 12:1–4.

———. 1948. Another account of the "dance" of the western diamondback rattlesnake. *Natural History* 34:1–3.

Graves, B. M. 1989. Defensive behavior of female prairie rattlesnake *(Crotalus viridis)* changes after parturition. *Copeia* 1989:793–94.

Jacob, J. S., S. R. Williams, and R. P. Reynolds. 1987. Reproductive activity of male *Crotalus atrox* and *C. scutulatus* (Reptilia: Viperidae) in northeastern Chihuahua, Mexico. *Southwestern Naturalist* 32:273–76.

Johnson, B. 1988. Combat and courtship of the eastern massasauga rattlesnake: Comparison of field and captive behavior. In *Proceedings of the Twelfth International Herpetology Symposium,* ed. M. J. Rosenberg. Thurmont, Md.: Propogation and Husbandry Zoological Consortium.

Keenlyne, K. D. 1978. Reproductive cycles in two species of rattlesnakes. *American Midland Naturalist* 100:368–75.

King, M. B., and D. D. Duvall. 1990. Prairie rattlesnake seasonal migrations: Episodes of movement, vernal foraging, and sex differences. *Animal Behaviour* 39:924–35.

Lindsey, P. 1979. Combat behavior in the dusky pigmy rattlesnake, *Sistrurus miliarius barbouri,* in captivity. *Herpetological Review* 10:93.

Lokke, J. 1985. A question of parental care in the timber rattlesnake, *Crotalus horridus. Nebraska Herpetological Society Newsletter* 6:4–5.

Lowe, C. H. 1942. Notes on the mating of desert rattlesnakes. *Copeia* 1942:261–62.

———. 1948. Territorial behavior in snakes and the so-called courtship dance. *Herpetologica* 4:129–35.

Martin, B. E. 1993. Reproduction of the timber rattlesnake *(Crotalus horridus)* in the Appalachian Mountains. *Journal of Herpetology* 2:133–43.

Murphy, J. B., and J. A. Shadduck. 1978. Reproduction in the eastern diamondback rattlesnake, *Crotalus adamanteus,* in captivity, with comments regarding taratoid birth anomaly. *British Journal of Herpetology* 5:727–33.

Nevares, M., and A. Quijada-Mascarenas. 1989. *Crotalus scutulatus scutulatus:* Mating behavior. *Herpetological Review* 20:71.

Price, A. 1988. Observations on maternal behavior and neonate aggregation in the western diamondback rattlesnake, *Crotalus atrox* (Crotalidae). *Southwestern Naturalist* 33:370–73.

Radcliffe, C. W., and J. B. Murphy. 1983. Precopulatory and related behaviours in captive crotalids and other reptiles: Suggestions for future investigation. *International Zoo Yearbook* 23:163–66.

Reinert, H. K. 1981. Reproduction by the massasauga *(Sistrurus catenatus catenatus). American Midland Naturalist* 105:393–95.

Reinert, H. K., and R. T. Zappolorti. 1988. Field observation of the association of adult and neonatal timber rattlesnakes, *Crotalus horridus,* with possible evidence of conspecific trailing. *Copeia* 1988:1057–59.

Schuett, G. W. 1992. Is long-term sperm storage an important component of the reproductive biology of temperate pitvipers? In *Biology of the pitvipers,* ed. J. A. Campbell and E. D. Brodie, Jr. Tyler, Tex.: Selva.

Schuett, G. W., P. A. Buttenhoff, and D. Duvall. 1993. Corroborative evidence for the lack of spring-mating in certain populations of prairie rattlesnakes *(Crotalus viridis). Herpetological Natural History* 1:101–6.

Schuett, G. W., P. J. Fernandez, D. Chiszar, and H. M. Smith. 1997. Fatherless sons: A new type of parthenogenesis in snakes. *Fauna Magazine* 1(3): 20–25.

Schuett, G. W., P. J. Fernandez, W. F. Gergits, N. J. Casna, D. Chiszar, H. M. Smith, J. B. Mitton, S. P. Mackessy, R. A. Odum, and M. J. Demlong. 1997. Production of offspring in the absence of males: Evidence for facultative parthenogenesis in bisexual snakes. *Herpetological Natural History* 5:1–10.

Sealy, J. B. 1996. *Crotalus horridus* (timber rattlesnake): Mating. *Herpetological Review* 27:23–24.

Shaw, C. E. 1948. The male combat "dance" of some crotalid snakes. *Herpetologica* 4:137–45.

Sutherland, I. D. W. 1958. The "combat dance" of the timber rattlesnake. *Herpetologica* 14:23–24.

Trapido, H. 1939. Parturition in the timber rattlesnake, *Crotalus horridus* Linne. *Copeia* 1939:230.

Wagner, R. T. 1962. Notes on the combat dance in *Crotalus adamanteus. Bulletin of the Philadelphia Herpetological Society* 10:7–8.

Wharton, C. H. 1960. Birth and behavior of a brood of cottonmouths, *Agkistrodon piscivorus piscivorus,* with notes on tail luring. *Herpetologica* 16:125–29.

TAXONOMY AND CLASSIFICATION

Auffenberg, W. 1963. The fossil snakes of Florida. *Tulane Studies in Zoology* 10:131–216.

Bogert, C. M., and W. G. Degenhardt. 1961. An addition to the fauna of the United States, the Chihuahuan ridge-nosed rattlesnake in New Mexico. *American Museum Novitates* 2064:1–14.

Cadle, J. E. 1982. Problems and approaches in the interpretation of the evolutionary history of venomous snakes. *Memorias do Instituto Butantan* 46:255–74.

———. 1988. Phylogenetic relationships among advanced snakes: A molecular perspective. *University of California Publications in Zoology* 119:1–77.

———. 1992. Phylogenetic relationships among vipers: Immunological evidence. In *Biology of pitvipers,* ed. J. A. Campbell and E. D. Brodie, Jr. Tyler, Tex.: Selva.

Campbell, J. A. 1979. A new rattlesnake (Reptilia, Serpentes, Viperidae) from Jalisco, Mexico. *Transactions of the Kansas Academy of Science* 81:365–69.

———. 1982. A confusing specimen of rattlesnake from Cerro Tancitaro, Michoacan, Mexico. *Southwestern Naturalist* 27:353.

Campbell, J. A., and B. L. Armstrong. 1979. Geographic variation in the Mexican pygmy rattlesnake, *Sisturus ravus,* with the description of a new subspecies. *Herpetologica* 35:304–17.

Campbell, J. A., and W. W. Lamar. 1992. Taxonomic status of miscellaneous neotropical viperids, with the description of a new genus. *Occasional Papers of the Museum, Texas Tech University, Lubbock* 153:1–31.

Christman, S. P. 1975. The status of the extinct rattlesnake *Crotalus giganteus. Copeia* 1975:43–47.

Crother, B. I., J. A. Campbell, and D. M. Hillis. 1992. Phylogeny and historical biogeography of the palm-pitviper, genus *Bothriechis:* Biochemical and morphological evidence. In *Biology of the pitviper,* ed. J. A. Campbell and E. D. Brodie, Jr. Tyler, Tex.: Selva.

Dowling, H. G. 1959. Classification of the Serpentes: A critical review. *Copeia* 1959:38–52.

Frost, D. R., and D. M. Hillis. 1990. Species in practice and concept: Herpetological applications. *Herpetologica* 46:87–104.

Gloyd, H. K. 1935. The subspecies of *Sistrurus miliarius. Occasional Papers of the Museum of Zoology, University of Michigan* 322:1–7.

*———. 1940. The rattlesnakes, genera *Sistrurus* and *Crotalus. Chicago Academy of Sciences Special Publication* 4:1–266.

Greene, H. W. 1994. Systematics and natural history: Foundations for understanding and conserving biodiversity. *American Zoologist* 34:48–56.

Grismer, L. L., J. A. McGuire, and B. D. Hollingsworth. 1994. A report on the herpetofauna of the Vizcaino Peninsula, Baja California, Mexico, with a discussion of its biogeographic and taxonomic implications. *Bulletin, Southern California Academy of Sciences* 93:45–80.

Harris, H. H., Jr., and R. S. Simmons. 1976. The paleogeography and evolution of *Crotalus willardi,* with a formal description of a new subspecies from New Mexico, United States. *Bulletin of the Maryland Herpetological Society* 12:1–22.

———. 1978. A preliminary account of the rattlesnakes with the descriptions of four new subspecies. *Bulletin of the Maryland Herpetological Society* 14:104–211.

Hoge, A. R. 1966. Preliminary account of neotropical Crotalinae (Serpentes, Viperidae). *Memorias do Instituto Butantan* 32:109–84.

International Commission on Zoological Nomenclature. 1985. *International code of zoological nomenclature.* 3d ed. London: International Trust of Zoological Nomenclature.

Julia Zertuche, J., and C. H. Trevino Saldana. 1978. Una nueva subspecie de *Crotalus lepidus* encontrada en Nueva Leon. In *Resumenes de Segundo Congreso Nationale Zoo.* Monterey, Nuevo Leon, Mexico: University of Nuevo Leon.

Klauber, L. M. 1930. New and renamed subspecies of *Crotalus confluentus* Say, with remarks on related species. *Transactions of the San Diego Society of Natural History* 6:95–144.

———. 1931. *Crotalus tigris* and *Crotalus enyo,* two little known rattlesnakes from the Southwest. *Transactions of the San Diego Society of Natural History* 6:353–70.

———. 1936. *Crotalus mitchelli,* the speckled rattlesnake. *Transactions of the San Diego Society of Natural History* 8:149–84.

———. 1941. A new species of rattlesnake from Venezuela. *Transactions of the San Diego Society of Natural History* 9:333–36.

———. 1944. The sidewinder, *Crotalus cerastes,* with a description of a new subspecies. *Transactions of the San Diego Society of Natural History* 10:91–126.

———. 1949. The relationship of *Crotalus ruber* and *Crotalus lucasensis. Transactions of the San Diego Society of Natural History* 11:57–60.

———. 1949. Some new and revived subspecies of rattlesnakes. *Transactions of the San Diego Society of Natural History* 11:61–116.

———. 1949. The subspecies of the ridge-nosed rattlesnake, *Crotalus willardi. Transactions of the San Diego Society of Natural History* 11:121–40.

*———. 1952. Taxonomic studies of the rattlesnakes of mainland Mexico. *Bulletin of the Zoological Society of San Diego* 26:1–143.

Knight, A., and D. P. Mindell. 1993. Substitution bias, weighting of DNA sequence evolution, and the phylogenetic position of Fea's viper. *Systematic Biology* 42:18–31.

———. 1994. The phylogenetic relationship of Colubrinae, Elapidae, and Viperidae and the evolution of front-fanged venom systems in snakes. *Copeia* 1994:1–9.

Knight, A., D. Styer, S. Pelikan, J. A. Campbell, L. D. Densmore III, and D. P. Mindell. 1993. Choosing among hypotheses of rattlesnake phylogeny: A best-fit rate test for DNA sequence data. *Systematic Biology* 42:356–67.

Liem, K. F., H. Marx, and G. B. Babb. 1971. The viperid snake *Azemiops:* Its comparative cephalic anatomy and phylogenetic position in the relation to Viperinae and Crotalinae. *Fieldiana Zoology* 59:65–126.

* McCranie, J. R., and L. D. Wilson. 1979. Commentary on taxonomic practice in regional herpetological publications: A review of "A preliminary account of the rattlesnakes with descriptions of four new subspecies," by Herbert S. Harris and Robert S. Simmons (1978. *Bulletin Maryland Herpetological Society,* 14(3): 105–211), with comments on other Harris and Simmons rattlesnake papers. *Herpetological Review* 10:18–21.

Pisani, G. R., J. T. Collins, and S. R. Edwards. 1973. A re-evaluation of the subspecies of *Crotalus horridus. Transactions of the Kansas Academy of Science* 75:255–63.

Radcliffe, C. W., and T. P. Maslin. 1975. A new subspecies of the red rattlesnake, *Crotalus ruber,* from San Lorenzo Sur Island, Baja California Norte, Mexico. *Copeia* 1975:490–93.

Simpson, G. G. 1961. *Principles of animal taxonomy.* New York: Columbia University Press.

Sprackland, R. G. 1994. Taxonomy: The making of scientific names. *The Vivarium* 6:14–17.

Tanner, W. W., J. R. Dixon, and H. S. Harris. 1972. A new subspecies of *Crotalus lepidus* from western Mexico. *Great Basin Naturalist* 32:16–24.

Underwood, G. 1967. A contribution to the classification of snakes. *Publication of the British Museum of Natural History* 653:1–179.

Underwood, G., and E. Kochva. 1993. On the affinities of the burrowing asps *Atractaspis* (Serpentes: Atractaspididae). *Zoological Journal of the Linnean Society* 107:3–64.

Werman, S. D. 1992. Phylogenetic relationships of Central and South American pitvipers of the genus *Bothrops (sensu lato):* Cladistic analyses of biochemical and anatomical characters. In *Biology of the pitvipers,* ed. J. A. Campbell and E. D. Brodie, Jr. Tyler, Tex.: Selva.

In the early morning light, all but a few inches of its tail remains until this San Lucan red diamond rattlesnake, *Crotalus ruber lucasensis,* is safely underground in a Baja California rodent burrow, having survived another night of hunting for prey, precious water, or a mate.

INDEX

Rattlesnake species and subspecies are indexed by common name here. Corresponding scientific names can be found in Appendix 1 (scientific names cross-referenced to common names) and in Appendix 2 (common names cross-referenced to scientific names). References to photographs are printed in boldface type.

advertisements, rattlesnakes in, 194–95
aestivation, 100–101, 102
Africa, 13, 14
Alabama, 150, 151
amphibians, den-sharing with, 96, 153, 155, 158
anatomy, 62–69, **77;** circulatory system, 70, 86, 87; digestive and elimination system, 84, 86; eyes, 67; fangs, 13, 134–35, 137; glottis, 81–82; head, 47; heart, 86; hemipenis, 105, 110, 114; jaw, **75,** 81, 82; lungs, 86–87; neck, 58; nostrils, **61,** 67; rattle, **53,** 55; reproductive system, 105, 110, 114–15; skeletal system, 81–82, 123–24, **124;** tail, **38,** 56, **57,** 116; venom-injecting apparatus, 13. *See also* facial pit; scales; skin; tongue
Angel de la Guarda Island speckled rattlesnake, **xxviii, 68**
animal rights. *See* roundups
antivenom therapies, 142, **143,** 144, 145–46
Argentina, 22
Argentinean viper, 14

Arizona, 18, **21;** conservation efforts, 200, 204; habitat, 24, 27, 35, **93, 95;** Poison Control Center, 146, 147; range of rattlesnakes, 8, 28, 32
Arizona black rattlesnake, **xi,** 24, 39, 40, 114, **115**
Arizona ridgenose rattlesnake, **xii,** 47, **49, 93**
Arkansas, 151
art, rattlesnakes in, **182–95,** 182–97
Aruba Island rattlesnake, 7, 9, **9,** 200, 201–2
Autlan rattlesnake, 28

Baja California rattlesnake, **30,** 32, **66,** 67, 129, **130–31**
banded rock rattlesnake: conservation of, 200, **201;** dens, **93;** effects of bite, **139;** feeding behavior, **72,** 73, **76,** 77; food sources, 77; habitat, 28, 35; hybridization, 7; mating, **107;** patterns and coloration, 39, **218–19;** predation strategies, **57;** sympatry, 27
barometric pressure, 89, 102, 108
behavior: burrowing, 47; combat dance, 109–10; cratering, 31–32, 70; defensive, 3, 39, 54, 56–59, **57, 58, 59,** 86, 124; drinking, 86–89, **87,** 95; feeding, 67, **72,** 73, 74, **74, 75, 76,** 77, 81–82; homing, 60; maternal protection, 115–16; the moon and, 101; reproductive, 32, 56, 69, 106, 108–14; side-to-side head movement, 62; soaking, 89; thermoregulation, 69, **70,** 71; the wind and, 101. *See also* locomotion; predation strategies; strike
blacktail rattlesnakes, 14, 17, 95, 124, 207. *See also* Mexican blacktail rattlesnake; northern blacktail rattlesnake; San Esteban Island blacktail rattlesnake
blood, 86, 87, 138, 180
body bridging, 59, **59**
brain, 62, 64, 67
breathing, 81–82, 86–87, 89

California, 13, 28, 40, 151, 177, 204
California kingsnake, 59, **59**

A coral color variant of the tiger rattlesnake, *Crotalus tigris*, whose range is within the Tucson Mountains region.